This book and its insights and practical techniques are highly recommended."

Rubin Battino
Author

"... suggests practical ways of helping people change their own models of the world. This book makes an important contribution to our understanding, and at over 400 pages, has a great deal to offer practitioners, family therapists, trainers, as well as everyone who is part of a family or group.

"*Social Panoramas* will delight those people who enjoy exploring other people's models of the world. The Social Panorama Model enables you to intervene appropriately and creatively in someone else's model of the world—when they are stuck and need help—by giving them an alternative point of view. It will also widen your own panorama of the world, and you could be surprised at what you find there!"

Peter Young
Author of *Understanding NLP*

Social Panoramas
Changing the Unconscious Landscape with NLP and Psychotherapy

Lucas Derks

Crown House Publishing Limited
www.crownhouse.co.uk

First published with the German title *Das Spiel sozialer Beziehungen: NLP und die Struktur zwischenmenschlicher Erfahrung* by
Klett-Cotta
© 2000 J.G. Cotta'sche Buchhandlung Nachfolger GmbH
Stuttgart

This English edition published by

Crown House Publishing Ltd
Crown Buildings, Bancyfelin, Carmarthen, Wales, SA33 5ND, UK
www.crownhouse.co.uk

and

Crown House Publishing Company LLC
6 Trowbridge Drive, Suite 5, Bethel, CT 06801, USA
www.crownhousepublishing.com

© Lucas Derks 2005
Translated from Dutch by Sue Hiller Smith

British Library Cataloguing-in-Publication Data
A catalogue entry for this book is available
from the British Library.

ISBN 978-190442403-1
LCCN 2003102131

Printed and bound in Great Britain by
CPI Antony Rowe, Chippenham and Eastbourne

Contents

i

Table of techniques

Foreword

A great many new ideas have crossed my path in the 20 years that I have been a practising psychologist. Beware of new ideas, they are horrific troublemakers, viruses infesting the magnificent conceptual tree of social science.

During my time as a student I learnt to defend myself against such alien concepts; at university they provided me with a 'new ideas filter'. It works like this:

First I look at the academic status of the person from whom the idea has come. Is he famous? Do I remember any of his books? If so, it will always be better than an unknown. A Nobel Prize winner beats everyone. A doctor is worth more than a graduate, who in turn is higher than a student. A layman is just below a technical college student. A North American is always better than a West European. Australians are worth more than Israelis or East Asians, who are closely followed by us, the Dutch. South Americans and black African scientists are at the bottom of this hierarchy. On a general level, seniors beat juniors and men beat women who, in turn, are way ahead of colleagues from 'wrong' adjacent academic disciplines.

If the source of a new idea is lower than I am I may safely ignore it, but when the creator of a new concept passes this automatically-functioning built-in status test I will be very upset. To escape these feelings I may try to convince myself that this idea is not new at all but simply an old notion in a new suit. In a small number of cases this will fail and I will have to start looking for another excuse.

Maybe I heard a reputed scientist call this new vision unprofessional, unscientific or even unethical. Or else I may make the effort of doing a lot of thinking and reading in order to try to disprove the new idea with logic – are there any internal inconsistencies to be found? If all else fails I may proclaim that this idea falls outside my domain of expertise so I don't need to consider it – it's none of my business, I don't know and I don't need to know. If the worst happens and territorial redefinition fails as well, I will be forced to let the new idea enter my intellectual world – and that is a very painful affair indeed!

Thanks to the widespread existence of this type of filter in the minds of psychologists, new ideas generally have no chance at all. If, by a miracle, they do make an impact, they are generally transmitted by 'pioneering' scientists with great reputations who can raise their profiles yet further by being the first person to launch (somebody else's) new idea. To do this they must give a speech at a conference, write about it in a scientific journal, or (even better) appear in an interview in the newspapers or on television. Only when your status in science is indisputable can you take the risk of promoting the idea of a student, a lay person or even a Dutchman!

In other words, a new idea stands or falls by the location of its originator in the social panoramas of the scientific community. Individuals who can embrace a new idea simply because they think it is good are truly great and independent spirits, and if you write a book like this you learn to appreciate them. Jaap Hollander organised my first Social Panorama workshop, Henriette Mol told me every day that it was a good idea and Walter Ötsch, Veli-Matti Toivonen, Wolfgang Walker, Richard Bolstad, Stefan Ouboter, Hans Meyer, Barbelo Uytenbogaerd, Tim Hallbom, Janneke Swank, Karl Nielsen, Denis Bridoux, Philip Boer, Roman Braun, Wassili Zafiris, Anneke Durlinger, Frank Görmar, Peter Winnington, Penny Tompkins, James Lawley, Benny Gelenbrecht, Michael Hall, Anneke Meier, Jeroen van Ewijk, Jan Rautner, Bernd Isert, Marja-Leena Savimaki, Nikolai Hozan, Alberich Pesendorfer, Grete Haas and Harald Brill all belong to a group of people who independently and publicly dare to say that they think that the Social Panorama Model is a good idea. It is thanks to them that this book is now here for you.

Fortunately, many people have reacted positively to my work. All these people are at my back in my social panorama, their support is the motor behind this project.

Lucas Derks
Nijmegen, June 2004

Preface

You are now holding a very special book, and for several reasons:

- It makes sense in a very simple manner of the way we relate to other people.
- Along with the Meta-States Model of L. Michael Hall and the Symbolic Modeling work of James Lawley and Penny Thompkins, it is arguably the most significant addition to the NLP field to emerge in the 1990s.
- It strongly links together the domains of social psychology, cognitive psychology (especially NLP), and cognitive linguistics.
- It is the result of well over 10 years of thoroughly documented research and field trials.
- It is extremely well referenced.
- Last but not least, it is brilliantly and engagingly illustrated by the author himself, who has a graphic arts background.

I first became aware of Lucas Derks' Social Panorama model through a series of witty and brilliantly illustrated articles which appeared in *NLP World* from 1996, first on the Social Panorama model itself, and then on its mystical corollary, the Spiritual Panorama, among others. These blew my mind! How could something so evident have eluded us? It made sense of so many aspects of our social modelling with such an economy of means! Another of Lucas' articles, on the Social Panorama Modelling of Slobodan Milosevic, quickly convinced me not only that NLP practitioners should learn this, but that *everybody*, from educators to managers, to politicians, to parents etc. should definitely learn about it also.

At that time, I was working on developing an NLP Master Practitioner course that would enable people to go beyond the standard model of NLP mastery and integrate not only the science of communication but also the art of communicating, and was on the lookout for leading edge material to incorporate into the training that would do just that. Derks' Social Panorama model was definitely going to fit in there! I got in touch with Lucas and we met early one morning during one of his visits to London. There he was, a very mild-mannered chap, with twinkling eyes and an engaging smile. We spoke for a couple of hours, I showed him how I would present his material and he gave me his blessing. Thank you Lucas.

A couple of years later Lucas then released a monograph of his work and I'll always remember receiving it through the post. There was so much more to the model that had not been presented in his articles. This definitely should be published, and sooner rather than later!

However, fate intervened and more years have passed before the much-awaited publication of this material than I would have liked. Lucas has not been idle though. He has used this opportunity to his advantage, not only to broaden his subject further, but also to link and cross-relate it with great cogency to all the other existing social psychology models and to ground it firmly in the Cognitive Linguistic models of George Lakoff and Mark Johnson.

So, here you are at last, with Lucas Derks' *Social Panoramas* in your hand. Enjoy, as you prefer, dipping into it or reading it from cover to cover. Get pulled in by the illustrations. It reads well, and you'll never think the same way again about the way you relate to people and they to you. That's a promise.

Denis Bridoux
October 2004

Introduction

Is passionate love only possible when our central nervous system has generated the right pictures, feelings, sounds, smells and tastes? Is sexual excitement exclusively dependent on sufficient external stimulation? Do you, as a participant-observer, have an answer to this question?

When I am lecturing about the subject matter of this book, this sort of question immediately catches the attention of any type of audience. Advertising executives, as a matter of course, put a little piece of nakedness in between the insurance and the washing powder in order to do so. For a while, if I may continue in the role of sex-educator: "Boys and girls, ladies and gentlemen, how do you actually make love to someone? What must you be aware of, what should you imagine and what do you tell yourself? In short, what steps must your brain take to create the feeling of love in your body?"[1]

However, once this has gone on for 10 minutes, questions are no longer sufficient – people want answers. Curious but already tired, most of my colleague psychologists in such an audience will want chi-squares[2] or PowerPoint pictures with tables and graphs. To accommodate them I offer the following:

People can love other people just as well when they are on the other side of the globe as when they are right next to them. Passionate love depends on the manipulation of social images held in the brain. These inner images – sounds, smells, tastes and feelings – must be in the correct proportions to one another in order to create love for someone. The mental constructs involved must match the requirements that the individual has put in place throughout his or her life. For example, if you think about loving someone yourself, you could notice that the 'love of your life' may

---

[1] Cameron Bandler wrote the first sex therapy handbook for therapists based on cognitive linguistics in 1987. Bolstad and Hamblett gave a presentation of the more 'tantric aspects' at the Finnish NLP Congress in 1997.
[2] A test of statistical significance to inform whether we should accept or reject a hypothesis.

become optimally attractive if you imagine him or her at the right distance (five centimetres/two inches away), in the right place (in front of you), in the right colours (orange and pink) and sur-rounded by the right smell (chestnut blossom) for example.

Are you beginning to worry that this might be a pornographic book? Let me reassure you, after this things start to get rather more serious. This book is about patterns in unconscious social thinking and cognitive therapeutic interventions to improve human rela-tionships in the broadest sense. In other words, it is about under-standing how people unconsciously see one another, and how the insight thus gained can be used as a problem-solving device. This is an extremely useful subject because people think almost con-stantly about other people, and also because most human suffer-ing is connected with social thought.

In this book you will read a large number of educated guesses about the patterns in unconscious social mental processes.[3] These guesses are based, in the main, on hundreds of case examples from my own clinical practice, from my therapy demonstrations in sem-inars and from many cases reported to me by my colleagues. A lot of additional data came from observing my students doing exer-cises in workshops, from daily life, from a few small-scale experi-ments and from browsing through the literature.

About the expression 'unconscious social cognition'

It would be splendid if this book were only about love, but it is equally as much about all the other varieties of social experience. It is about emotions such as irritation, hate, togetherness, loneli-ness, self-confidence, isolation, discrimination, loss, shame, pride, authority, loyalty, subservience, etc. As a social psychologist, I would say that this book is about structures in social cognition, where I define social cognition as: 'All the mental processes on which our social lives are based.'[4]

---

[3] Approximately 534 clients have been involved in the development of the techniques in this book. About another 150 cases come from demonstrations in workshops.
[4] See Greenspan (1997) who seems to mean 'social-affective' whenever he writes 'emotional'.

The problem in tracing these patterns of social cognition is precisely the fact that they are largely unconscious.[5] In other words, if you are in love with someone the only thing you will actually be aware of is the fact that you are in love. This conscious part, namely the feeling of being in love and knowing with whom, is, however, only the tip of the iceberg. Below the surface of your consciousness many hidden processes are at work. All the evidence suggests that, although they remain unnoticed by your conscious mind, these hidden processes are the ones in control of your experience. In this book I assume that our social behaviour is driven by unconscious social cognition, in which patterns can be found at individual, cultural and universal levels.

Theory and practice

To give you a quick idea of the sort of experimentation that has given rise to my social panorama theories I will begin with a small experiment. To do this, I will ask you to create a few experiences. If you have the luxury of having someone with you, ask him or her to read out this paragraph to you, because it works best that way. If you are alone, just read slowly…

To begin with, think of humanity, the greatest social whole that exists. Think of it in your own usual way.

How do you perceive it? Do you see the whole of mankind at a distance or do you experience all the other human beings as surrounding you? About one third of my subjects spontaneously take the distant view. Are you one of them? If you are, try to put yourself in among the rest of mankind and then step into your 'self'. I want you to imagine that you are in the middle, amongst everyone else in the world. Experience yourself as a person surrounded by all the others. Once you have that, then let your thoughts turn to a person you really love and care for. We will call this person your 'loved one'.

Think of your loved one, and make sure that you create a strong feeling of love for this person. Feel only love. I'll wait a moment…

---

[5] In this book I use 'unconscious' in the way Milton H. Erickson started to use it in the 1950s, and not in the way that is common in psychoanalysis.

Have you chosen someone? Are you feeling intense love for that person? Yes?

I expect that your feelings are very clear, but that your awareness of the other senses may be very vague. For example, the visual aspect, if present at all, may be nothing more than a few weak shadows. This vagueness is quite common but it may cause many people to become uncertain during this experiment, as they wonder if they are doing it 'right'. But, as I said, all this doubt is exactly on the mark; this is precisely the point where the research into unconscious social cognition begins, and it is the reason that this research is still on thin ice from a scientific perspective. Social cognition is vague and difficult to get hold of... but is its exploration an impossible project? I think not.

Another question: Were you able to experience an intense feeling of love? If you were, you can be 100 percent certain that this was a product of your own thought processes. Also, feeling a strong sense of love in this way is evidence of the fact that you do not require the physical presence of the object of your love in order to love him or her. It seems that your imagination is all that is required and this, in its turn, suggests that feelings of love can be completely independent of any external stimulus.

The general idea that social cognition is not dependent on external stimuli was discussed by Leo Pannekoek and Jerome Singer in the 1980s but, in the above example, it was I who suggested to you to think of a loved one in the first place. In this case, of course, I triggered the process. However, social thoughts often appear without any noticeable external causes. This is not to say that social thoughts don't need stimuli at all. They all have to start somewhere, although these beginnings often remain hidden within the swarm of unconscious mental processes.

Please return to that feeling of love for a moment and think about *where* in your mental space your loved one is located. How far away and in what direction do you experience the sense of him or her? Let the answer seep quietly into your consciousness. And if you're not sure, make a guess – which spot did you think of first when you heard or read the question 'where'?

Now think about the position of your loved one more precisely. On which side of your body do you sense his or her presence? Left, right, in front, behind, inside of you or somewhere else?

Recently, I asked 239 subjects for the locations of their loved ones.[6] Of all these people, about 94 percent had their loved one within arm's length. Of these, 29 percent had their loved ones on the left and 33 percent to the right-hand side of them. Twenty-eight percent had their loved ones straight in front of them while half a percent found their loved ones within the contours of their body. The remaining three-and-a-half percent had them behind, all around, in double or multiple locations or elsewhere. You may want to ask yourself what it means if your loved one is much farther away than arm's length – is your relationship really intimate or is there another person who is closer?

As soon as you know for sure where your loved one is located, you are ready for the next stage of this experiment. For this, first notice in what direction your loved one is looking. Once you know that, try to turn your loved one a quarter turn clockwise, so that the direction of gaze changes. What does this change in direction do to your feeling of love? Does it become more or less intense? When you have done that, turn your loved one back to the original position. Perhaps you are now beginning to discover the importance of 'glance direction' in social imagery. The barely conscious pictures we make of people almost always have a clear front and back, as well as a direction of glance and eye level.

Let us play another game with your loved one. Place your loved one five centimetres/two inches further away from you. Okay? How does that make you feel? What occurs at 20 centimetres/ eight inches or at three metres/10 feet? And what happens at 10 metres/30 feet?

I expect that moving your loved one further away had the same effect as with almost all of my subjects: it reduced the intensity of the feelings. Did that happen to you, too? This experiment shows that changing the positions of social images can influence the feelings associated with them. Imagine how a family therapist can make use of this knowledge!

---

[6] The experiment was conducted at the 15th Conference for NLP on 3rd April 2004.

Now move the image of your loved one to the opposite side (from left to right or from front to back) and 30 centimetres/12 inches further away. In this book, that process is known as 'a shift of location'. It probably radically changes the character of the relationship. For example, the person may change from a loved one into a family member or a good friend. These changes, often dramatic, support the theory that mental space is vitally important to the creation of meaning.

In the writings of Gilles Fauconnier (1997) the notion of 'mental space' is central. He describes how language triggers pictures and schemata that are subconsciously projected in the imaginary space that surrounds a person. Meaning is created within these mental spaces, so we live inside a three-dimensional theatre where we can see, hear, feel, smell and taste what is spoken or written about. The thing is, the intensity of most of what is played for us in this mental theatre is below the threshold of consciousness. We know what is spoken or written about, but only now and then do we notice fragments of the 'pictographic' level of experience. Fauconnier states that all subjective experience is primarily spatial in nature.

In this book I focus on how this is true also for social experience. The social panorama is a landscape of social images that generally remain unconscious. Without even noticing it, we live our lives in the middle of this panorama. Whether we are aware of it or not, it functions as our one and only map of social reality. It is the guidebook for our day-to-day travel through the human world.

Let's try another little experiment. Think about a neutral person, a postman for example. Imagine this person in the exact spot where your loved one is located. What happens? Try to keep the postman in this position, and make him 20 centimetres bigger and bathe him in bright sunlight...

Hey!... have you by now fallen in love with the postman? That's theoretically possible but it is more likely that you have experienced a strong resistance as if this position is only reserved for a very special person. In this way you may discover that you are not completely free to change social experiences; such changes are limited and bound by your own internal set of rules. In the chapters ahead of us we will examine some of these rules.

While playing with the image of the postman you may have discovered the most important principle of the social panorama model, *'relationship equals location'*. This means that the emotional quality of a relationship is governed by the location in mental space in which the image of the person is projected. I wrote 'relationship equals location' for the first time on a flipchart in 1993. That was the birth of the Social Panorama Model.

Okay, just to be on the safe side, put your loved one and the postman back in their original locations. I'll wait a moment...

Research into the unconscious

Thirty years of intensive research into cognitive psychology and cognitive linguistics have brought to light the fact that most thoughts are high-speed activities that whiz past and through each other at very high velocity (Schneider and Shiffrin, 1977; Kunda, 1999). In this respect they agree with the work of William James in the nineteenth century and Milton Erickson in the 1950s. Unconscious thoughts are too fast and too complex to be noticed by our conscious minds in the same way that the individual frames of a movie are invisible to the audience. We notice only the slowest aspects of our thoughts, and then almost always only when a process becomes stagnant (Mandler, 1979) – we only see the single frames of film when the film breaks down.[7]

Our consciousness functions as the brain's monitor; it only gets involved when there is a problem or when some improvement is required. All it does is to bring problems, questions and choices to our attention. The rest of our thoughts disappear before we know they exist (Derks, 1989).

Psychology

The elusive nature of most of our thoughts makes psychology a nerve-racking business. Unlike scientists in most other disciplines, we psychologists are unable to directly observe the majority of the

---

[7] See Derks and Goldblatt (1985) on the way in which information is consciously and unconsciously processed. Also in Derks (1989).

objects of our research. Physicists need equipment that costs billions and massive amounts of effort and perseverance to witness the existence of basic particles or black holes, but they find themselves in a wondrous position when compared with psychologists trying to research unconscious thought processes. Thoughts are ephemeral and never the same. Thoughts can be spoken of or written about but these are words and not really thoughts at all. Thoughts stay hidden within the neural tissue and flash by in milliseconds never to reappear in the same form.

Nonetheless, like all other scientists, psychologists are keen to formulate and test their theories. Our conscious, rational, analytic, scientific mind desires nothing more than the opportunity to understand and explain unconscious thought, but the battle seems lost before it begins – Terry the Turtle versus Harry the Hare. The conscious brain is too unwieldy and too slow. By the time our consciousness has noticed something, the unconscious mental processes involved are already miles ahead. Our brains are full of unconscious thoughts in the same way that the ether is full of radio signals but we don't have the right 'radio receiver'. In fact, the only 'receiver' we have is the brain itself, and all that contains is a 'fault detector' – the conscious mind. So it seems that research into unconscious social thought processes is a hopeless endeavour and it is foolish even to try! But no matter how ridiculous and stupid it is, many colleagues and I are still incapable of accepting this as a fact. It may be foolish and doomed to failure but even if it is impossible, we still want it!

Luckily, we are not alone in this struggle for knowledge.

Cognitive linguistics

The same problems that psychologists have encountered with unconscious thought structures have also been found in the study of linguistics. The mental processes that lead to language production and understanding are just as fast, complex and unconscious as social cognition is. The writing on this page is language – and there are certainly quite a few sentences to be read here! Sentences that, logically speaking, I *must* have thought about. However, I have absolutely no idea how I created them. Am I stupid? Am I dyslexic? No. No more than average. My inner language factory produces sentences without the knowledge of my consciousness. Although I imagine myself to be the commander of my language factory, I can only glimpse a tiny part of the production process. I am usually aware of mistakes, but if things go well I notice nothing. So I don't actually know how I write and speak.

The already mentioned pioneer of cognitive linguistics, Gilles Fauconnier (1997) wrote the following:

> There is a steady flow of talk in the world, and it looks very easily available indeed. What is more, people who study language signals happen, because they are humans, to come biologically endowed with very good technology for receiving and processing such signals. But this technical prowess will not immediately impress other human beings, who are equally gifted for this particular technology and are admirably equipped to use the received signals to produce rich mental constructions with such ease that the entire process does not seem to them especially complicated or mysterious.

In the same way, social psychologists can miss the unbelievable complexity of social cognition, simply because they never really reflected on it. The world is just as full of social activity as it is of language. That is why we think about it so little.

As a psychologist I see language as a by-product of unconscious thought, and not as thought itself. We no longer make the mistake of stating that *thought is nothing more than inner talk* (Solokov, 1977). Thought involves activity in all the senses. Spoken words seem to be much like the clicks of a computer mouse that can awaken meaningful mental constructions, but these constructions can also become activated without any words at all. What is written and spoken becomes the indirect expression of the lightning-fast multi-sensory 'pictographic' activities in our brains (Ötsch, 2001).

Applying linguistics

The cognitive linguists, George Lakoff and Mark Johnson (1999), have come to three conclusions that, in my opinion, are also essential to my own research. They suggest that most of our thoughts are unconscious, that abstract concepts are metaphorical and that the foundations of thought are developed from bodily and physical experiences. In short, our thoughts begin in our bodies and then become translated into metaphors that are used almost completely unconsciously.[8]

From this vision, Lakoff and Johnson went in search of the unconscious thought constructions that all people must create in order to live. What is the minimum that a person must know? They state that what we experience as common sense feels so 'natural' just because it is derived from bodily sensations that we all shared during our childhood. On the basis of this common but implicit knowledge we build logic and philosophy. In short, philosophy is in the flesh.

Lakoff and Johnson discovered, for example, that everyone learns the difference between 'in' and 'out'. A very simple difference that we learn as a baby though our experience of the world: in the mouth…out of the mouth…in the cradle…out of the cradle…in the bath…out of the bath. Such general and universal experiences lead to a framework of 'basic concepts'. From these basics the individual can build an individual thought-world. The ability to reason logically, according to Lakoff and Johnson, is based on the acquisition of these cognitive building blocks. The basic concepts are 'primary metaphors' inasmuch as they are image schemas of sensory-motor functions that are used in conjunction with other concepts. For example, when the bodily experience of 'inner-outer' is applied to 'family' (in the family and outside the family), 'science' (within a science or outside a science) or 'system' (within the system or without the system) – it's as if the family, science and systems are boxes one can put things into. So what we learn as sensory-motor concepts in the cradle can later be applied to every other concept.

For the development of the social panorama we must look even before the cradle, in the womb. There, an embryo must start to notice that there are parts in its environment that it can move, feel and control and parts it cannot. This difference may be the start of the concept of 'here and there'. I am here and the rest of the universe is there.

---

[8] See my 1995 article in *NLP World* on the distinction between metaphor and non-metaphor within the context of the social panorama.

According to Lakoff and Johnson, the analysis of such universal building blocks of thought offers a 'way in' to the structure of unconscious cognition. For, as soon as they are learned, these basic concepts start to play an unconscious, automatic and self-evident background role in our thinking. Of course, despite this research into basic concepts, the unconscious remains just as difficult to reach as before. What Lakoff and Johnson's ideas do offer is some insight into what *must* be going on in the unconscious. Ideas like 'inner and outer' and 'here and there' can be found in everybody's operating system – if not, the person will be extremely handicapped.

Referring to Narayanan (1997) and Bailey (1997), Lakoff and Johnson wrote:

> Primary metaphors are part of the cognitive unconscious. We acquire them automatically and unconsciously via the usual processes of neuronal learning and may be unaware that we have them. We have no choice in this process. When the embodied experiences in the world are universal, then the corresponding primary metaphors are universally acquired. This explains the widespread occurrence around the world of a great many primary metaphors.

Lakoff and Johnson's theory about primary metaphors relates directly to my approach to the social panorama. I believe that the panorama is made up of social basic concepts that are analogues to primary metaphors and can be combined into complex social meanings. Every baby will experience the difference between its own and other people's bodies. Such basic experience will result in a primary 'self and other' metaphor. Everybody learns the difference between 'self' and 'other' in roughly the same way. Almost everyone learns that other people feel warm to the touch. This basic sensory experience can be transformed into the primary metaphor of 'warm contact'. This is a metaphor that almost everyone understands, because they have had the bodily experience.

Introspection and population modelling

In the same way that linguists use parts of speech and fragments of text as the basis of their research, my data come from experimental subjects and therapy clients speaking about their social lives. What people report about their own social inner world forms the majority of the material for my research.

But that is the primordial method of introspection! Isn't that a terrible step back? Introspection is the old-fashioned method used by Wilhelm Wundt and William James in the 19th Century. The behaviourists Pavlov, Tillman, Watson and Skinner all criticised introspection for being *unscientific*!

With hindsight, we can say that these behaviourists threw the baby out with the bathwater. I believe that introspection is still the only method that brings us close to unconscious thought, certainly if we use the right techniques for its exploration. These techniques stem largely from hypnotherapy and 'imagination-therapy'. The highest standard of precise exploration of subjective experience can be found in the work of Richard Bandler and John Grinder (1975a, 1979, 1982; Grinder and Bandler 1981, Bandler 1985). Most often, their subjects sit with eyes closed while they are questioned in detail about their inner images, voices and feelings. Bandler and Grinder talk about 'modelling', which is to explore the subjective experience of one person in order to teach their mental skills to others. The classic idea of 'modelling' consists of the painstaking examination of the patterns in the thought processes of one single expert. This type of modelling process is finished when the patterns are clear enough to be imparted to some motivated students who hope, by those means, to obtain similar results as the expert.

The introspective exploration of unconscious social thinking is unusual for a social psychologist like me. We social psychologists tend rather to arm ourselves with questionnaires and observation tools. In my case it was a special fascination with hypnotherapy – which began around 1978 – that brought me to it. The connection with social cognition came much later.

Somewhere before 1993 I discovered that when clients were brought into a light hypnotic trance they were able to give explicit descriptions of their inner models of social reality. Since then I have worked with many hundreds of subjects and bit by bit the universal, cultural and personal patterns in people's social panoramas have become apparent. By using Bandler and

Grinder's tool of modelling on a great number of subjects, I evolved a qualitative-quantitative type of research, which I called 'population modelling'.

Clinical field research

My Uncle Bill taught Guatemalan radio technicians in record time by locking them up in a workshop full of broken radios. They learnt in what we would call an experimental setting. "Within two weeks all the radios worked," said my Uncle proudly, "and the boys knew more about electronics than after a year in college." In the same way I learnt a great deal by trying to help people improve their social lives. I closeted myself with psychotherapy clients who had 'social problems'. Data collected in such a manner seldom reach the level of verifiability that quantitative researchers require. As Albert Einstein put it, "Not everything countable counts. And not everything that counts is countable." The lack of statistical certainty in this study is compensated by the robustness of the reported phenomena. In general, I hope that this book adds to the development of a methodology for what Charles Faulkner insists we should call "applied cognitive linguistics".[9]

A great number of techniques that bring difficult interpersonal problems within the reach of short-term psychotherapy have been developed from the social panorama project. To my surprise almost all my clients benefit from this type of work. I experienced a radical shortening in therapy duration after I started to use these methods at the beginning of the 1990s and the techniques have been improving ever since. From 1996 to 2001 my clients' average treatment time dropped even further from five-and-a-half hours to four hours and five minutes.[10] Besides such an improvement in efficiency, the social panorama concept has enriched my psychological insight enormously. I hope it will do the same for you.

---

[9] Faulkner argues that cognitive linguists have the same vision as followers of NLP. However, they have little familiarity with the practical application of their knowledge. Cognitive linguists are able to maintain a connection with the academic world. This link is lost with NLP.

[10] This average comes from a sample of 203 therapy clients over a period of five years.

Chapter 1

The building blocks of the social world

1.1   *Personifications like you and me*

This book is about a number of challenging questions. For instance, how do I think about you and how do you think about me? More generally, how do people create the thoughts they have about one another? Or more academically, what are the recurring patterns within the structure of unconscious social cognition?

In this book we explore these patterns not only for the sake of increasing our knowledge, but each time we gain some insight, we will also look for its practical use. The demands for practical applications are enormous because, as you might have discovered yourself, the world is full of social-emotional misery. The primary reason for writing a book like this is that its content can add to the quality of human life in the broadest sense.

In this chapter we try to reconstruct the building blocks of unconscious social thinking. Many child psychologists are working on related questions. At the beginning of this quest we focus on the fundamental difference between social and non-social cognition. So, if it exists at all, what does 'non-social' mean?

You don't need to search for the answer to this question in the psychological literature.[11] 'Non-social' cannot be found within science; at most you might find 'antisocial'. Most of my colleagues find it 'quite common' that there are many theories dealing with social cognition without anybody knowing what non-social means. Many assume 'non-social' to be the same as the never-used expression 'physical cognition'. But what is 'quite common'? In psychology the greatest miracles hide behind what is considered to be 'just ordinary'.[12]

1.2   *One must recognise one's own kind*

So, what may commonly be meant by 'social'? In nature, we observe a strong inclination to treat one's own species differently

---

[11] See Buunk and Meertens (In Meertens and Von Grumbkow, 1992) on searching for a definition of 'social'.

[12] 'It comes naturally' or 'normal' are expressions that indicate unconscious competences.

from other organisms. To make this possible, plants and animals must be able to recognise other members of their species. Lions know how other lions smell, look and sound; they hunt together, mate together and socialise with one another, but they don't do those things with leopards, crocodiles or hyenas.

So, at first glance, this ability to recognise one's own species is essential for reproduction, and this might help to define what we call 'social reality'. In the first place it is the world of human gene carriers. The difference between social and non-social seems to be a reflection of a biological necessity, coupled with the unconscious ability to differentiate between people and non-people; most humans can do that, thanks to our unique vertical stature. That is why we don't generally fall prey to a careless hunter during a walk in the forest. People see people as fundamentally different from all other animals; even most cannibals believe that human flesh is an unusual dish.

However, if we look a little longer at the animal kingdom, we see that the mental programs designed to recognise other members of the same sort don't always function faultlessly. Butterflies some-times flit around each other, wondering 'can we do business?' Dogs sometime see people as super-dogs and follow their owners as if they were pack leaders. Ask yourself, is that because dogs cannot hear or smell the difference? No! Are they stupid then? Dogs might offer the excuse that the wide variety of dog breeds makes matters very difficult for them. If a St Bernard and a Chihuahua are both members of the same sort, isn't it under-standable that some dogs find more similarity between themselves and their owners? In debates like this, dogs might defend them-selves by saying that their owner is a 'leader' rather than a 'mate', and they might argue that many people, like shepherds, avalanche rescuers, explosives experts and blind people, in their turn often give the lead to a dog – without having to copulate with it. Now let us get serious again.[13]

---

[13] This paragraph is inspired by the work of biologist Midas Dekkers (1997).

1.3   *How we turn 'objects' into people*

The fact that humans can breed with each other means that we are genetically one species, but that does not automatically mean that we encode each other as equals in our minds. Once upon a time in the state of Massachusetts (remember this), a law was brought into force forbidding the shooting of wildlife in the streets, with the exception of wolves and Indians. At that time Indians were not generally regarded as people. To become part of another person's model of the social world, to be human is not enough. To make that happen, the other person needs to perform a cognitive operation called *personification*. (For a more in-depth explanation, see Mithen, 1996.)

Ötsch (2001) states that to think of a 'thing' is only possible if we know how to 'objectify' something. For a 'thing' to be an object in our mind, we need to ascribe a number of properties to it. A thing needs to be somewhere. A thing needs to have volume. A thing must be thought of as having a surface. A thing needs weight, size and colour. A baby will only be able to deal effectively with things when it has mastered the skill of 'objectification' – assuming all these properties to be present in any object. Luckily, most children have no problems on this level. The properties that must be in place to make something into a thing can be called 'objectification factors'. If any of these factors is missing, for instance, if a thing has no surface, then it cannot be a thing. Or if the thing is without a location, if it is nowhere, it cannot be thought of as something that really exists at all.

Since every person is a thing but not everything is a person, we may conclude that the cognitive operation of creating a person takes more steps than that of creating a thing. This brings us back to the process of personification.

The verb 'to personify' is defined in the dictionary as: "Thinking and speaking of a non-human object as if it had human qualities." In other words, treating a non-person or a thing as a person.[14]

---

[14] The practice of speaking about concrete things as if they have human characteristics stems from Greek rhetoric.

However, in order to construct a useful map of our social reality, we need to represent humans as people and not things. What this implies is the following: The process of personification only attracts our attention when we do it, erroneously, with non-human things. The thought pattern used in creating a person in our minds was disregarded in social psychology. The activity of personification was only noticed by a few linguists in cases where it was falsely applied to objects, animals, mountains, abstractions, etc. Social cognition as a science starts with the recognition that the same cognitive process of personification is commonly used to represent real people in exactly the same way. Up until recently this seemed much too normal for social science to take any notice of.

Maybe you wonder why you never noticed personification? I suggest it is for the simple reason that the personification of a real person is so obvious, common and habitual that it takes place fully automatically. Personification is a dramatic example of unconscious social cognition. Without thinking about it we create thought structures that represent objects and because of the special way in which we have constructed them, they become people to us.

The number of dogs personified by people is without doubt equal to the number of people accepted by dogs as their own kind. As stated before, all things such as abstract ideas, cars, money, plants, symbols, organisations, rocks, nations and political parties can be personified. But more than anything, the animals of the species Homo Sapiens are cognitively treated in this fashion. As soon as people in their first years of life learn the art of personification, they can personify everything with the greatest of ease.

The result of all this 'personifying' is the existence of 'personifications'. Translated into the brain-computer metaphor,[15] we can regard a personification as a memory file in which all our information about a person is retained according to a specific structure.

1.4   *A personification awakens*

When I see my colleague, Frits, in the office, the personification that I created of him (the one that to me *is* him) is activated. More generally stated, as soon as I see a real person, my personification of that person is awakened. A passive element of my memory is stimulated and becomes active through perception and recognition. The neural activity involved can vary greatly in intensity, and generally remains below the threshold of consciousness. But no matter how weak the mental activity, my inner visual image of the person is still called into action. To illustrate: to me it's as if Frits were a figure made of thin neon tubes that are switched on as soon as I meet him. But the switch has a dimmer and it is almost always set to a very low level. That is why Frits radiates very weakly in my inner field of vision. He may just be visible, but the light is usually so dim that I'm not conscious of him. The information that my external senses register – for example, Jane, the secretary from the acquisitions department – drowns out my inner Frits like a Boeing taking off overwhelms the chirping of a grasshopper along the runway. As I go about my daily activities the image of Frits is completely forgotten, but still this almost invisible image determines everything that I feel about Frits.

---

[15] Many psychologists try to avoid using the computer metaphor, but I find it very useful for getting an idea across quickly, so I use it throughout the book.

If I relax, close my eyes and direct my attention inwards, I can sometimes see this dim light which is Frits; I can just make out what the image is made of. Under certain emotional conditions however, this image can appear to me to be as clear as day. This morning Frits was appointed my new boss!

1.5 Organising personifications

The unavoidable consequence of all this personification in our brains is that more and more of these cognitive structures become stored in memory. How to handle this overload? For instance, can I ever get Frits out of my mind? Because today I would rather like to 'delete' him from my social panorama! No. What a pity. I can't get rid of him. Why not? The answer will be given in Chapter 6. Once they are formed, personifications cannot be removed; they can only be transformed or moved around in the social panorama. So Frits will stay in my mind forever.

Because the brain cannot process millions of individual personifications, it turns to the process of generalisation for assistance. By sorting personifications into categories we arrange our social reality. We bundle similar sorts of people together to store them in the same place, melding them together into a 'type'. Today Frits is clustered with 'bosses'.

Besides the bundling of personifications into categories, most people also make use of 'distance'. They create an intimate circle around themselves that is exclusively reserved for lovers, children, parents and the personifications of exceptionally important entities like spirits, gods or angels. The larger space around this intimate circle is filled with less significant people, like friends, neighbours and colleagues. The images of people in this area are generally grouped together, although they are all recognisable as individuals. On the outer spheres of the social panorama one finds the group-personifications like 'the party', 'the factory' and 'the government'. This morning my unconscious mind has moved Frits from the close zone of 'colleagues' to the distant domain of 'directors'.[16]

---

[16] The discovery of the social panorama came out of analysis of categorisation in terms of the submodality model of Bandler (1985). 'How do we categorise human beings?' was the main question.

By listening to his parents' conversations, for example, a small boy can discover that the difference between rich and poor plays a very important role in life. Possibly he will also learn some of the external signs with which to distinguish the rich from the poor. But what he needs to find out for himself is how to give shape to such a difference in his own mental software.

In the operating system of his mind the difference between 'here and there', 'high and low' and 'close and far' will already be solidly engraved. On the base of this type of primary cognitive distinction, the boy will start to create his own new mental program that deals with the rich and the poor. This then becomes an 'idealised cognitive model' (Lakoff, 1987), an abstract prototype.

In such a prototype the distinction between the categories 'rich' and 'poor' can be made by means of putting them in different corners of mental space. For example, the boy may put poor people low and rich ones high. In the same way someone may encode trustworthy people nearby and untrustworthy people far away, fortunate people on the left and unfortunate on the right or his own folks all around him and his enemies far away.

1.6   *Five types of personification*

We use the noun 'personification' to indicate the mental representation of a 'somebody'.[17] In this book, we differentiate between five types of personifications:

- Self-personification – the representation of the self.
- Other-personification – the representations of other individuals.
- Group personification – the representations of groups and large social complexes that are bundled together into single cognitive units, such as parties, nations, factions, clubs and organisations.
- Spiritual personification – the representations of dead and non-human social entities such as ghosts, spirits and gods.

---

[17] In Dutch the verb 'to personify' (personificeren) does not appear in the Van Dale dictionary.

- Metaphorical personification – invented personifications (such as characters in a book), physical objects, abstractions, animals, plants, symbols, processes and non-human-non-spiritual entities to which are ascribed human-like qualities.

We invent all these different types of personification. We create an image, put it in a particular place, attribute feelings, drives and a wealth of other features to it and then save the whole thing in our memory. After that we start to behave as if the thing in our mind is a real flesh and blood person. From that moment on we believe that this person really exists in the way that we have created them.

1.7 Assumption 1: Personifications are parts

Bandler and Grinder (1979) do therapy by communicating with mental functions called 'parts'. For instance, they may work with the part that makes the person happy or the part that protects the person against disappointment, etc. In Bandler and Grinder's practical psychology, the human personality is regarded as a collection of goal-directed units – a set of personality parts. Any relevant unit of neural activity can be defined as a part if it needs therapy. The therapeutic effect of this approach stems largely from the act of personifying these parts. By having the client visualise the part in the shape of a version of himself or in another human-like form, things in therapy become more alive. As soon as abstractions, problems or mental functions become personified, something very important starts to happen – a huge quantity of extra mental software will be mobilised for assistance. Everything the person has learned about how to deal with people can now be applied to what is, in fact, a non-social problem. The power of the unconsciously working 'social operating system' will add tremendously to the capacity to solve problems of any kind.

Conclusion: personifying non-humans can be very useful.

A totally different relationship between parts and personifications has to do with the demarcation between self and other – who is who in the social panorama model?

Personifications consist, by definition, of activity in neural tissue. They are stored in someone's memory. They are owned by the person in whose brain they are represented.

The logical implication of this is that our personifications of others (the knowledge we have about them that is neurologically laid down in our minds) are also parts of ourselves. Although other human beings exist as real physical objects in the world, we know only as much about them as our own neurology can represent. So the real flesh and blood others are in fact only occasions for us to compose our personifications. Although we know only our self-constructed representations of other people, we (mistakenly) tend to presume that it is the real ones we know – ignoring the fact that the person we 'know' is no more than an activity in our own brain.

Conclusion: All the people, organisations, gods, groups and creatures that we know are parts of ourselves. Thus people surround themselves with a circle of self-created personifications that are, to them, the only knowable social world. That means that a change in their social panorama is a change in their social reality.

1.8   *People, animals and personifications*

During the social development of their children parents may have to interfere once in a while, "No, Johnny, don't bite that boy, you'll hurt him!" So now Johnny will learn that other children do also feel. "Don't do that, Johnny, kittens have feelings, too!" However, the fact that animals can feel doesn't make them equal to us. So what does?

Do you still remember the people in Massachusetts who were forbidden to shoot wildlife in the streets? They considered Indians not to be human because they did not believe in God. These people thought that only the right spiritual connections made people into humans. In that respect many things have changed over the last century. These days even the opinions of Westerners about other primates have turned completely around. Nowadays primatologists such as Jane Goodall see no categorical difference between humans and the great apes. What category of competence should we look for?

Research shows that orang-utans are conscious of self and can recognise themselves in a mirror. They can make their own feelings and motivations known to each other and to their human carers and are able to imagine situations from other creatures' point of view. Chimpanzees seem to communicate with each other with a beep-like language, while gorillas can learn to understand spoken language and logical reasoning and have demonstrated a sense for past, present and future. Bonobos have made flint tools and can operate computers and telephones. Some primates even outperform intelligent humans on number recognition tests and computer games that require fast reflexes. These days no one needs to have any doubt that great apes possess complex emotional lives, so a child might well include them in their own species. Do apes believe in God? Do all humans? In other words, the borderline between people and non-people is not easy to draw on the basis of what they can do. Still, this theme has kept scientists busy for ages. Science-fiction books and movies are also illustrative. *Star Trek* is full of debates about the status of robots, humanoids and aliens. How to deal with these? Is it ethical for a human to throw an old but still operating super-intelligent robot away, if there is a better one? What if this robot says he loves you, weeps and promises always to be your slave? Personification has been and always will be a subject for ethics.

1.9   *Personification factors*

In the wake of William James (1890) most psychologists call the closest and most continuous stream of perceptions the *self-experience*. This experience forms the non-stop background to all else that is going on inside us. As soon as the brain is able to record data, the self-experience will be laid down in our neural connections. Habituated to it as we all become, we only notice our self-experience if there is something different happening to it, such as inner conflicts, emotional breakdowns or fundamental shifts in our personality.

Many scientists believe that in the course of human development this experience of self must precede the experience of others. The latter starts off when, after birth, we are dropped into the middle of the social world. For multiple births this is a little different. They have already met the other(s) before birth. But still their lives may start around a core of kinaesthetic self-awareness. As soon as we arrive in the world of others we are confronted with the fact that they provide a far more variable pattern of stimulation than we are to ourselves.[18]

In this text I will call the generalisation that is derived from this ongoing self-perception the 'self-concept' and more often 'self-personification'. This self-personification constitutes a dramatic example of unconscious cognition. We know who we are and we know that we know. We often know only vaguely what the content of our self-knowledge is. When someone asks us, 'Who are you?' it may take minutes before we finally become aware of a clear impulse that enables us to answer. Often people who are asked this question just stare silently in front of them, trying to grasp their inner signals.

The unconsciously functioning self-personification is very crucial in social life. It consists of a complex of images and feelings that tell the person who he or she is. It is their identity. You need to know who you are in order to play the appropriate roles in society. Your self-image helps you compare yourself with others. Your self-feeling lets you know what your position is in the group.

When people grow up, they collect more and more content for their self-personifications; they learn to know themselves ever better. But the acquisition of self-knowledge is not the only function of the self-personification; it is also the primary example for how to conceive of others. When we believe that others are similar to the kind of creatures we are, we may use our knowledge about ourselves to come to understand them.

That is how the self-personification becomes the template for all other sorts of personification: it is the prototype for all social constructions. In the terminology of Lakoff and Johnson we can call the self-personification 'the model' for other-personifications, group-personifications, spiritual-personifications and metaphoric-personifications. When we believe that others, groups, spirits or

---

[18] It is a sad fact that hypnotic age regression is just as unreliable a source of information as hidden memory testimony in forensic hypnosis. Otherwise we might be able to discover the antenatal and postnatal experiences and build our theories about early development on hypnotic facts.

objects are similar to us, in the sense that they house the same categories of subjective experience as we do, we are ready to construct them in the same way as we have previously done with ourselves. Thus we will project on others what we see in ourselves.

In the experience of the self, people tend to use a number of natural categories, which I will call 'the personification factors'. These categories are the building blocks of personifications. All techniques of therapeutic intervention in this book are based on influencing one or more personification factors. These factors are the key to the changing of personifications and to the changing of social systems in general. The following list of personification factors first names the factor, and than tells us what this factor means for the self.

Nine personification factors – and what they mean in self-personification

*   Location – my awareness that I am here and others are there.
*   Abilities – my awareness that I can do things, such as moving, talking, reasoning.
*   Drives and motivation – my awareness that I want something.
*   Feelings – my awareness of emotions, bodily sensations and pain.
*   Self-awareness – my knowledge of who I am among others.
*   Perspective – my awareness that I see things my way; my beliefs.
*   Spiritual connection – my awareness of my connection with the whole.
*   Perceivability – my awareness that I can be seen, heard and felt.
*   Name – I know what I am called.

Thus, when I create a personification of another person, I unconsciously assume that they have the same categories of awareness as I do. In addition to the above list of nine, I have an idea of what needs to be there in a personification in order to turn it into a representation of a human like me. This list will suffice for the purpose of therapy and working for change, but can, of course, be extended to include a great number of other factors that, to many scientists, are also typical for humans. For example, language, creativity, reason, logic, use of symbols, use of analogy, art, consciousness, use of tools, rituals, etc. It would be a pity if the discussion about what should or shouldn't be on this list were to occupy readers too much.

As social scientists we must assume that people create personifications with great ease and speed without even thinking about it. In general, we automatically assume all nine factors to be present in a single process but that does not mean that we will have content in every category – some may still be empty. For instance, we may have no clue about the other person's self-awareness but we still assume that this person does have some experience of self. In the same way, we may know that the other person must have his or her own perspective, but we may have no idea about what his/her view on reality is like.

But what happens when one or more of these factors fails in the concept of another person? What about when this person is thought of as having no name? No feelings? Or no abilities whatsoever? In such cases the person is seen as less than us; as strange, weird, ill, inferior or alien.

Consciousness comes into play only if something unusual is noticed; it is attracted to any rarity and an alarm bell will ring if one or more personification factors are missing.

What missing personification factors mean to our concept of another person:

Factors	What I believe about the other if this is missing
No location:	The other is non-existent, is nowhere.
No abilities:	The other is powerless and incapable.
No motivation:	The other has no will of her/his own.
No feelings:	The other is unfeeling or unemotional.
No self-concept:	*The other is socially incapable, plays inappropriate social roles.*
No perspective:	The other has no opinions.
No spirituality:	The other has no spiritual connection.
No perceivability:	The other is a ghost, spirit or god.
No name:	The other is anonymous.

Some violent sociopaths assert that they are unable to see other people as part of their own kind (Greenspan, 1997). Often they see themselves as very superior to their victims. Soldiers in wartime are often drilled to see the enemy as a lower kind of creature: as invertebrates or the excrement of invertebrates. When in a social concept one or more personification factors is omitted, we may call this 'de-personification'. The non-persons who have been created in this way will be located outside the social panorama (where they will meet wolves and Indians). In cases of ethnic conflict, we see that, when the feelings, motivations and perspectives of the members of the other group are ignored, it becomes much easier to be violent and abusive to them.

Children who are bullied at school often react by pretending not to feel hurt, by ignoring name-calling. Mol (1998) believes that this strengthens the idea in the minds of the bullies that their victim has no feelings and is weird in that way. Bullied children can be taught to react with their emotions to break this cycle of bullying.

Diener's (1980) experiments with objective self-awareness show that the quality and intensity of someone's self-image can be influenced by, for example, looking in a mirror. A look in the mirror prevented experimental subjects from aggressive behaviour towards others. This implies that knowing who you are may prevent you from forgetting who the others are, making impersonal attitudes unlikely. The social psychologist Zimbardo (1970) was fascinated by the way in which some people can treat others as identity-less numbers. He manipulated the perception of experimental group members by dressing them up with paper bags with peepholes on their heads. He discovered that maltreatment only happened if the victim was perceived as being non-unique and having no self-awareness.

In our reconstruction of the unconscious building blocks of social cognition, we may conclude that personifications do have a structure. The information content about the person is sorted out in a number of 'normal' categories that don't surprise us. As personifications are, however, very dynamic cognitive structures, adding or omitting personification factors is a normal unconscious faculty. Because of the fact that most social cognition stems from self-generated software (or, in other words, the person has made it all up by himself without the guidance of parents or teachers), it is logical that great varieties do occur. The more complex a level of social development we look at, the more diverse the individual repertoires will be.

1.10 Why the personification factor location comes first

Most developmental psychologists agree with Piaget (1965) that in the beginning the embryo must be completely self-oriented, without knowing the difference between itself and the rest of the world. But even in the womb a child touches on the first border and begins to develop self-experience. It will discover the fact that some aspects of its experience can be manipulated and felt from the inside, while other parts are seemingly out there and uncontrollable.

According to Lakoff and Johnson (1999) this process leads to the realisation that the self is 'here' and everything else is 'there'. The bodily experience in the womb will turn location into the foundation of thought in general. That is why Fauconnier (1997, 2002) stresses 'mental space' and Lawley and Tompkins (2000) 'mindspace'. But it was Julian Jaynes (1976) who pioneered the spatial dimension. He demonstrated its relevance with the aid of the concept 'cat':

> Where do you see it? In front of you? To one side or the other? Above or below eye level? What is your emotional response to this cat? Where are you experiencing the sensations of that feeling? If you have an inner dialogue about the value of owning a cat, where do the words appear to come from? Do they seem to be spoken from the inside or the outside of your head?

Coming to understand that I am in a different location from everything else that exists seems to be the most fundamental cognitive task. Lakoff and Johnson (1999) say this concept will be generalised into 'being is location'. Everything that exists has its own place in the universe and anything without a place does not exist at all. Everyone seems to learn this very early in life. Piaget's (1965) theory about 'object-permanence' points to the same phenomenon; when a child is aware of the fact that things continue to exist when they are out of sight, it will search for objects it has lost. Piaget also notes that, for that to happen, the object must be represented in the child's memory.

However, for social cognition to start, a child needs to grasp the concept of 'other people' too. 'I am here and the rest of the world is there' is probably learned long before a child understands that 'the others are there as part of the rest of the world'.

Some developmental psychologists (Greenspan, 1997) believe that children stay unaware of the difference between themselves and their mothers for several months. Embryos, in fact, share their location with their mothers. It is after birth that individuals are ready to discover their own unique position in the cosmos.

Schaffer (1996) has performed experiments that suggest that children learn to regard themselves as humans among other humans after the first few months of life. So, as well as learning the position of the self in regards to the others, the notion of belonging to a group of a similar kind is an even higher level of basic social knowledge. My findings show that most individuals finally represent this understanding in the shape of a sphere of personifications around the self located in its centre – their social panorama.

1.11   *Learning to personify*

Social cognition is learned in stages. One way to determine the developmental phase of a child is to look at the way it plays with a doll. For example, does your daughter use her doll to hammer on the ground while she bites its legs? If so, she probably has not yet personified the doll. If she begins to talk to the doll, giving it its own 'voice', then personification – Piaget (1965) calls this *animation* – has almost certainly taken place. I know a baby of 18 months who already does this.

Learning to create personifications is not an 'all in one go' process, but will be mastered step by step. It starts with slowly coming to the conclusion that others are similar beings to oneself. At the same time the personification factors will get clearer outlines. These categories are neither transferred genetically nor are they learned from other people. They will primarily be extracted from spontaneous individual discoveries. A person develops his own 'theory of mind' – as many scientists today call the unconscious knowledge about one's own and others' thinking. As Lakoff and Johnson see it, the personification factors are derived from bodily experience and other confrontations with the world. Maybe some additional parental reinforcement is useful in learning to discriminate and name them. Finally they will be generalised into basic concepts that live their lives under the surface of awareness. Research by Markus, Smith and Moreland (1985) shows a general tendency for people to apply to others the concepts they apply to themselves. The personification factors form the foundation of this social cognitive pattern.

For the personification factor 'feelings and emotions' to occur, the ongoing stream of kinaesthetic information that reaches the child's brain from its body must be noticed. Without ever having given it the slightest thought, a child may assume that every person has this inner experience too. Hunger, thirst, pain and comfort seem to have already existed in the womb; no wonder that a child, without any contemplation, will assume that this will be the case for everyone.

Baldwin (1987) believes that children develop the idea that others have feelings within their first year of life. According to Greenspan (1997) children will at first believe that their mothers feel identical emotions to their own, but to their surprise they find out that this is only occasionally the case. It is enchanting to imagine a child lying drowsily on its mother's lap, smelling her odour, feeling her warmth, sensing her breathing, feeling her movements and also sharing her emotional state. Then, after this sense of being unified, it suddenly feels discomfort and begins to cry, while its mother goes on reading a novel. Instantly this turns into a confrontation between mother and child in which a great divide in emotions, motivation and perspective may become apparent.

The reconstruction of the basic building blocks of unconscious social cognition takes us from the generalisation that 'we are the same but on another spot' to its very opposite. In a later phase of social development the child learns (if everything goes well) that 'everyone is different but shares the same planet'. This lesson comes naturally in the confrontation with others with different abilities, motives, emotions, self-concepts, perspectives, spiritual connections and names.

1.12 Learning who we are

Was George H. Mead (1934) right when he said that interaction with others is a necessary condition for the development of 'the self'? Indeed, does the confrontation with others create the stimulus for the self to bloom? Greenspan (1997) suggests that the affective quality of relationships with others (the parents) is crucial for the coming into being of a stable and positive self-concept. So is it true that at first you are nothing until the others make 'someone' out of you?

In doing this study I had to conclude that when everything works out the way it should, a child in the womb will form a strong kinaesthetic core of self. Later, and especially in puberty, complex knowledge about roles and positions will be organised into the 'self imagery'.

Working with clients who have problems with their self-concepts has shed light on the structure of the self-experience. Endless experimentation resulted in the point of view that a 'feeling of self' on the one hand must be distinguished from an 'image of self' on the other. In one's 'self-image' a person sees him or her self in the way they can see others, as if seen from the outside at some distance. It is a generalised picture showing how others may see us. But such a self-image is a fantasy by necessity because a person cannot see himself that way. Even a view in a mirror, photograph or video will not show our selves objectively. To create a self-image we must compose something new in our mind's eye. The question that will be central in Chapter 3 is: If the self-image is a fantasy, what fantasy works best for a person? This is an important question indeed, because a self-image makes it possible to compare oneself with others, and by so doing it enables us to value our abilities in relation to others: are we good, mediocre or hopeless in the things that we do? By orienting ourselves with the aid of a self-image, we can find our place in hierarchical structures. It dictates our position, status and social roles.

Chapter 3 is entirely devoted to the implications of the critical function of the self-concept within the social panorama model (as its core). There we will see how a therapist can influence these unconscious elements, how one can treat clients who complain about a lack of self-esteem, or who are confused about who they are or who fail to play their role in life.

1.13 *Acquiring higher social skills*

The deeper we dig into the structure of unconscious social cognition the greater the gap between the theoretical complexity we encounter and the great ease with which we practise these mental activities ourselves in our daily routines. What I mean by that will be clear to you if you follow me into a cinema. Someone watching a film creates countless personifications without raising an eyebrow. You see a man with a poker face on the screen for no more than two seconds. Even though he does nothing but stare, you say, "that is a serial killer looking for a victim." Modern cinema forces the spectator to assemble entire personifications out of a few frames of film and a word or two. Film directors often work their hardest to get their actors to do nothing at all. On the big screen and in close-up any sign of emotion seems to be too much and is called overacting.

Only if the actor shows no emotion will the audience be amused. When the actor does not show his feelings, it is the spectator who must supply them. The audience must guess what goes on inside the character, and that keeps boredom away.

Most people watch a film in a sort of trance, far less conscious of themselves than usual. This condition is ideal for identification. Without even noticing it, the audience creates new personifications into which, a minute later, they will step. The viewer becomes that character, and will be feeling the feelings they project on the image of the actor. An artfully shot and edited film will mobilise most of someone's social cognitive abilities.

On the Internet we see personification skills demonstrated in another way; people have chatting relations with individuals who are completely 'virtual'.

On the level of social cognition there is no difference between a relationship with a virtual lover and a real flesh and blood idol. However, an intelligent individual will ensure that a virtual lover

is sufficiently differently represented in his social panorama from the real thing (smaller, farther away and dimmer), to ensure that reality and fantasy do not mix. Are you that intelligent?

My friend Theo recently said. "I'm very close to my Mac." Most people are able to personify surprisingly well, and most people would also immediately understand what Theo means. For those who don't, try following the instructions below for personifying your computer, as I modelled them from Theo.

Technique 1: The personification of your computer[19]

Indication: If you feel lonely at work

1. Give your PC a name (Theo's secret name for his Mac is Maggie).
2. Visualise your computer somewhere in mental space. If you want a tight relationship, put her close to you; so close that no one else can come between the two of you (no partners, no children and no pets).
3. Think about all the things that your computer can do – unlimited possibilities.
4. Step into the shoes of your machine. Begin to imagine that for a moment you are her and think about what she wants, how she feels, what she thinks of herself, visualise her perspective on the world and notice to what spiritual entities she feels connected (she is connected to the world wide web).
5. Stay within your computer and also experience her social emotions. Enjoy some warm sensual feelings. That is what she feels for you!

In the literature on social intelligence, we often encounter the themes of assertiveness and empathy. Merlevede, Bridoux and Van Damme (2001) believe that both abilities are based on being able to notice very slight differences in one's own inner experience and to notice the signs of the same in others. Being able to recognise one's own emotions (Cameron-Bandler and Lebeau, 1986) and to define one's own position (Goleman, 1996) are both necessary in order to be assertive. To be empathetic, it is necessary to put oneself into the experiences of another and understand their feelings and perspectives. In other words, to be empathetic is to take the position of the other for a moment.

By studying the spatial aspects of the experience of empathy, it became apparent that we need to imaginatively 'step into another's shoes'.[20] To accomplish this one must pretend to be in

---

[19] This is included in the book as a means of clarifying the principle, but not as something seriously advised to the reader. However, it was based on historical fact. My friend Theo's love for computers overshadowed his social life.

[20] There appear to be cells in the brain, called 'mirror neurons', that facilitate the imitation of the behaviour of others.

the position of the other. The location in the social panorama where the other is projected marks the spot to move to. Our mind can easily travel through mental space and take any position. The identification with another individual means to move one's own centre of self to where one believes the other's self-feeling is located. The translocation does not need to last long. When somebody identifies, a small portion of their mind moves across and returns, before you know it, with the required emotional information. In psychodrama, Gestalt, and hypnotherapy, people are asked to shift from one seat to the other. This literal change of position is used to reinforce the identification process when the person cannot do it on their own. This also makes the discovered feelings more intense. Most people can do this without any assistance, incredibly quickly and purely within the world of imagination.

I assume that most socially intelligent people can make these mental moves, but they are generally only aware of the emotions that they unleash in this way. For example, my mother may say, "My neighbour is afraid that her in-laws are ashamed of her". When I ask my mother how she arrives at this insight she replies, "I just feel it". After 88 years of social training she can *just feel it*. To be able to stand successfully in the shoes of other people one must have full access to one's own archive of emotional experience.

Some researchers (Schaffer, 1996) suggest that a child who has experienced intensive physical contact with its parents is better able to move 'into another' later in life. Lack of physical contact is thought by many developmental psychologists to be the cause of an inability to empathise (Greenspan, 1997).

1.14 Limited social skills

Research seems to indicate that genetic factors are responsible for the fact that women are generally more socially able than men. Is that a result of the similarity and dissimilarity of the sex hormones in the womb? I wonder who will test this hypothesis in an experiment. Most of us will conclude from our own experience that social abilities are graduated, and that women do better than men. At the furthest male end of the spectrum we find people diagnosed with autism. Autistic people find insight into the thoughts and feelings of others extremely difficult (Baron-Cohen, 1991). Baron-Cohen, when looking at the dramatic (1% female and 99% male) gender difference in autism, points at 'the female superiority in folk psychology and the male superiority in folk physics'.[21]

The question is, are autistic problems unchangeable? Greenspan (1997) assumes that a child with biological problems only requires the right social training in order ensure successful social development. He is of the opinion that vital additional socio-emotional experience should be offered – gentle conversation, touching, stroking and cuddling – to support existing basis experiences. He has written about a number of cases where this approach has been successful.[22]

---

[21] At the opposite end, children affected by Williams' syndrome, a genetic disorder, are extremely good at socialising but poor at reasoned cognition. They appear to be predominantly female.

[22] A number of pedagogical experts are convinced of the genetic (and consequently incurable) nature of autism. They are so convinced that even when a child that was formerly diagnosed as being autistic loses this diagnosis, they would rather speak about a diagnostic failure than about a cure.

A logical question within the framework of this study is: can the slow social development of autistic children be related to short-comings in their self-personification? Do they fail to notice their own emotions, for example, or their own perspectives or feelings of self? If you cannot recognise drives in yourself, it's not so likely that you will easily recognise motivations in others. Lacking personification factors in the self-personification must result in systematic omission of these in other-personifications. If that is the case, then autistic children must first train themselves to differentiate and personify themselves in order to be able to learn to do so with others. There is some evidence that autistic children can improve their ability in this respect with sufficient support (Lamers, 2000; Mol, 1998). Furthermore, we currently see a differentiation in the diagnosis of autism and Asperger's syndrome. On the one hand there are autistic people who are mentally retarded, while on the other hand there are creative geniuses amongst them. Fitzgerald (2003) names Wittgenstein, Valera and Ramanujan as examples of the latter – great objectificators with little interest in personification.

1.15 Concluding remarks

The social panorama model is a tool for analysing and solving problems in social life. The model has the images of people, called personifications, as its elements. Change in a personification will be brought about on the level of its components, the 'personification factors'. Location is defined as the primary personification factor; a change in location will necessarily change the relationship involved. Quite often a therapist needs to change one of the other personification factors first in order to make a personification move in someone's social panorama. The personification theory, as discussed in this chapter, describes the basic elements which compose unconscious social cognition. This chapter also sheds some light on the implications of this theory for day-to-day social life and its use in therapy.

In a way this chapter has been rather philosophical. The ensuing chapters will be, in contrast, very practical indeed.

Chapter 2
The social panorama model

2.1   *Personifications in mental space*

When I conceived the central idea of this book, I considered names like 'socio-sphere', 'psycho-topography' and 'socio-geography'. In the end I preferred 'Social Panorama' – a 360° landscape full of social images.

In Chapter 1 I introduced the elements that compose this land-scape: the five types of personifications. I also explained that these elements derive their socio-emotional meaning from their location in mental space. This chapter is about the specific spatial patterns to which this leads and what these patterns imply for social life and how it may be improved by therapy.

Before I understood these patterns, I saw clients suffering from incomprehensibly complex symptoms and I didn't have a clue about what to look for or what to do about them. I was totally unaware of the social cognitive creations that were hiding right in front of my eyes and I never imagined what my survey of this landscape could mean for education, coaching and psychotherapy.

Recently I met a client called Frederique who suffered from a gen-eral phobia for life, a state of depression and an extreme lack of self-confidence. I immediately began to explore her mental space. With the aid of the social panorama model I found out that she had four personifications located within her body limits, her mother, her father, her abusive grandfather and her boyfriend. Over the last decade I have come to understand that this can cause the sort of severe symptoms that Frederique was suffering from. The best thing about the current state of the social panorama is that it gives clear directions for helping to solve such an enmeshment.

2.2   *The centre and the scale*

The size of the universe exceeds even the imagination of such extremely large-scale thinkers as, for instance, the physicist Stephen Hawking. He is an expert on the age and size of the uni-verse – it is an estimated 14 billion light-years across, plus or minus three billion light-years or so – but if we were to ask him for the dimensions of the mental space in which he represents humanity, he will probably be able to tell us far more exactly and, if we apply the right imagination techniques with him, he will also be able to pinpoint the exact location of every single personification. Given this technical condition, it is possible for practically anybody to give a precise description of his or her social panorama.

But even if we just ask a person, 'Where do you sense your Dad, your boss or your mum?' we will usually get useful answers, for example, 'Yes ... up here', 'In here', 'Over there' or 'About seven metres in front of me,' and all such answers will be supported by clear nods and gestures.

Several years of systematic questioning have taught me that many people are surrounded by hundreds of cubic metres of social representations, while a few exceptions have compressed the whole of mankind into the tight limits of their own bodies. In the course of my observations I have come to the conclusion, as yet untested, that the size of a person's social panorama is a basic personality trait that corresponds with their position in society. However, before we can test such an idea, we must first determine what constitutes the point of origin for the social panorama, the point from which to measure.

As in Frederique's case, many clients project other-personifications within the boundaries of their own body. This observation forces us to conclude that the core of the social panorama is smaller than the body. It also raises the question of whether there is a natural centre in people's social panoramas. Is it perhaps the spot they tend to point to when they talk about 'me'? Is it the same location from which they experience their relationships? Is there a spot that functions as the subjective middle of it all?

In order to answer this, I asked everyone round me for the location of his or her 'self'. From this research emerged the notion of the 'kinaesthetic self', which, in common language, is called the 'feeling of self' or the 'centre of self'. The kinaesthetic self is the area in the body that has the strongest association with the experience of 'me' and is most often to be found in the stomach or the chest. This spot is the point of origin. It is the nucleus of our social cocoon or, in astronomic terms, we may call it the sun in our social solar system. The planets in this configuration, however, are relatively stable, generalised social images, which, in contrast to the physical planets, are fixed in place – they do not spin, turn or cycle.

Once this was established, it was clear where the centre was as their social panorama now included a 'me'. We will elaborate on the implications of including the self in the social panorama in Chapter 3.

2.3   *Finding the location of a personification*

We are constantly thinking about people, and when we do, images and internal dialogues are accompanied by feelings which, in their turn, can give rise to new waves of social cognition. Our heads are like puppet theatres in which hundreds of personifications play their parts in endless variations.

The close involvement of memory in all social thinking brought social psychologists to the concept of 'person memory' (Fiske and Taylor 1991; Martin and Clarke, 1990; Ostrom, 1989). This concept suggests – probably without justification – the existence of a special portion of the brain that is occupied with social information.

The theory about 'person memory' confronts us with the ravine between academic research and therapeutic practice. Knowing that people remember one another is of very little help to therapists in their work because, except in geriatrics, amnesia is seldom the issue. The human inability to forget the personifications that are bothering them is what causes most problems. Once a puppet is in the theatre, you can't get it out. When a client is hampered by such an unforgettable personification, the first thing to do is find its location. Once you know where it is you can start to look for ways to remove it from that spot. Most interventions in this book are simply ways to move personifications to better places in the client's social panorama. Thus the primary diagnostic tool in social panorama-based therapy is finding the locations of the problematic personifications. That is why a recurring question in this book is, 'Where is this problematic personification located? Where do you see, hear or feel him or her?'

Finding out where a certain personification is located in someone's social panorama can be very simple. Without even being asked, the subject may spontaneously point to the spot while speaking about the personification, or it may be the direction of their gaze that signals the answer. But, as stated above, we can often get reliable information by simply asking, 'Think of John. Where do you see him in your mind?'[23] If you want to be sure, make use of Techniques 2 and 3.

Technique 2: Finding the location among all mankind

Indication: Spotting personifications

1. Determine for which personification (for instance John) you want to find the location.
2. Ask the subject to close his or her eyes.[24]
3. Ask them to imagine all the people in the world.
4. Ask them to imagine being among all the people in the world.
5. Ask them to think of the relevant personification (John) among all the others.
6. Ask the subject, before they open their eyes, to point to the location at which they sense that personification.

Technique 3: Using the context and the problematical feeling to find the location

Indication: Spotting personifications

1. Determine for which personification (for instance Judy) you want to find the location.
2. Ask the subject to close their eyes.
3. Ask them to notice the relevant social context of the relationship with the personification (Where is it that Judy bothers you? In the family, at work or in kindergarten?).
4. Ask them to call up the (problematical) feeling that belongs to the relationship with that personification.
5. Ask the person to focus on this (problematical) feeling.
6. Ask the person where they sense (see) the personification.
7. Ask the subject, before they open their eyes, to point to the location at which they sense that personification.

---

[23] For information on the disadvantages of this method see Chapter 6.

[24] You could use a short hypnotic induction here, or say, "Imagine you are in your most favourite place." From such an imagination into a favourite spot, the step towards the exploration of the social panorama is easily made: "Sit down. Think of all the people you know ..."

31

As a follow-up to both approaches it is useful for the researcher to walk to the indicated site and to ask the subject to guide their hands and fingers to the exact location of the personification; the precise distance, direction, eye level and direction of gaze. The best way to get really reliable data is for the researcher to move his or her hands intentionally off the mark so that the subject is provoked to correct, 'A little higher … No, no, that is too high!' At such moments people show their level of unconscious certainty. More often than not, social panorama sessions start off with clients who are entirely uncertain about what to see or feel, but before they know it, they are no longer in any doubt and can explain accurately, to the centimetre, where important personifications are located.

2.3.1 Explanation of Techniques 2 and 3

Technique 2. When you use 'all mankind', the subject should be stimulated to feel themselves among all the people of the world (associated) and prevented from observing this from a distance (dissociated).[25] Using the steps of Technique 2, the subjects are taken from the general domain of mankind to the concrete example of a single personification. This procedure enables the subject to 'zoom in' to the right level of abstraction, which is the level of 'relationship'. This is the critical level for most social panorama work. Relationships, however, have no physical existence – they are mental constructions in the shape of generalised concepts that are derived from concrete, day-to-day interactions. For example: Remembering a mental picture of your brother at the moment he married his now ex-wife is quite concrete; it is a mental photograph of an historical moment of interaction. You may also have a general sense of 'my brother as a human being' that is not tied to place and time. This latter can be said to be a broad generalisation about who your brother is. So if you want to work with your relationship with your brother, you need to find this generalisation. 'All the people in the world' helps you to tune in to the right level of abstraction.

---

[25] In terms of Bandler and Grinder (1979) it is a visual-kinaesthetically associated experience.

Technique 3 (using the context and the problematic feeling) is currently the most popular among therapists, though the client must be able to remember a clear example of the problematical social emotion – like for instance: the anger about Judy's behaviour, a particular jealousy or a particular feeling of love. Within most therapeutic contexts these feelings are easy to find.[26]

What happens when we apply Technique 3 is quite complicated. When we help the subject to access the problematic feeling (step 4), we can be sure that this feeling is associated with the relevant pictures. Current cognitive theories suggest that an image of a person will always be activated when we talk about him or her. This picture may, however, be below the threshold of consciousness and will not necessarily be in the location of the personification; in fact it can be any image of that person. When a person focuses on the problematic social emotion (step 5) they will need to access the relevant picture first. Once the feeling is boosted, it becomes easier to get conscious glimpses of the actual images that drive the feeling (Dilts and DeLozier, 2000; Bandler and Grinder, 1979). The location can be clearly spotted from an intensified 'problem feeling'.

2.4   *But it is not always that easy*

The use of Technique 3 can be confusing in that the problem feelings are 'mixed feelings' resulting from inner conflicts. Then one finds double representations, images inside the body limits, blurred or moving images.[27]

In other situations when a person has difficulties sensing the location, this can often be the result of one of two things. Either:

1.   the person didn't understand the questions, or
2.   the person tries too hard to open themself up to the unconscious information and that makes them fail to become aware of it.

---

[26] A frequent error is to ask, "Where do you **put** John?" leading the client to think about 'the active putting' rather than 'passive finding'.
[27] In such cases we must include the possibility of more locations.

Restating the question in different words may solve the first problem. Lowering the criteria will solve the second one, all the therapist needs to do is to say something like, 'Just loosen up a little', 'It's not that important', 'See what comes up', 'That's okay with me', 'Give your best guess' or 'That's good enough' while making sure that this is accompanied by relaxed non-verbal signals.

Quite often I made the mistake of thinking that a client had mis-understood my questions because he gave weird answers. Again and again it turned out that the client had understood me perfectly well and had given a very accurate answer but it was an answer that didn't fit my too-narrow expectations. These days I tend to take any answer seriously. I have come to believe that, in mental space, one can encounter personifications all over the place.

When you are looking for the locations of personifications with your clients, the exactness of unconscious social cognition will probably surprise you as much as it still surprises me. After hav-ing been surprised so many times, one has to assume several things. Firstly, that the unconscious social operating system gener-ates social panoramas for every relevant context. The question, *'Can you imagine being at work?'* helps to tap into the social panorama from that specific context. Secondly, besides assuming social panoramas to be recorded by 'context' we must assume that they are embedded in the life history of the subject. Social panora-mas develop and change throughout one's lifetime; not only does the social operating system create new up-dates, but it also seems to keep records of all earlier versions. Try this out for a moment: Remember your 5th birthday. Explore where you find the person-ification of your mother in between all mankind.[28]

It is not difficult for most subjects to imagine being younger and to remember their social panorama from that time. I must say that after 10 years I still find it hard to believe the accuracy and the amount of detail that subjects usually demonstrate. My conscious mind simply cannot grasp that the unconscious mind really does have such a rich and detailed knowledge.

The question, 'Where is your mother?' is sometimes answered by, 'Over there', 'Cooking in the kitchen', 'She's sitting beside me at the table' or 'She lives in Amsterdam and that is over there to the North'. This type of answer includes concrete historic descriptions in which the topography of countries, towns, houses, gardens and tables blur our view of the social panorama. The subject is not functioning on the abstract level of relationships but on the

---

[28] See 'shared location' in Chapter 6.

concrete one of interactions and historic or geographic situations. It is crucial for researchers or therapists to notice this.[29]

It may take considerable effort on the part of the therapist to dislodge a person from this concrete level, especially when they have learned in other types of therapy that the focus should lie on the reliving of concrete traumatic experiences.

Sometimes you need to explain the difference and ask for the 'general idea of mum'. On other occasions it helps to turn the subject 180° and ask them again, 'And where is your mother now?' When the personification involved has also turned, it may indicate that the location is on the level of relationships. In other words, the social panorama with all its personifications is turning as the person turns – if his Mother is at the front of it she will move so as to be still in front of his nose.

MIX!

In many cases, even though I had strong doubts about the level of abstraction, I decided to go on as if the location given was the right one. More often than not the client corrected himself a little later and everything was clarified. It is better for the therapeutic relationship never to disqualify anything the client says or does. Even when you are sure that the answer is wrong, accept it, praise the client and move on from there in the right direction.

Some general advice to any practitioner who wants to work with the social panorama: first to ask your clients to find the locations of unproblematic personifications. Once a person has found the location of their best friend it will be easy for them to find that of more troublesome people because they will already be tuned to the right level of abstraction.

In the introduction to this book, I asked you to find the location of a loved one. This is one of my favourite ways to introduce the social panorama to clients as well as to groups. A direct therapeutic application of this is to be found in the counselling of couples. Both partners, standing with eyes closed, are instructed to find each other's personification. When they have found the social panorama locations of their partner in the here and now they should try to do the same historically. For that they will need to remember the feeling of being in love, as they were at the start of their relationship. By comparing the changes and differences in locations, clients are often able to find out which spatial position will be the appropriate one for the future.

2.5   *Recognizing patterns in social panoramas*

The social panorama model came into being mainly through clinical data. The systematic exploration of a particular aspect (in this case the social aspect) of the subjective experience of a great number of therapy clients is a mixture of quantitative and qualitative research. This type of information gathering has been called 'population modelling'. Not all questions that arise about the spatial dimension in social cognition can, however, be answered in this way.

Lakoff and Johnson (1999) suggest that when human beings share a particular class of bodily experiences, they will create identical basic concepts out of these and thence construct similar metaphors to live by. From this view comes a challenging question: is the social panorama a common psychological phenomenon? Do, indeed, all humans represent social reality in a similar fashion?

As a social psychologist I wondered if I could design experiments to test whether social panoramas were universal, and also to find out how one could count and measure the similarities and differences within a population, so I geared a number of quantitative pilot studies to these questions. I have described them here in order to support the reader's understanding and as a starting point for colleagues who want to research the field of unconscious social cognition.

On May 23, 1993, I carried out the first experiment. My subjects were 24 therapy students, none of whom was familiar with the concept of social cognition and spatial representation. They were asked, as a group, to localise four kinds of people (disagreeable, kind, weak and strong) in the space around them and then to mark out the corresponding locations on a specially provided diagram. This diagram consisted of a schema in which the self was drawn centrally. The subjects could indicate with a letter in the area

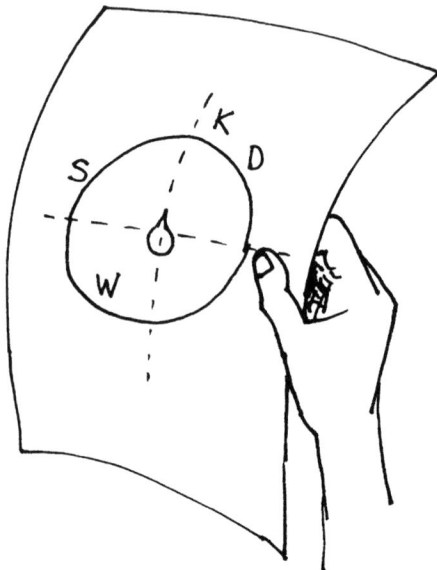

around the self where they experienced these different categories of people. To make it possible to show how far above or below eye level these four kinds of people were experienced, a wide circle around the self was drawn to mark the horizon.

Three out of 24 subjects found themselves unable to express this clearly enough in two dimensions. Twenty-one of them did succeed but they did have difficulty in differentiating between high and low and far off and close by.

The question put to them was, 'Where would you locate disagreeable, kind, strong, and weak people, left or right, far back or in front, high or low, far off or close by? Use the letters D, K, S, and W to mark the spot'. I allowed them plenty of time to think about it. I refused to answer any questions about what exactly was meant by, for instance, 'strong' – I wanted their responses to be determined only by their own interpretation of the words. The pattern of results for 'strong' people is shown in the illustration.

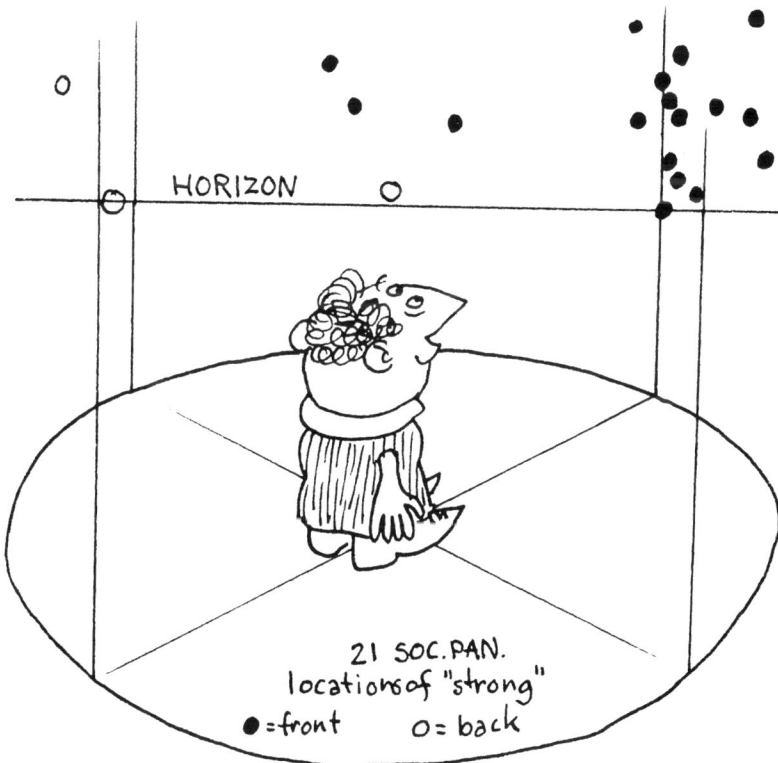

21 SOC.PAN.
locations of "strong"
● =front   O = back

Half the subjects placed disagreeable people in front, and the other half placed them at the back. The disagreeable people at the back were placed lower than those in front, and only two out of 11 were situated below the horizon. Everybody put kind people in front, with a two-thirds majority placing them on the right and fairly low.

Nineteen out of 21 put weak people below the horizon, of whom 16 located them on the left behind them (low). In contrast 11 of the 21 located strong people in the middle, high and in front.

In June of the same year I repeated this exercise with a group of 51 trainees who were likewise unfamiliar with the concepts. The question they were asked had been slightly adjusted and was formulated as, 'Which point in the space around you – left right, far back, up front, high, low, far off, close by – do you associate with disagreeable, kind, strong and weak people'. The results were similar to those of the first pilot study. Here, too, subjects encountered the difficulty of expressing a three-dimensional subject in a two-dimensional drawing.

On December 2, 1993, and March 11, 1994, I carried out two other experiments. On these occasions I made use of a paper ring on which subjects could write on the inside.

The subjects had to imagine themselves at the centre of this ring. A horizon was drawn in the middle on the inside and four directions were indicated, front, left, right and back. This paper ring made it much easier to indicate the correct direction. I asked them to estimate distance in so-called 'mental metres'. The subjects responded with a letter (K = kind) and a number (5 = five metres away). In both experiments this method produced much clearer data. The results were, however, quite similar in character to those of the earlier pilots.

2.6   General patterns

The above pilot studies and my other observations allow me to draw the following conclusions:

1.   The instruction to characterise people by their location is easily and intuitively understood. That, together with the spontaneous surfacing of spatial descriptions of relationships by clients in therapy and people at large, supports the hypothesis of a general tendency to encode the social world in mental space.

2.   The similarities between individuals suggest the existence of universal patterns in how the social world is represented. These patterns have in common that they appear to be 'very obvious' to most people. They seem to result directly from the way social reality presents itself to all of us and how repeated and prolonged exposure causes us to generalise about it from early childhood.[30]

Beside universal patterns that apply exclusively to the social domain there are several others of a more basic nature that do apply to the physical domain: to the world of things. We could call them 'the universal patterns of objectification'. We already briefly discussed objectification (Ötsch, 2001) in Chapter 1. There, personification was introduced as a special case of objectification: People are things of a special kind. 'Objectification' is the name given to the mental representation of objects. And in Chapter 1 we

---

[30] See Greenspan (1997) on developmental psychology.

discussed the objectification factors: What properties need to be there to make some concept the representation of a thing? We stated that in order to be considered as a thing, a concept should include a location (it must be thought of as being somewhere in the cosmos) it needs to be seen as having volume, a surface, weight, size and colours. If this is the case, the concept will also conform to a set of other rules which are based on these. These rules we call the universal patterns of objectification. To name some of these universal patterns:

- The size of an objectification depends on distance and height.
- Big objectifications draw more attention than small ones.
- The more centrally an objectification is represented, the more important it is.
- The closer the objectification is represented, the more impact it will have.
- An objectification in the foreground receives more attention.
- Objectifications tend to be represented as resting on the ground.
- A part of an object represents the whole thing.

These common patterns are strongly related to Richard Bandler's (1985) description of 'submodalities', to the 'Gestalt laws' from Gestalt psychology, and to the laws of eidetic imagery of Akhter Ahsen (1968, 1972). All these suggest that there is evidence to formulate a set of rules to which all cognitive content conforms.

In this study we make a start by describing an additional set of patterns that only applies to personifications. The discovered commonalities in the way in which you experience people in your mind are:

Distance
- People whom you love and care for are experienced as close to you.
- You can sense the body temperature of people who are close to you.

The centre of attention
- Important people draw your attention and will be put in the centre.

Size
- Big strong people can force you into a powerless position.
- Big strong people can protect you.
- Big strong people can take things away from you.

Staring eyes and orientation
- People who want something from you will look at you.
- People who support you often stand behind you.
- People with a similar goal stand beside you.

These experiences are shared by most individuals and lead to a common system in the way people represent personifications in their social panoramas. Also the opposite of these patterns are generally true, for instance: People you don't love and care for are envisioned further away. In other words, distance, size and orientation each have a great social meaning in all of us.

2.7 *Changing basic social panoramic dimensions*

Satisfying one's own curiosity or getting better contact with other people are very good reasons for studying social panoramas, but management advisors, coaches and psychotherapists may have many other reasons for doing so. Amongst those is the fact that some clients have very limiting attitudes to mankind at large. For instance, a client may feel totally isolated or alienated from all mankind or deserted by it. Some may constantly feel powerless and dependent, inferior to everyone. Others may be the complete opposite: they will behave arrogantly and consider themselves to be superior to everyone.

An investigation of such clients' social panoramas may show exactly how they create this type of troublesome general attitude. Their distance to the bulk of mankind or the elevation of all people in relation to their own height can easily be related to their attitude. Logically such insight will lead to ideas about how things can be improved.

In this section I will briefly describe how the basic dimensions of a person's social panorama can be altered. These techniques are

quite simple and build directly on what has already been discussed, but what kind of techniques are we talking about?

Richard Bandler (1985) developed a method of changing the qualities of any kind of subjective experience (he called it sub-modal-
ity work). For that he made use of direct suggestion (Andreas and
Andreas, 1989). For instance, when colours are needed in a certain
image, the therapist may just suggest to the client, 'Now, why not
add some more colour to that picture'. Or when the distance must
be reduced, 'Bring it closer'. The success of such direct suggestions
does depend on the client's ability to follow them, but, as the work
of tens of thousands of therapists all over the globe has demonstrated, the human ability to change these sensory qualities seems
to be almost unlimited.

We must assume that people automatically change the sensory
qualities of their mental images whenever a change in meaning
occurs to them. This implies that humans are constantly making
things bigger, more colourful, brighter, etc. Obviously, this also
includes their social imagery: they draw personifications closer,
shift them to the sides or change their height whenever relationships change. However widespread and profound the human
potential for changing the sensory qualities in their own subjective
experience is, this potential frequently fails to work and people
need assistance. There are two reasons for this:

a. People take their mental images for granted and cannot easily
   control them consciously. Therefore they often need somebody
   else to suggest the changes.

b. The other reason why people cannot easily change their own
   mental imagery has to do with inner coherence. We may state
   that as every aspect of a person's mental software is involved
   in the way they see things the way they do, everything a person believes, wants, values or fears plays a role in the shapes
   their mental images take. Cognitive content is systemically
   interconnected in such a way that a change in one part may
   alert other parts which then object to that change. The forms
   and shapes mental images have taken in the course of a person's development are the result of a kind of 'consent'
   between all subsystems of a person's mental software; any

change in sensory quality (colour, distance and size, etc.) will give an image another meaning and there may be personality parts that will resist a change because they object to this new meaning. Changes in the sensory qualities of a certain image may cause instant conflicts with other personality parts that will try to 'undo' the change if they can.

When such inner resistance occurs, a client will notice that a particular shift in sensory qualities does not last. For instance, a personification that was put closer will immediately shift back as if it were on an elastic cord. This tells the practitioner that some opposing part has its hands on the controls.

Bandler and Grinder (1979) introduced the word 'ecology' in this context. An 'ecological' change works instantly and lasts a long time because it does not cause any new problems or inner conflicts. With social panorama interventions our object is to achieve such ecological change.

As we have said before, consciousness functions as the mind's monitor. It is also the place where problems and inner conflicts make themselves known. If a change does not completely suit all parts of a person, chances are that they will become aware of this in some way. It may be no more than a dim awareness and that is why the therapist or coach often needs to amplify it. For this the therapist will ask, 'Do you notice any objections from within?'

When I asked Paula for her social panorama, she said that she saw all the people of the world at some distance in front of her. She saw mankind at large slowly parading from left to right. She felt like an outsider, a bystander who was not taking part in life. Her husband, however, was right in the middle and Paula immediately explained, 'I think it all looks like this because my husband has a job, and I don't. He is in the middle of life.'

The logical direct suggestion was, 'Paula, now step into the parade and join it!' Paula's face puckered as she tried her best, but she clearly encountered a lot of resistance in herself. She said that she could not change this view until she had a job herself. However hard she tried to step into the crowd she could only do so for a few seconds, which proved that this was not an ecological option for her. She explained to me, 'The part of me that prevents this change wants to force me to look for a job and not be a bystander. I can only take part in life when I take real action. You know, I lost confidence and that has made me passive.'

Technique 4: Changing general social attitudes

Indication: To demonstrate to individuals or groups how one creates one's place in the social world

Sit in a relaxed manner and think for a while about all mankind, all the people in the world. Do this in your own way.

If you are observing all mankind from a distance (dissociated), make sure you now step into that image. Experience yourself as part of mankind and feel yourself surrounded by all the other people. Observe what you see and feel while you try the next set of changes one by one.

1. Have all people of the world come five steps **closer** to you. Examine the emotional effect this has on you, and then put everyone back to where they came from.

2. Move all people of the world 30 centimetres **upwards.** Again, notice the effect. Put them back where they belong.

3. Move all people of the world 10 metres **farther away** from you. Notice how this feels, then change it back.

4. Make all the people in the world 50 centimetres **lower** than you. What does this do to you? Put them back where they were.

5. Make all the people in the world turn (look) away from you.

Take a minute to draw your own conclusions.

This, Technique 4, may have convinced you that attitudes to humanity at large are mainly a direct function of the horizontal and vertical dimensions of the social panorama. If you feel alienated, insignificant, inferior or superior, this necessarily results from the dimensions of your social panorama.

Another conclusion might be that all sensory qualities responsible for general social attitudes can be changed. For instance, when a person experiences a cold area in the social world it is worthwhile telling them to make it warmer, or, when it is too dark, to make it lighter.

I hope that all of you who experimented with Technique 4 also noticed some form of inner resistance.

2.8 Deeper into the social panorama patterns

Pattern recognition is said to be the core activity in modelling (Bostic St. Clair and Grinder, 2001). A pattern can be defined as a recurring similarity within a class of phenomena. Here, a pattern is a clearly reappearing trend in how a number (at least three) of subjects described aspects of social representation.

Recognising these patterns is, in a way, like the discovery of air; it is seeing beyond what is obvious and examining something that is often entirely habitual. These patterns show a world of experience that was up to now hidden within our collective unconscious knowledge.

INTENSITY AND ABSENCE

Personifications surround people like a translucent veil or a cloud of mist. The amount of social stimuli strongly influences the density of this sphere of social images. At a party, gathering or other social event the awareness of others surrounds you like a thick blanket. When a person is on their own this thin veil gets denser by directing attention to their social life. A personification can remain in the background, vague and fragmentary, even when it is given full attention, or it can become so clear that it obscures the perception of the outside world. In psychiatry and hypnosis this phenomenon is known as 'positive hallucination'. Skilful hypnotic suggestion may help a subject to get fully absorbed in the voices, images and wishes of personifications. Such trance phenomena are common in social panorama therapy and no specific trance induction is needed. Quite often the client is so occupied with their internal world of personifications that the therapist sitting next to them may be totally forgotten.

When two people are engaged in normal conversation, the awareness they have of each other's inner image is not always clear. This is why people are often mistaken when they think that they are responding fully to the physical person. Although the perception of the real flesh-and-blood person may occupy consciousness, it is the mental representation shimmering in the background that governs social behaviour. *Representation dominates interaction.*

Most people start to think about people as soon as they wake up. As long as they are awake their social panoramas seem never to be switched off. It would be of great interest to apply the so-called 'thought sample method', in which subjects report what they think every five minutes (Klinger, 1978) to social cognition to test to what extent this constant social activity is universal.

Clinical data suggest that some personifications remain active all the time. For instance, many clients have father-personifications in front of them all the time, criticising and looking angrily down on them from above, which makes them uncertain in all corners of life. The images of children and lovers, dead or alive, in or outside the body limits, may also be of constant influence. People can become sick and tired of such permanent personifications – some clients seek real solitude and become complete hermits in order to get away from people whom they will actually never escape because they exist only in their minds.

There are stories of mountaineers who went alone to the farthest, highest and loneliest spots, only to find themselves still engaged in dialogues with individuals who were tens of thousands of miles away. At high altitudes some lonely climbers start hallucinating companions. In contrast, we hear reports from individual desert travellers or sailors who single-handedly cross oceans, who have experienced what the French foreign legionnaires call 'the shower of loneliness'. Sheer lack of stimulation seems to cause them to lose all activity in their social panoramas.[31] The experience of

---

[31] As happens to the main character Teusje in Derks' (1999) mini novel about the social panorama with the Dutch title *Spoken in de kop* ('Ghosts in the Head').

loneliness that arises from this may cause fits of panic or it can result in an unforgettable spiritual experience (see also Chapter 7). Native Americans practise 'vision quests', which involve staying alone in the wild for several days. People who deliberately seek solitude are often searching for reconnection with 'nature', 'the real world' or 'physical reality' or, in the terminology of Chapter 1, with the non-social domain.

HARD-TO-FIND PERSONIFICATIONS
There can be several reasons for the inability to answer the question, 'Where do you see John?' The most common is the unconscious nature of social cognition. We also encounter unconsciousness in relation to certain personifications but not others. Personifications can be repressed, suppressed or blocked out. As early as 1892, Freud wrote about 'counter volition' that later became known as 'repression'. Thanks to Singer (1990) these phenomena have received their rightful place within cognitive psychology.

If 'my disagreeable foster parent' cannot be localised, we should be aware that this personification may be repressed. This problem can often be solved with variations of Technique 6.

BI-LOCATION
A common pattern in social representation is the so-called bi-location, which means that the same person is being represented in two spots in the social panorama. Such a double representation makes it difficult for the subject to decide 'where' a personification is located. Confusion and a delay in response are the primary signals to note. Whenever the subject hesitates the researcher can offer the possibility that there may be more than one location for that personification.

Bi-locations result from inner conflicts. The client has doubts about the true nature or appropriate social role of the person in question. Most role conflicts become clearly visible when one explores the social panorama.

AGE AND TIME

As previously stated, every stage of a person's development will have its own social panorama. By means of hypnotic age regression one can enable a person to explore even very early versions. Since deeply rooted social behaviour stems from how the social world was mapped out in early childhood we will, in Chapter 6, apply this tool for changing it.[32]

The practitioner who makes use of the social panorama technology will wisely always to take age into account. For instance, when we talk about the location of a personification we need to know to what age the client is regressed. This regression may come naturally without any special instruction. When the client talks about an event from childhood and we ask for the location of a personification within that frame, we will probably get an historic answer. When the client is reliving a past experience the social panorama from that age will automatically become reactivated.

ASSOCIATION/DISSOCIATION

In general, a person can think of his social panorama in two distinct ways. He can either imagine himself to be in the middle of it, or see himself in it from a distance. This is the classic (Bandler and Grinder, 1979) distinction between visual-kinaesthetic association and visual-kinaesthetic dissociation. These terms define the difference between thinking about something in the role of observer or thinking about it in the role of protagonist and actually experiencing the associated feelings.

Being the observer enables the person to avoid experiencing the unpleasant feelings. Being 'in the act', on the other hand, gives an opportunity to experience emotions and feelings fully. '*I can see myself* in the middle of all the people...' expresses an observer's position. In this mode of thinking social emotions will be reduced to evaluations.

Observing one's social panorama from the outside means distancing oneself from humanity in the same way, in which people can

---

[32] See on NLP and Psycho diagnoses (DSM-V) Derks and Hollander 1996, Chapter 24.

distance themselves from groups such as their family, their team or their nation. If they do that continuously they will feel that they do not belong to that group, 'I am an outsider.' In this chapter we will also look at the dissociation of the kinaesthetic self, which results in an experience of a lost sense of self.

DISTANCE

Distance is crucial to the experience of both objectification and personification. We may ask a subject, 'When you feel yourself to be surrounded by all mankind, where do you sense the nearest others? And who is closest to you?'

The social panoramas of some people begin far away. I say 'far away' when the closest personification is at a distance of more than three mental meters, measured from the kinaesthetic self. For many people with such social panoramas, 'loneliness' will be the keyword. Other people see the nearest representations of people quite close, on the skin or partly or completely inside their body. Their complaints will often be dependence, identity problems and fear of being manipulated. Many of these clients' problems will be solved as soon as everything is moved outside of or farther away from their body. Personifications that are inside the body are difficult to observe and control. The traditional term for this condition is 'possession'. More often than not these personifications are predominantly kinaesthetic in nature, but may become visible and controllable when moved outside.

The question, *'who is closest to you?'* proves to be of great diagnostic value in therapy. Imagine what it means if the closest personification is a rapist, a murderer, a dead ancestor or a secret lover?

It is a general principle that the intensity of a social emotion increases as the personification responsible for it comes closer. It is a common mental skill to be able to feel, by means of kinaesthetic imagery, another person's presence even when they are nowhere near. 'Even when you are miles away, I still can feel you near me' is a cliché in many love songs and most people have no trouble understanding that. Kinaesthetic imagery often accompanies visual representations of these people, but not necessarily. The converse of 'I can feel you but I can't see you' can also be true,

'Even when we kiss, I can't feel you' (Sing along: Far away, you're so far away!).

An individual's personal 'scale of proximity' (Hall, 1966) has, without doubt, a tremendous influence. Some people represent the whole social world in a box, while others need a cathedral to depict even their most intimate circle.

The trend in someone's use of distance governs general social feelings like social pressure and loneliness. How can a person feel isolated when they see and feel everyone they know very close to them? They can't. No one can! The 'technique' for feeling lonely demands that other people be represented so far away that nothing of their presence – no warmth – is felt. In the same way we may find that crowd phobia is caused by the others being felt and seen so close that no room whatsoever is left – so close that the crowd pushes directly on the skin and prevents one from breathing.

FRONT–BACK

We may encounter people who have personifications only at the front. This seems to be associated with great interest in the behaviour of others and, sometimes, with mistrust: 'I don't want them behind me, because there might well be vampires among them,' one lady told me. Other individuals thrive with many people at the back, maybe because they feel themselves to be socially supported, 'backed' by colleagues, family or friends.

UP FRONT

Straight in front, at 'twelve o'clock', is always an important spot. Who is there? In Chapter 3 and 8 we will see that this location is the place where the self-image is normally positioned; any other-personification on this spot can blur a clear view of what you are.

Personifications that are straight in front tend to be loved ones when they are within the intimate circle (within arm's length) and competitors when they are further away. Also we find people who symbolize the things they do not want to be right in front, often several metres away and a little above themselves. This kind of personification leads up to counter-identification (see Chapter 8) with all its dramatic symptoms.

VERTICAL

Personifications that are above eye level tend to be of great influence. Eye level offers a stable point of reference for measuring the elevation of personifications, 'Is this person below or above your own eye level? Do you have to look up or down?' In the far distance we can use the horizon for the same purpose. Any personification whose eyes are seen above the horizon is experienced as being taller than the subject is. The vertical dimension is very critical; a few centimetres higher or lower can make a great deal of difference. Status, social power, authority and dominance are all connected to the vertical dimension. This will be explored in Chapter 4.

Besides status, the distinction between living and dead personifications can be coded in the vertical dimension – heaven and earth. This will be the subject of Chapter 7.

Not only do we measure the level of single personifications, we may also look at the general level of the eyes of mankind at large. A social panorama in which mankind is seen very low means something completely different from a panorama in which it is placed above the self. The latter appears to be a clear indicator of low self-esteem; we could even say that self-esteem is defined by the general trend in the vertical dimension.

HORIZONTAL

The left-right dimension is often used for differentiating between good and bad or nice and nasty personifications – with the left being often regarded as negative. But there is far less universality to be noted on the horizontal level. Compare your intuitive understanding of the following sentences: (1) 'John is close to me' (2) 'John stands above me' and (3) 'John is on my left'. The relational meaning of expressions one and two seem quite clear, but the third sentence is open to debate. Not for everyone however. On the island of Bali, for instance, most people would find the third statement as clear as the first two. In Balinese Hinduism, evil is on the left and good on the right.

The closest left and right positions are often reserved for loved ones. Many spouses are represented within hand's reach and on one side or the other. Some therapists (Hellinger, 1995) assert that a typical gender difference exists, the female on the right-hand side of the male and vice versa. In the same manner, the location of the parents is believed to be bound to particular sides; father on the left, mother on the right. I tend to be very wary about these generalisations; I have seen too many contradictory examples.

DARKNESS AND LIGHT

The left-right coding of good and evil often comes with dark-light coding too. Darker and lighter personifications signify evaluative categories. A group that is disliked may be dark, while a group that is admired will often look bright.

In Chapter 5 we will deal with social attitudes and in-group/out-group phenomena such as racism. Colour is often combined with size, distance and temperature.

A light and radiant self-image indicates a positive attitude to the self. In Chapter 3 we use this fact when we want to improve some-one's self-confidence.

TEMPERATURE

Positive and negative social attitudes are often characterised by means of temperature and many subjects can distinguish warm and cold areas when asked to do so. Repressed personifications tend to have a cold aura around them. We will encounter the chill-iness of evil spirits and ghosts in Chapter 7, which deals with the spiritual dimension of the social panorama model.

MOVEMENT

Real people walk around, stand still, turn, gesture, breathe, sit down, wink, turn their heads, nod, blink, disappear and return. When humans are completely still they are either in a coma or dead. Human movement must be a major element of our basic experience, but to fix a personification in a certain location in the social panorama is an artificial cognitive step that seems to be necessary in order to create a serviceable map of social reality. It reduces the complexity of the social world to a level that we can handle easily. However, some personifications are represented as being in motion: they keep on moving in a certain manner while staying in one place – like athletes on a treadmill or cycle machine.

Moving personifications are expressions of changing relationships. They may show a tendency to approach or recede. The movement can also be kinaesthetic, as when people feel variations in attraction or repulsion. Quite remarkable are heads that turn to indicate different directions of attention. Some personifications move around in the social panorama by going back and forth on the same trajectory; others can travel anywhere.

ORIENTATION

A personification will be looking in a certain direction. Some personifications can look in several directions or alternate between directions. How personifications are oriented in relation to one another is also significant: who is paying attention to whom? Everyday language has many words for orientation: closeness, confrontation, backing up, supporting, turning their backs on each other, looking up or down on each other. In Chapter 6, where we deal with families, orientation will be a very important variable.

CLUSTERING OF PERSONIFICATIONS

A cluster of personifications in the social panorama will often be generalised into a single group-personification: 'my parents', 'the leadership' or 'the defenders'. When a person talks about a group, it will be the result of a generalisation of many individuals as if there were only one. Personifications that are close to one another often operate as one single unit; when the group members have the same orientation they will form a social force within the social panorama.

2.9 *The social panorama and communication*

Sceptical colleagues have repeatedly brought the next criticism to the fore. It is inspired by Heisenberg's idea about the influence of the perceiver on the object that is perceived. 'Does the therapist not himself actively create a social landscape in the mind of his patient when he asks for the sites of personifications? Do those requests not operate as implicit suggestions?'[33] In other words, is it the researcher who creates the object of research by speaking about it? If this were true, the locations found that way and even the whole concept of the social panorama would be an artefact.

SUGGESTION
The criticism mentioned above is in opposition to the idea that it is the therapist who brings something into awareness which already exists beneath the surface of consciousness. Though I strongly adhere to the latter vision I still want to discuss the influence of implicit suggestion on social life.

Both practitioners and scientists may have a strong desire to understand how people influence one another's social attitudes. How does one child turn another into the black sheep of the class? How do politicians create opinions about the opposition in their followers? How do parents transfer preconceptions to their offspring? How do you learn to love somebody by just hearing others talk about him?

It becomes apparent from observation of the interactions within groups and families that social opinions are transferred fast and subtly. People will seldom use clear, straightforward messages; you are unlikely to hear, for instance, 'Now I want you to start regarding your mother as stupid and seeing me as magnificent.' Implicit suggestion is far better understood these days – thanks to Erickson (1967, 1983) and Grove (1998) – we now know that it must play a major part in social life because the exchange of relational messages seems primarily a matter of unconscious non-verbal channels.

---

[33] Unintentional suggestions by therapists are the reason why Grove and Panser (1989) focus on what they call 'clean language'.

2.9.1   *The channels of social communication*

Only with the help of our insight in the spatial nature of social representation was it possible to analyse what goes on when one person influences another's map of the social world. By reducing social representation to the level of the locations of personifications it became apparent that a change in opinion must coincide with a change in location. The question was; how do people influence these locations?

For day-to-day work with the social panorama it appeared to be sufficient to distinguish four types of social communication channels:

1. *The naming of relationships.* In this channel relationships are typified by the words provided by normal language. For instance: 'You are my brother.' 'This is my wife.' 'You are my reader.' Most people have enough universal and cultural knowledge about where in their social panorama brothers, wives or readers must be represented to be able to place them. This channel does not need any further explanation.

2. *Talking about locations.* In this channel relationships are characterised by speaking of them in terms of spatial positions. For instance: 'He is standing beside me.' 'You are going in the opposite direction.' 'She was looking down on me.' This channel will be explored in the next section.

3. *Showing locations.* This is a non-verbal channel in which gestures, nods and gazes point to locations in mental space. For instance, I may look up when I talk about my boss or focus close by when I speak of my child. In this chapter we will help the reader to develop more sensitivity to expressions within this channel. Hands often paint social panoramas in the air around them.

4. *Metaphors about relationships.* For instance: 'We are on the same train.' 'He is trying to put me out in the cold.' 'She is fishing for my attention.' The use of metaphor in social life plays a role throughout this text. The images raised by a metaphor necessarily contain spatial positions that will automatically, on

the basis of analogy, influence the spatial representations in the person's social panorama. To take the first example, the train moves in one direction and is relatively narrow, which will bring the personification of the person to whom the metaphor applies closer and oriented in the same direction.[34]

The great human ability to think about relationships is paralleled by our ability to communicate about them. Social communication has its unconscious nature in common with social cognition – even the effect of communication within these four channels can escape our attention. It may work like this: Your neighbour is gossiping to you about another neighbour. She called that other neighbour a stupid worm and while she was speaking she stared at the ground. Without your being aware of it for even a second you moved both neighbours downwards and further away.

2.9.2   *Invisible communication creates magic*

The four channels of social communication provide you with some answers to the question, how is social influence possible? But is that good enough for you? Our scientific minds crave clear and well-defined explanations, models and theories, but can you be satisfied by an explanation based on communication that is too fast and subtle to be noticed?

When we change social images in therapy we often encounter very strong and strange effects. For instance, a man hated his brother. When he changed the image of his brother into something neutral, his real flesh and blood brother suddenly responded with unheard of friendliness. How was that possible? Was it magic? Was it telepathy, did the brother pick up the other brother's brain waves? Did they meet or call each other and did the brother unconsciously and non-verbally receive the messages that were, also unconsciously and non-verbally, transmitted to him by his brother? No, all that happened was that their mother mentioned the one to the other on the phone.

---

[34] An up-to-date and in-depth study of the use of metaphors can be found in Lawley and Tompkins (2000) and Derks and Hollander (1996).

An issue that recurs throughout this book is that because of the unconscious nature of social cognition and social communication we are often faced with incomprehensible phenomena. Much more seems to happen between people than our conscious mind can keep track of. More importantly, it exceeds the scope of our scientific imagination so our rational thinking cannot believe what our unconscious mind is capable of.

Most magical thinking arises from this rational inability to understand and believe what your own or another's minds (and bodies) are capable of. When irritated by the lack of sufficiently simple explanations, your reason starts to create new concepts out of thin air. In general humans will search for all kinds of external causes when they cannot grasp their own abilities. We invent causes such as energy fields, systems, collective knowledge, goblins, systemic forces, spirits, gods, telepathy, mystic channels, chocolate power, morphogenetic fields or whatever....

If we cannot believe that a psychic surgeon can cunningly manipulate chicken blood and tissue in front of an audience to suggest that he removes a tumour, then we must believe in magic. If we cannot believe that it is possible for a magician to do things too fast to be noticed, then his magic must be real. If we cannot believe in the social virtuosity of the human unconscious, then we social scientists have a problem.

We will return to this discussion in Chapters 6 and 7.

2.9.3 *Talking about locations*

When talking about relationships, people use words like high, low, behind, close and far, all of which describe relative locations. Temperature, brightness and colour often play second fiddle. One could say that the widespread use of spatial vocabulary is linguistic proof of the existence of the social panorama. Such a proof, however, only proves something to scientists such as cognitive linguists, who believe that such expressions represent the actual subjective experience of the speaker.

For therapeutic practice this latter view offers great possibilities. It implies that a therapist only needs to register how a client describes the spatial constellations in their problem state for the diagnosis to be made. The next activity is to intervene with similar spatial expressions which, when taken on by the client, will offer them more choice in their social life.

It is not a common practice among psychologists to regard verbal expressions as literal descriptions of subjective experience. Most of my colleagues tend either to fail to notice these expressions or to believe them to be of a more indirect, metaphoric nature. The different points of view that result from that can be clarified by the following example.

When a person says, 'John is against me', this may mean two different things, depending on the theoretical frame of the psychologist:

a. the speaker applies a saying that is commonly used within his language community as a standard metaphor, or

b.   the speaker expresses what he sees, hears and feels subjectively in words that fit his inner experience.

In the first theoretical viewpoint (a) it would make sense for a therapist to respond with, 'How do you know that John does not agree with you?' (Bandler and Grinder, 1975a). When one adheres to the other opinion (b), it is completely logical for the therapist to say: 'Then put John to one side' (Bandler, 1985, Derks, 1996).

The difference between these views occupied me greatly at the beginning of my social panorama research project (Derks, 1996, 1998a) because I thought that only viewpoint (a) supported the social panorama theory. Before I explain what changed my mind, I want you to experiment with spatial language yourself. To that end I have provided a number of sentences that will help you to sharpen your ears for spatial expressions.

The following examples make it clear that many spatial expressions do have both properties (a) and (b):

'He is at the top of his field.'
'The left and right wings have come closer to each other.'
'She is against us.'
'The upper classes have been torn down.'
'He puts himself on the same level as the staff.'
'It is lonely at the top.'
'We were driven apart.'
'The world is at your feet.'
'They lowered themselves considerably.'
'The children came between us.'
'They were in the way.'
'I have put my husband and my children first in my life.'
'The workers are behind us.'
'People felt closer to one another in those days.'
'He is racing up through the department like a comet.'
'I need your support.'
'Don't confront me.'
'He isolates himself.'
'Which side are you on?'
'I have put my German heritage behind me.'
'People are always after me for something.'
'I need a lot of space.'

These are all sayings that have been learned and are well under-stood within a language community. They can also describe actual subjective experience. Thanks to people like Lakoff and Johnson (1980, 1999) we can see that shared bodily experience leads to the existence of standard metaphorical expressions. However, when these expressions are applied they are still connected to the abstracted bodily source experience.

2.9.4 *Showing locations*

The words, 'my mother, you know… and this guy…' came slowly from Jimmy's lips but I knew exactly what he meant because, when he pronounced the words 'my mother', he looked down at his left hand, which was flat on his lap and moving slightly. Then, precisely at the moment he used the words 'and this guy' he held his right hand as a kind of umbrella in the air, just above the level of his eyes. For half a second he shook this hand powerfully. In this way he expressed his father's domination over his mother and the whole family.

Jimmy is Showing Locations

By using his hands Jimmy was *showing locations*; he made visible how his mother and his father were located inside his social panorama. His inner experience may possibly have been larger than the space of 30 × 30 × 30 centimetres in which his hands did their dance.

When Theresa, another client, talked about her colleague she glanced and nodded a little upwards and to the right. I pointed with my finger in the same direction, and asked her, 'Does he know he is blocking your creativity?' Theresa's response made it clear that she indeed visualised her colleague at this location and that she, in turn, understood my pointing finger.

The examples of Jimmy and Theresa illustrate how non-verbal communication expresses the social experience. People often glance in the direction in which the people they talk about are located. You may also notice that gestures, stance and all kinds of movements signal the structure of their social panoramic experience.

My colleague Frits Schoon noticed that some of his clients' postures suggested that they were involved in imaginary interactions, some of which seemed to have a permanent character. 'Is there someone on your tail?' Frits asked one client who moved very carefully and timidly. 'Yes,' answered the client, 'I walk like this because as a child I was always expecting my father to start yelling and hurting me.'

Once you are familiar with the idea of the social panorama, these non-verbal signals 'showing locations' are easily recognised.

2.10 Cultural patterns

According to Pinker (1997) and Lawley and Tompkins (2003) it is reasonable to regard the spatial representation of knowledge as a universal human – and maybe even mammalian – attribute. Social cognition is in no way different.

At the time of writing, all the ethnic, national and cultural groups that have been encountered apparently have social panoramas. It is reasonable to assume that various cultures do have their own patterns of creating their social maps.

Such cultural patterns must be based on both social experiences that are typical for that group, and the way people within that culture are taught the social rules and etiquette. In other words, the cultural transfer of social panorama patterns may be either implicit or explicit. For instance, in a culture where there are relatively few elderly people, a child will notice the respect with which the old are treated and know that they have a special position. Nobody needs to tell such a child that it should give way to old people – this is implicit cultural transfer. If the child is told that 'older people come first', then that would be an example of explicit cultural transfer.

It can be very useful information for a businessperson travelling to Tokyo to know that the Japanese are very hierarchical and that their company presidents are seen as godlike emperors. But is it true? The field of intercultural communications is, by definition, caught in the dilemma between the formulation of functional generalisations about groups on the one hand, and reinforcing unwanted prejudices about them on the other. For instance, bearing in mind the generalisation that all Africans listen better to older males, it may be helpful in business meetings to choose a senior chairman when you are dealing with Africans – but this will also confirm a prejudice, so what should one do?

The social behaviour of the members inside organisations, or any other type of social system, is based on each individual's social panorama. Although only existing in the minds of individuals, people may talk and act as if groups share social panoramas. 'Collective representations' were first discussed by the French sociologist Emile Durkheim, but it was Moscovici (1983) and Augoustinos (Augoustinos and Innes, 1990) who demonstrated that such collective social representations exist and are open to statistical analysis.

Individuals belonging to the same culture or subculture will be inclined to make use of common social categories; they will use verbal expressions and metaphors relating to social norms and values that will help to build their social panoramas along similar lines. If you want to communicate well with members of another culture, it is helpful if you can model some of the shared features of their maps of the social world.

When a sample of, say, Japanese social panoramas is compared with those of the Dutch it may provide us with useful transcultural insights. How, for example, do you behave when you visit Saudi Arabia? If you had an outline of the collective social panorama of Saudis along with you, it would tell you where they tend to locate Christians, their royal family, foreign aid workers, the military, terrorists, Bedouins, fundamentalists, Americans, Iraqis, Israelis, or oil technicians. This will be a helpful tool for establishing and maintaining rapport.

My colleague and I were invited for dinner. At five o'clock, the appointed time, we entered the neat home of our hosts in the outskirts of Kathmandu. The couple who had invited us asked us to sit down in a nice room with simple but comfortable furniture and showed us their art collection. Tea was served, and the four of us talked for an hour about a variety of topics. Then the lady asked if we were ready for dinner and we said 'yes'. Off to the kitchen she went and returned before long to lay the table. A short while later she brought two plates of food and, to our great surprise, she and her husband both left – we had to eat the meal, which was delicious, alone! It was 30 minutes before our hostess came back in to ask if we would like some more. Exactly three-quarters of an hour later they both returned, but only to say goodbye. At nine we were back at our hotel.

Our minds were buzzing with questions about Nepalese dining habits. Was their knowledge about how Westerners eat gained from a visit to a restaurant, where the waiter leaves you alone? Was this an example of a major cultural mismatch? Where did they put us in their social panoramas that made them treat us that way? Was it too high or too low? Were we too far away? If we wanted to eat together on a next occasion, what could we do to accomplish that? Should we meta-communicate and joke about it and say: 'Hey, Genshei old sport, let's all munch in the kitchen today!'

2.11 *Changing social emotions*

The audience in the puppet theatre of social images hardly notices the continuous shows that are run in there. The familiarity of their own inner processes will make these spectators' attention drift away, even when the puppets are singing and dancing for all they are worth. But they will all be startled awake as soon as the show raises negative emotions.[35] Problematic social emotions can at times become overwhelming, even unbearable and if any emotion reappears frequently it will limit a person's functioning. This will drive some to seek professional help; they will be implicitly asking the therapists to take this disturbing social emotion away from them.

No therapist can ever extract hate, loneliness, shame, guilt, submission, or dependence from his clients. Emotions are not liquids, bones or tissue. Social emotions arise from thinking about people but most social emotions don't involve thinking about other people in isolation, as those other people need to be thought of in relation to the self. It is the connection between self and others that is crucial.

To recap: the social constructions that create social emotions can be easily understood in terms of the social panorama. The self is in the centre and other people are located somewhere in the surrounding space. The sensory qualities of these two elements, together with their relative position, largely determine the emotional experience involved.

In Chapter 3, which is about the 'self', we will deal extensively with the self-part in this and we will recognise that some social emotions include very strong contributions of the self. For instance, emotions such as envy or shame cannot be experienced without the self being included. In these emotions the self functions as a background. In contrast, a feeling of pity can exist entirely independently of one's self; it may consist exclusively of the image of the person for whom the pity is felt.

The therapeutic techniques in this book are mainly categorised on the basis of two types of indication of which *disturbing social*

---

[35] The differentiation between emotionality on the one hand and cognition on the other is currently ignored by most psychologists. More and more one starts to regard emotion as being a part of intelligence. The Gray-La Violette-model suggests that the more varied someone's emotional expression, the more complex someone's cognitive representations. See Sommers (1982) in Ferguson (1990) on emotion as an aspect of intelligence.

emotions is the first. When clients complain about bad feelings that are associated with others, themselves or a combination of the two, we may simply assume that 'relationship equals location'. The problematic personification is in the wrong location; a better feeling will result from moving it to another site.[36]

Deeply rooted social behavioural patterns form the other type of indication for the application of the techniques. In Chapter 6 we will focus on automatic behaviour that was learned early, within the family of origin. A fundamental change in the images of early family life will give the client a choice in situations where he or she has previously been acting compulsively.

In the remainder of this chapter we will deal with techniques for changing *disturbing social emotions*. The pioneering work in this area was done by Steve and Connirae Andreas (1989) who, along similar lines, helped clients to change feelings of shame, guilt and loss.

2.11.1 Changing the pain of love

The opening lines of this book deal with the role of social images in the experience of love. For the treatment of love-related problems we need to look at this relationship in more detail. We will examine the landscape of love by means of examples to show you the general principles behind all problematic social emotions.

What is the emotion 'love'? Rubin (1970) wrote that it is composed of dependency, altruism, care and intimacy, while Demer and Pyszczynski (1978) proved a close connection with sexuality. Some people consider it spiritual, supernatural or sacred. For many years psychologists collectively assumed that it was not suitable for scientific analysis and that is why the word 'love' is absent from the glossaries of most social psychological textbooks. Words that can be found are 'affiliation', 'altruism', 'attraction' and 'sexuality'. Researchers who studied the psychology of love were, until recently, relatively rare.

---

[36] The simplicity of this proposition provides it its power. Pragmatism is the philosophy underpinning this way of reasoning. If somebody calls out, "It cannot be that simple!" they talk about reality, not about application.

In the last decades, love was studied primarily by biological psychologists like Walsh (1996), who clarified some of the hormonal and genetic aspects. Now we know that the smell of pheromones guide both butterflies and humans to their mates. The role of the older anatomical structures of the brain was emphasised by Lewis, Amini and Lannon (2000). They write, 'Words, good ideas and logic mean nothing to the limbic system and the brain stem, though the latter always tip the scales in decisions about love.' Yet these neurological structures make use of a kind of reasoning that belongs just as much to unconscious social cognition as the social panorama does. In their book *The Great Baby Wars*, Baker and Oram (1998) explain that we can only understand love when we see it as the result of the individual urge to reproduce oneself. Everything we decide and do in love is directed towards producing as many descendants as possible. We pick our mates because we expect to succeed in reproducing ourselves with them. When love makes us suffer, this is because our expectancy and investment in creating offspring is frustrated.

Before these biological psychologists started their work, love was the exclusive domain of psychoanalysts, novelists, poets and songwriters. 'Is this love; is this love; is this love that I am feeling?' (Bob Marley). Libraries and theatres are filled with stories about the pain of love. Is there beauty in tragedy? Or is it therapeutic (cathartic) to see and hear others suffer from the same old misery?

The Dutch psychologist Leo Pannekoek first revealed the complexity of love to me when I took part in his 'Sympathy Research Project' in 1983. There, the central issue was the subjective experience of affection. Although only a few colleagues considered this 'too phenomenological' project worthwhile, I found it new, fresh and non-conformist.

Pannekoek, using guided fantasies, managed to induce quite strong feelings of love. In semi-hypnotic procedures he gave suggestions to feel love for somebody else, for oneself and for creation in general. The fact that Pannekoek's subjects did at times report having very strong sensations proved love to be a mental skill. It also demonstrated that one does not need the stimulus (love's target) to be present in order to feel love. Love can be regarded as a mental activity based on imagination and we may say that people

vary in their 'competence to create the experience of love in themselves'.

To love, you need to see, hear, feel, smell and taste the other person in particular sensory qualities. When you feel love for a person you do something special with that personification in your mind, something that lets you know that this person is different from the people whom you only like.

Let us listen to the very detailed description given by Sandy. I asked her, 'How do you make yourself feel love for your boyfriend when he is not around?'

'When my boyfriend is not around and I want to experience my feeling of love for him, I look *upwards* and see a burst of mental pictures showing him in various situations. While these images *pass by* I experience a wave of warmth that moves quickly upwards from my pussy to my chin. This all happens in a split second. From all these images one picture will jump out and stop the flow of pictures. I keep seeing that image and experience a warm, round feeling in *the centre of my body, somewhere behind my belly button*. This feeling radiates out in all directions; it's hard to describe its *exact location* because it seems as if it is *everywhere*. Then I feel an urge to express my love for him and several internal dialogues may start *in my head*. These dialogues will probably consist of fragments of conversations from the situations I visualise. At the same time, other inner voices may start to negotiate about what to do; they will tell me all the options I have to express my feelings – writing a letter, calling, packing all my things and catching the *train to go to see him,* and so on. These ideas alternate with thoughts about things that would be more useful and productive to do, like finishing my work. When the internal dialogues start, the flow of images begins again and, depending on the power of these voices, the images of my boyfriend interchange with pictures of the things I should do. Then again one picture will dominate, and I will start feeling the feelings that belong to this picture. I will experience feelings of love as long as the images of my boyfriend stand out. The intensity (the measure of roundness, radiation and the feeling of completeness) of my feeling varies with the colours/brightness/movement of the dominant image. When my boyfriend is there, my feeling of love for him can be activated in a similar way by what I see of him or by something he says.'

In this account there are many words that point at the visual, kinaesthetic and auditory senses but nowhere do we hear much talk about locations. The evaluative feelings dominate; Sandy describes them well but we still need to ask more questions:

1. Where do the pictures of your boyfriend appear in your visual field?
   (Sandy: Centrally, slightly to the right and a little above the horizon)

2. How far away do you see him?
   (Sandy: He comes closer and closer until I can easily touch him)

3. Where do you hear the conversations?
    (Sandy: Whispering inside my head, usually on the right-hand side)

4. What is the critical difference in sensory qualities between a person you like and one you love?
    (Sandy: A person I love comes much closer, looks brighter and I feel connected to him as if a cord connects our bellybuttons; that gives me a warm round feeling around my stomach that spreads through my whole body. A family member I love feels connected in a more diffuse way and is also more distant.)

Sandy's example makes it clear how complicated it can be to model social emotions. Actually, it is as complicated as you make it; you can dissect an emotion into as many pieces as you like. For instance, one strategy is the sequence in which the senses are involved. One can look at all the sensory qualities of every representation in all these sensory systems. And there may be numerous beliefs, values and linguistic structures involved.

The basic distinction Pannekoek made with respect to love is between the giving and receiving sides of love. He found that giving love requires a clear and positive self-image on the part of the lover. The lover's mind should not be occupied with worries about who they 'really' are, whether they are good enough to give their love or whether their love will be accepted. If a person with such problems completely adores another person anyway, they may lose their autonomy and in the end this love will hurt.

People do not need a professional psychologist to tell them that love may often turn into something painful, but can a therapist really help? I will answer this question by describing a number of cases in which the social panorama technology was applied to help take away the pain of love.

MIRIAM
Miriam, a client of mine, had just found out that her husband had been having an affair for six months. She told me that she was too dependent on her husband, she had no pleasure in their relationship and that she made far too many adjustments in her life to

71

please him. In addition, Miriam believed that her dependency had driven him into the arms of another woman.

I started by asking her, 'Imagine yourself in the middle of all people... where do you sense your daughter?' Miriam told me that her daughter was two metres in front of her, to the right. Having made sure that she understood me I asked her, 'Where do you see Harry [her husband]?' Without any hesitation she told me that he was two and a half meters in front of her. She added that he was this far because of what she just found out about him so I asked her, 'Where was Harry located before you knew about this affair, say six months ago?' Miriam laughed, and said, 'Twenty centimetres away, straight in front. I look up to him ...'

A most dramatic change occurred after I suggested, 'Why not move Harry to the side? Which side would you prefer?' She placed him on her left-hand side. She felt much better immediately. I went on by asking her, 'Why not make him a little shorter?' Miriam thought deeply for a moment. When her attention returned to the here and now she told me, 'I can't make him small; if I do, I can't respect him, and I need to respect him to be able to love him.'

Nevertheless, part of Miriam still wanted what she called an 'equal relationship' and for that she would need a shorter husband. Here I used the Bandler and Grinder (1979) *V-K Squash* technique. One hand represented the part of Miriam that wanted 'equality' and her other hand contained the part that wanted to love and respect him. Although her hands could not completely merge to integrate the two wishes, they did come closer to each other.

Now Miriam saw Harry become slightly smaller but she could still respect and love him. To Miriam's surprise he turned green. She had to smile when this happened. 'Now I can have fun again,' she said.

An alternative approach to decreasing the size of the loved one is to enlarge the self-image of the lover. My experience up to now has shown that whichever approach one takes, both things will happen anyway; when one arrives at an ecological solution the self-image will be improved and the loved one will become of more or less equal size.

JOANNE

Joanne, another client of mine, complained that she could never fully give herself in her current marriage. 'To give yourself fully is an intense experience,' she said, and she knew what she was talking about. I asked her how she knew and she explained that she had once fully surrendered herself to someone. His name was Nicholas, her first date. She was 15 and had been totally obsessed by this young man, whom she adored above everything else. The relationship with Nicholas had lasted nearly a year, and then he had suddenly left her. That was 19 years ago, but in Joanne's social panorama Nicholas was still central, very close and tall – he was even 30 centimetres closer than Joanne's present husband! Joanne confessed: 'I still love that boy. I see him in my mind the way he was, slender, tall and doing what he thought was best. I can feel it again!'

I asked Joanne if she remembered how she had taken the break-up with Nicholas. She explained that since her parents were not able to support her – her father was her mother's first date too – she had to get over the loss all by herself. After a year of soul-searching she came to the conclusion that 'surrendering to someone leads to loneliness' and she said that she had known loneliness all too well in her early youth. This limiting belief appeared to be at the heart of Joanne's problem. Surrendering to her husband would leave her lonely, 'like a discarded apple core.'

While working with Joanne I discovered that her parents had neglected her. This had left her with a weak sense of self, 'It can crumble at any time', she told me, 'I admired Nicholas when I was 15 because he had a lot of self-confidence and personal power.' In fact, her love for him was also directed to acquiring these qualities herself. She had hoped that by loving him she could establish a solid self too but this attempt did not work at all. Being in love with Nicholas did not give her a grain of self-confidence, and when they broke up the opposite happened, she lost a truckload of self-esteem.

In the ensuing therapy session Joanne managed to bolster her sense of self (Technique 13). She changed the limiting belief (Technique 17) that 'surrender leads to loneliness'. She modified her personal history (Techniques 42, 43 and 45) in such a way that she would not have fallen in love with Nicholas at all, and would have enjoyed her childhood longer. After that, Nicholas moved out of her intimate circle to a place where he was no more than 'a nice person from the past'. Eventually, after all these changes had taken place, she acquired enough certainty to give in to passion and could feel it for her husband of 10 years' standing. During the changes he had moved much closer to her.

2.12 Basic techniques for the improvement of relations

This book combines scientific discourse with practical applications. To bridge the gap between the domain of discussion, observation and hypothesis and that of therapeutic tools for real people, we need to assume several things to be true. Such assumptions are chosen beliefs, they help to create certainty where in fact there is none. By doing that they serve a pragmatic purpose: they simplify reality to enable the practitioner to make decisions.

Assumption 3: *Personifications cannot be deleted but can only be transformed by changing personification factors (mainly location, abilities and perspective).*

The third assumption of the social panorama is that one cannot discard a personification once this has become part of a person's model of the social world. This is a biological fact that has its roots in our neurology (Sinclair, 1982). It is impossible to delete a file from our mental hard disk, but such files can be relatively easily relocated or improved. That is why you will encounter two major methods of intervention in this text:

a. Moving personifications to better locations by means of direct suggestion (e.g., draw it closer, make it lower, and push it sideways).

b. Improving personifications by means of widening their abilities or changing their beliefs. (Most often this is done by 'transferring resources'.) Formulated very briefly: 'What ability do you believe this personification misses?' 'Where do you have that ability yourself?' 'Send this ability to the personification.')

Both techniques 5 and 6 are the necessary ingredients in most successful social panorama change work.

Technique 5: Moving to a better location with the aid of a reference personification

Indication: All relationships that need improvement

1. Feel the feeling that is connected to the problematic relationship.
2. Find the location of the problem personification X (see Technique 3)
3. Feel the feeling that belongs to your relationship with personification Y – an individual or group to whom the client has the kind of attitude that the client would prefer to have to the problem personification.
4. Find the location of that reference personification Y.
5. Move the problem personification X as close as possible to the location of reference personification Y.
6. Evaluate the feelings, the stability of the image and search for resistance against using this new location during future encounters (Help solve all additional problems).
7. If all is well, proceed by having the client click the personification onto its new location and clean the old spot.

Problems you may encounter with Technique 5 and their possible Solutions

P: The problem personification X does not reach the intended location.
S: See whether this is sufficient progress for the client. If so, leave it like that. If not, see Techniques 6, 7 and 8.

P: Some parts (remnants) of the problem-personification stay on the original location.
S: Suggest repeating the movement several times, and cleaning up the old site. If this is not sufficient, use Technique 6 on the persistent parts.

P: The problem personification gets involved in non-productive interaction with the reference personification. (They quarrel about positions.)
S: Suggest that the reference personification goes to sleep; it was only needed to find the location to which to move.

P: The problem personification is a dominant authority.

S: Empower the self-image and shift the authority down (see Chapters 3 and 4).

Technique 6: Improving a personification with the help of additional abilities

Indication: All relationships that need improvement

1. Find the location of the problem personification (use Technique 3).
2. Explore what **abilities** (resources) the problem personification is **lacking,** causing them to be on the wrong spot. Name these missing abilities. (The problem personification cannot X.)
3. Find an example from your own life, where you were able to do exactly that what the problem personification can't do (named X).
4. Step into this memory of you using ability X. Make this as lively and intense as possible. What do you focus on? What is important to you? What exactly are you doing? What do you feel? How do you breathe? What do you say to yourself and/or to others? As soon as the intensity is at its peak, pick a colour to associate with this ability. Imagine yourself to be in the middle of a cloud of this colour that means the ability X.
5. Now send the ability X in the shape of a coloured beam of light to the problem personification. Continue this until it appears to be enough.
6. Evaluate the emotional influence on the relationship. Try imaginary future encounters with the problem person. What objections can be found against interacting in this way?

Did the location of the problem-personification change?

Tips

If the problem-personification cannot absorb the ability X, see if it first needs another ability to make it receptive – a conditional resource Y.

If the problem personification deflects the ability X, apply Techniques 7 or 8.

2.13 Overcoming very intense negative social emotions

Techniques 5 and 6 are often sufficient, as they repeatedly demonstrate a great potential for change, particularly when used in combination. In many cases, however, a client will feel a strong resistance that stems from a deep negative social affect like fear or hatred.

If it is hatred that stands in the way the easiest thing to do will be to match the client's aggression as in Technique 7. Other deep feelings can be approached with Technique 8 where the personification is given more abilities at an early age – in the cradle. Observing the enriched personification grow up will help to change its image into something very stable. This procedure will prevent the client from staying fixated on his previous image of the personification.

Technique 7: The single-sided improvement of very bad relationships

Indication: To neutralise feelings of hatred

Characterise your relationship with the problem-personification on a scale of (1) neutral to (10) intense hatred:

1 2 3 4 5 6 7 8 9 10

Where in your social panorama is this problem-personification located?

1. Visualise a movie screen. See yourself on it as a powerful cinema hero, equipped with everything that might be helpful to deal satisfactorily with the problem person.

2. Stay in the role of observer. Imagine scenes in which you see yourself taking revenge.

3. Repeat the scenes until it starts to become boring or you begin to feel pity.

4. Ask yourself, 'What inner, psychological abilities does the problem person lack that make him or her behave so badly? Write your answers down:

The problem personification is short of:

(a) The ability to ...
(b) The ability to ...
(c) The ability to ...

5. Think about the first missing ability (a) and ask yourself, 'When did I possess this ability very strongly?'
Find a memory of such a situation; make it a specific occasion with the exact time and place.

6. Relive having this ability (a) as intensely as possible, experience the time, place, sights, sounds and odours. Concentrate on the feeling of being fully occupied with ability (a). What are you doing? What do you say to yourself? What do you notice?

7. Keep the ability (a) in mind and choose a colour to fit it. Surround yourself with a cloud of this colour while at the same time exaggerating the experience of using the ability.

8. Send the ability (a) perhaps in the shape of a beam of coloured laser light towards the problem person. Make sure this person is filled with it. Go on until you see that the problem person has enough of ability (a). If the laser light is deflected, you need to use a stronger calibre laser.

9. You can repeat the same procedure for the other lacking abilities (b) and (c) etc.
How did this affect your feeling for the problem person?
Where in your social panorama is this problem-personification now located?

Reassess your relationship:

From neutral (1) to intense hatred (10).

1 2 3 4 5 6 7 8 9 10

79

Technique 8: Taking on a problem-personification as a baby

Indication: To improve long-term problematic relationships

Where in your social panorama is this problem person located?
Assess your relationship with the problem-personification:
From neutral (1) to intense hatred (10).

1 2 3 4 5 6 7 8 9 10

1. Ask yourself, 'What inner, psychological abilities does the problem person lack that makes him or her behave so badly?' Write your answers down:

    The problem personification is short of:

    (a) The ability to …
    (b) The ability to …
    (c) The ability to …

2. Think about the missing ability (a) and ask your self, 'When did I possess this ability very strongly?'
3. Find a memory of such a situation, make it a specific occasion with the exact time and place.
4. Relive having this ability (a) as intensely as possible and experience the time, place, sights sounds and odours. Concentrate on the feeling of being fully occupied with ability (a). What are you doing? What do you say to yourself? What do you notice?
5. Keep the ability (a) in mind and choose a colour to fit it. Surround yourself with a cloud of this colour while at the same time exaggerating the experience of using the ability.
6. Imagine the problem-personification as a baby. See it in its cradle. Send the ability (a) in the form of a beam of coloured laser light towards this baby.
    Go on until you see that this baby has enough of ability (a) for the rest of its life. Repeat this with any other missing abilities.
7. Imagine this baby growing up with the abilities. See how different a person it will become.
8. Test by imagining meeting the problem person again. How will this affect your feelings for him?
    Where in your social panorama is this problem person now located?

Reassess your relationship with the problem-personification:

From neutral (1) to intense hatred (10).

1 2 3 4 5 6 7 8 9 10

2.14 Concluding remarks

Helping people to improve their social lives with the aid of the techniques from this chapter is a wonderful way to learn about unconscious social cognition. I would advise all academic readers to do some hands-on testing of what you have read.[37] The latter type of experimentation is responsible for the existence of the social panorama model. The content of the following two chapters also stems largely from trial and error in therapeutic practice.

---

[37] I myself was trained as an academic researcher and did social psychological research for several years. To start testing things on real people outside of the laboratory was always a very big step for me and my colleagues.

Chapter 3

Self-awareness

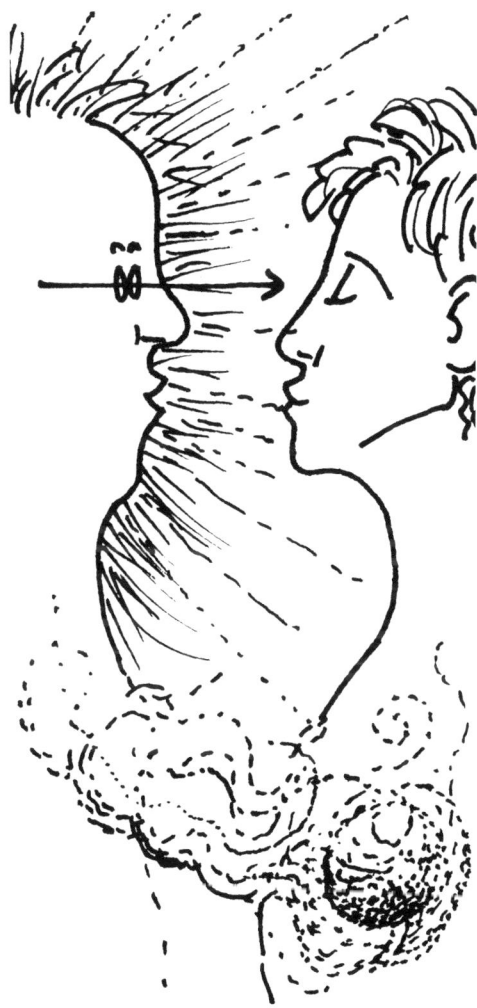

3.1   *I am the centre of the social world*

In Chapter 1 we introduced self-awareness as one of nine essential personification factors. The core of the experience of the self was said to be the 'feeling of self' or 'kinaesthetic self'. This spot in the body functions as the nucleus in a person's social solar system – the kinaesthetic self forms the centre of most people's social panoramas. This is the place in mental space in which relationships are given shape. Normally, someone's self-image accompanies the feeling of self like a satellite – a cloud of imagery hanging in front of the person. You may visualise it in such a way that, if your body were a projector, it would project self-images in the space in front of it. These projected self-images are generalised schematic pictures that are usually too vague for conscious perception. But however vague self-images are, they have a profound influence on social life because they dictate our position and role.

In this chapter we will study the dynamics of self-awareness within the context of unconscious social cognition. As soon as we have mapped the rules of self-experience within social life, we can have a look at their therapeutic applications. These applications are in all areas where people have problems with self-confidence, social roles, inferiority or superiority complexes, negative self-images, authority, identity or a weak ego.

3.2   *Talking about and changing self-awareness*[38]

The familiar notions of 'self' and 'identity' are both parts of a complex of related meanings. Together with the ideas 'I', 'me' and 'myself' they form a system of meaning for which it is difficult to define boundaries. This difficulty has through the ages given philosophers and psychologists endless grist for the mill of debate. They asked one another questions like: 'What is the nature of the self?', 'What is the ego made of?', 'Does the soul really exist?', 'What is identity?', 'How do people develop self-esteem?' and 'Is consciousness identical to self-awareness?'. One of the high points of this debate is found in the 'self-psychology' which came from

---

[38] See Lawley and Tompkins (2000) on symbolic modelling.

the work of William James (1890), a central theme of which was the difference between 'I' and 'me'. Accurate philosophical analysis does not necessarily result in methods of changing things but the confrontation with a lot of suffering on the level of identity has made psychotherapists hungry for such methods.

Prochaska (1984) made an inventory of what the different psychotherapeutic trends were doing in the field of 'increasing self-esteem'. He came across very few techniques specifically directed at the self. In contrast to the shortage of existing therapeutic technology, the diagnostics of personality disorders (Boon and Draaier, 1995) are highly advanced. Psycho-diagnostics is a monster head in which the therapist can find very little of practical value in guiding someone to a better functioning self. Among the few methods that Prochaska discovered, was Ellis' (1973) rational-emotional therapy. Ellis tries to boost self-esteem by encouraging the client to stop asking himself all sorts of irrational questions about his 'self'.

Imagine you are a therapist with a client who claims to have lost himself. What incantation can you use to recall a self that has disappeared?

This practical question remains unanswered in the work of the philosopher Gergen (1998), though he has had a lot of influence on the post-modern view of the self. Among other things he claims that in this time of social chaos the concept of a stable identity is an anachronism. In other words, if someone loses his 'self' in these troubled times, then he's right.

From their point of view, Lakoff and Johnson (1999) point at what they call the 'folk theory of essences'. This generally accepted common-sense view suggests that people have a 'true', 'real' or 'essential' self. This 'folk theory of essence' has been fuelled by generations of theologians, gurus and therapists who have preached such concepts as 'the soul', 'the mind', 'the true self', 'the higher self' or 'the centre of being'.

Instead of some 'essence' being present, people use a whole complex of conceptual metaphors for the self. According to Lakoff and Johnson, people think (and speak) of their 'self' as if it were a tangible, concrete object. If someone says, 'I've lost myself', everyone will understand what they mean because this ties in with: (1) the universal basic experience of losing things, and (2) the universal conceptual metaphor of one's self as a thing. In short, people project basic experiences they have with objects onto experiences with 'non-objects' like the 'self'.

Lakoff and Johnson present a series of conceptual metaphors, which they see as characterising the various aspects of the 'self'. The most important are:

1. You possess a self just as you can possess an object.
2. You can control your self in the same way you can control an object.
3. Self-control takes effort and strength, just as you would need to manipulate a heavy object.
4. The self is sometimes identified with the body. Self-control is in that case the same thing as body control, which again is derived from the basic experience of manipulating objects.
5. Forcing yourself into action is the same sort of thing as overcoming the inertia of a heavy object.
6. You can take possession of someone else's 'self' just as you can take an object from them.
7. You can look at your self and have an opinion about it, just as you can judge an object.
8. Self-control also means control of the attention. Attention is also looked on as an object that you can relocate.
9. The self has a specific location just as an object can be kept in a specific place, and it can be lost.

So, from the point of view of cognitive linguistics, people talk (and think) about the self in a way that shows that it is made up of a number of mental constructions which are based on elementary experiences from infancy. If you have lost yourself, then you are using the "self-as-a-thing-in-a-place" metaphor.

The burning question, 'what is my real self?' may be nonsense from the linguistic and philosophical point of view, but it can still ruin lives. Psycho-diagnostics, philosophy, self-psychology and linguistics don't seem on the face of it to be able to give us the tools to help replace a 'lost' self. It is also difficult to discover a technique which helps find the 'real' self or to strengthen a weak one.

A number of such techniques have been initiated in the pragmatically based neuro-linguistic therapy of Bandler and Grinder (1975a). In particular we find some methods of changing aspects of the experience of self in Leslie Cameron-Bandler's so-called 'imperative self workshops'. She assumes that people live according to a 'core question' and finding this question helps to ascertain central themes in their experience of themself. These identity-defining themes can be brought within the reach of conscious choice – do you really want to spend the rest of your life asking yourself "Does my Mummy love me?"

Dilts and DeLozier (2000) and Andreas (2001), in the same neuro-linguistic tradition, were more interested in the descriptive side of identity. They answered the difficult question, 'What is someone's identity?' simply by saying 'Whatever a person believes it to be.' As they describe it, the self is a system of beliefs, which means that they favour belief-changing techniques to influence it (Dilts, 1990). The fact that beliefs about identity are seldom easily expressed through language makes this approach difficult; the client who can describe exactly who he is belongs to an elite. Faulkner (1994) recognised that these beliefs often take the form of a metaphor so, by searching for these metaphors ('so you are like a ...?') and by better adapting these metaphors to the needs of the client he developed a simple and practical approach which also plays a part in this chapter. Thus a metaphor such as, 'I am a researcher,' or 'I am the rising sun' can strongly influence someone's experience of self.

3.3   *Exploring the world of self*

I began my field research by listing the answers I received to the question, 'Who are you?' A pattern emerged straight away in all answers that started with 'I am...' First of all, such identity definitions often begin with 'I am a...' or 'I'm like a...' or 'I think I am...' People often produced a whole series of expressions of identity one after the other, as in the following fragment:

Lucas: 'Anita, can you tell me who you are?'

Anita: 'Oh, gosh… I'm…. (long silence) How can I put it into words? (more silence) It's a feeling! (silence) It's just… I was me, long before I knew that I was a person or a girl. Yes, I still see myself as a girl… Now I'm a secretary… and I think I'm a faithful wife. (laughs) It's an image, too… I think I'm elegant and attractive… and I'm assertive. I'm Anita (laughs). But first of all, I'm me. You know, just me! Like I always was' (laughs, satisfied).

The answers people give to this question have a number of typical forms:

> I am X (X is a synonym for 'I'. e.g. I am me, I am myself).
> I am Y (Y is a name. e.g. I am Peter).
> I am Z (Z is a metaphor. e.g. I am a night tiger).
> I am U (U is a quality. e.g. I am flexible).
> I am E (E is for emotional state. e.g. I am happy).
> I am a V (V is a social category. e.g. I am a teacher).
> I am a n-V (n is a value within the social category. e.g. I am a bad teacher).
> I think I am W (W can be any sort of identification. e.g. I think I'm bad, I think I'm the god Ra).

As well as these forms of identity definition we also come across answers that refer to a sensory experience without being specific. In other words, the answer refers to a feeling, picture, sound, smell or taste. As in; 'I'm… eh… um… it's a feeling.'

We also often hear expressions like; 'it's just …', 'it's an idea', 'it's just something you know', 'it comes naturally', 'it's obvious', 'it's a feeling inside' which all point to the unconscious nature of self-awareness. Such expressions seem to be used when someone is confronted with an unconscious mental construction on which he cannot consciously focus, even though he is absolutely certain that he knows its content.

In the work of Bandler and Grinder and their colleagues (Derks and Hollander, 1996a) there is a lot of attention paid to the structure of the sensory experience. Like Fauconnier (1997) and Grove

(1998) they believe that all meanings take the form of three-dimensional sensory mental constructions. In addition to the words people use to describe their self-awareness, they postulate the existence of a layer of sensory experience projected in space which usually escapes conscious appreciation. Self-awareness is therefore primarily something that is unconsciously felt, seen, heard, tasted or smelt in and around a person.

Just as we described personification in Chapter 1, we need to see 'self-awareness' in terms of the most basic of human experiences. Logically, it needs to be based on the universal primary experience 'I am here'. It is, however, rather a large step from the deduction that such a thing should exist to exploring it in living beings (How do you know that you are here?).

Fauconnier's ideas (1997) suggest that the words 'I' and 'myself' help to activate (like a mouse click) the subconscious mental construction. By assuming that the 'self-construction' was, in one way or another, experienced in sensory qualities in mental space, I was ready for my first experiments with clients. I began with the following questions:

1. Can you focus your attention on yourself, your 'me'? Say something like 'I' or 'myself' to yourself. Have you got that?
2. What do you feel? Where do you feel it?
3. What can you see? Where do you see it?
4. Do you hear anything? Where do you hear it?
5. Can you taste or smell anything?

A few patterns quickly emerged. First of all, it was quite possible to get people to focus attention on their experience of self. Secondly, they didn't always find it easy to put this experience into words, though the accompanying body language was very meaningful. In particular the hands often indicated the exact locations in mental space where something was felt, seen or heard. I gained much apparently reliable information by either (if it was some meters from the client) walking to the indicated location or (if it was closer to the client) asking the client to indicate the exact spot with his fingers.

3.4   *Patterns in the awareness of self*

It was a logical step with many clients, while exploring their concept of themselves to experiment with changing it. Suggestions for change enhance the degree of consciousness of the aspects of the experience of self. Change clarifies the image and solidifies the feelings. In other words, while just finding your feeling for 'self' produces a fairly vague idea, once something is changed there follows a moment of more intense consciousness (an orientation reaction) which clarifies both the old and the new situations.

In this book, in the interests of compactness, I will present the patterns I discovered in therapeutic and exploratory work as a whole. The cohesion between the feelings, pictures and sounds of the self will be dealt with as they come up.

3.4.1 *Patterns of feeling in self-awareness*

Thanks to Gershon's research (1998) we have come better to understand our 'gut' feelings. According to him we have a second 'brain' in our stomach which consists of the enormous amount of nerve cells which surround the intestines. We need to realise that metabolism is the most important function in the development from embryo to suckling. The stomach and intestines constitute an intelligent biochemical factory long before the senses start stimulating the brain. The feeling of self probably originates somewhere in the intestines and is linked to the brain at a later stage. The question that arises from this is: is there a universal basic experience we could call 'I am my stomach'?

Perhaps we should interpret the link people have between their awareness of self and their self-image as a reflection of the link between Gershon's 'intestinal brain' and the mind. The importance of gut feelings in social life may well trace its origins to the role that mothers play in the maintenance of the digestive system. Should we also postulate a 'mother is food' basic experience?

The instruction to 'feel your "me"' is enough to draw attention to the kinaesthetic aspect of self-awareness. The experience usually intensifies when people are kept focused on this. In the course of research three main types of 'self feeling' have emerged:

1. *The kinaesthetic self.* This determines the location of the self-awareness: it is the site of the self.
2. *Emotions arising from self-evaluation.* Positive, neutral or negative feelings that are the result of self (image) evaluation.
3. *The familiar sensation of self.* This consists of a continuous stream of background emotional, visceral and self-perceptive sensations.

Not every test case or client can differentiate between these feelings, and we cannot claim that everyone experiences all three types, but these classifications are very relevant to therapeutic practice. Complaints about the 'self' always fall into one of these categories. For instance:

'I have lost myself' – Loss of the kinaesthetic self
'I'm sick of myself' – Negative self-judgement
'I feel strange' – Something wrong with the familiar sensation of self.

3.4.1.1   The kinaesthetic self

The kinaesthetic self is the seat of our existence. When asked about it, people usually point to their stomach or their chest. However, this is not mentioned in the standard psychological literature, probably because of a combination of the great mobility of the location, its unconscious character and the dynamics of its intensity. This is in contrast to Eastern psychological traditions, which give great weight to the phenomenon. The Chinese speak of the 'Chi point'; the Japanese the 'Ki point' and Yogis call it a 'Chakra'. In the theatre, people like Johnstone (1990) speak of the 'centre'.[39] People in the alternative health sector (those who work with energy and holistic medicine) and practitioners of the martial arts

---

[39] Johnstone (1979:179) cites Michael Chekhov (1953) who writes:

So long as the centre remains in the middle of your chest (pretend it's a few inches deep), you will feel that you are still yourself and in full command, only more energetically and harmoniously so, with your body approaching an 'ideal type'. But as soon as you try to shift the centre to some other place within or outside your body, you will feel that your whole psychological and physical attitude will change, just as it changes when you step into an imaginary body. You will notice that the centre is able to draw and concentrate your whole being into one spot from which your activity emanates and radiates.

Johnstone advises to experiment:

Put a soft, warm, not too small centre in the region of your abdomen and you may experience a psychology that is self-satisfied, earthy, a bit heavy and even humorous. Place a tiny, hard centre on the tip of your nose and you will become curious, inquisitive, prying and even meddlesome. Move the centre to one of your eyes and notice how quickly it seems that you have become sly, cunning and perhaps hypocritical.

have discovered that the location of this point plays an important part in a person's well being. When people feel good, the kinaesthetic self is often inside, just above or below the navel. When they feel less good it is usually higher up in the body.

When I ask 'Which part of your body feels the most like 'me'?' most of my clients can point straight to their kinaesthetic self; others find it easier if I indicate my own torso with my hands. The disadvantage of such gestures is that they can have a misleading suggestive effect. Adding 'inside your body or outside?' can restore the openness of the question.

LOCATIONS

To my surprise I found a lot of variation in the locations of the kinaesthetic self. The Eastern traditions often have different standard locations. In the light of the variation that I have found I prefer to assume individual differences. Though the feeling is usually within the body itself, I have also come across cases where it was partly outside the body or up to a metre away from it. In the course of the years my clients have pointed to spots in the front of the head, beside the head, at the back of the head, in the neck, at the top of the chest, just in front of the chest, round the shoulders, in the middle of the chest, round the heart, above the navel, behind the navel, on the navel, below the navel, in the stomach, in the thighs and in the feet. I have also often seen double locations; these always indicate internal identity conflicts. The 'average' kinaesthetic self is to be found at the front, just above the navel.

Practitioners of the above-mentioned (Eastern) schools of body-centred therapy believe that too high a position of the kinaesthetic self is associated with unbalanced personality and bodily functions. These practitioners are also of the opinion that locations which are too far forward, in the neck, or in the back should be corrected. They do this by using direct suggestion and special exercises, which in this context are called 'centring exercises' or 'grounding'. For instance, 'Stand on your toes, tense your stomach muscles, breathe in deep and keep your breath for a few seconds, then breathe out and feel how your centre of gravity drops as you stand back on the soles of your feet.'

ABSENCE OF THE KINAESTHETIC SELF

If a client cannot point out a location for his 'me' when asked, it probably has an important diagnostic meaning. I have encountered a number of very characteristic cases of clients who failed to locate their kinaesthetic self even though all of them could easily locate other personifications. These cases resulted in the formulation of the following hypotheses:

1. An absent kinaesthetic self comes with a tendency to put oneself in the place of others: 'that's my problem, I don't know my own place...' 'I am afraid of people in general, I cannot tolerate them closer than four metres; when they come closer I don't know what to do anymore. I become absorbed by the others.'

2. A person without a kinaesthetic self will sometimes prefer to fill his centre with identity feelings that belong to someone else. They will probably identify themself with one of the strong personifications in their intimate circle – e.g. their partner/spouse, their twin or even Jesus Christ. This may lead to pathological identification, role confusion or identity loss. People with a weak kinaesthetic self often take on the stronger role of another. In Chapter 4, which is about authority, we come across the dominance pattern. People become dominated when they combine a weak self-awareness with a very prominent other-personification. People without a kinaesthetic self will totally lose themselves in relation to dominant personifications in their social panoramas.

3. It also often happens that people cannot point out a kinaesthetic self because they have a multiple awareness of self. This can happen in the 'multiple personalities' described by Boon and Draaijer (1995). The so-called 'bi-location of the self' indicates inner conflicts on the level of identity.

4. The absence of a feeling of self can also indicate a very negative self-image. The negative judgement of the self is so associated with dysphoric emotions that a person finds it necessary to suppress their kinaesthetic self. I had a client who hated himself because of previous homosexual activities. Such denial of self is often accompanied by 'not wanting to be

there'. Without a kinaesthetic self a person is subjectively absent, and is playing a sort of social-emotional hide-and-seek.

5. I am convinced that all out-of-the-body experiences, such as those that are studied in psychiatry and parapsychology, indicate insufficient activity in the kinaesthetic self. Many people find the suggestion, 'just leave your body' easy to follow. We see this capability to 'leave the body' used therapeutically in the 'Time-line Therapy' of James and Woodsmall (1988), and when Erickson (1967) talks of 'the brain floating in the middle of nowhere'. The kinaesthetic self can be missing in dreams, too, as in many unusual states of consciousness (Mavromantis, 1987).

6. Visceral feelings of strain or pain can overrule the kinaesthetic self. If these feelings result from negative emotions, we see people identify with these emotions. They may 'become' their fear or anger.

OTHER-PERSONIFICATIONS IN THE KINAESTHETIC SELF

In theory, the kinaesthetic self must take the central position in the social experience and the social world should turn around this 'me-feeling'. In therapeutic practice one may encounter some clients projecting other-personifications in their centre. This seems to be the result of identification on a permanent basis. The kinaesthetic self of the self-personification is then beside the body centre, to the left or right of the spinal cord. Sometimes the kinaesthetic self cannot be found at all. An interesting example of this was the 'cold hole inside' which came into being after a client of mine had lost a beloved partner whose personification had been in the middle of her social world.

The presence of other-personifications within the body limits tends to cause confusing identity symptoms and if such a 'possessing' personification is in the central position it has a very strong distorting effect indeed. This does not necessarily mean, however, that the person is completely socially handicapped; I was surprised to find that people can live very well with it, although they are aware that there is something odd going on –

'sometimes I just don't know who I am'. Please understand that in 10 years of practice I came across only a handful of such cases.

INTENSITY

The intensity of the kinaesthetic self can be subjectively measured by asking people to give it a value between one and 10. High intensity is almost always experienced as positive – an ego-kick! It will be accompanied by a smile, a sigh of relief and an upright posture. As the intensity increases, so does the volume of the area of the body where it is housed and it will approach the standard location in front of and above the navel. Many therapeutic interventions for increasing the self-confidence are indirectly aimed at increasing the intensity of the 'feeling of self'. In this way therapists can quickly learn the non-verbal distinguishers of a weak 'kinaesthetic self' from a strong one. Popularly put, a strong 'feeling of self' is accompanied by an increase in personal magnetism and presence.

THE KINAESTHETIC SELF IN RELATION TO THE SELF-IMAGE

The awareness of self consists of at least two components, the kinaesthetic self and the self-image. These two are usually to be found at different locations, sometimes tens of metres apart. A long distance between them will divide a person's attention between the two points. The highest intensity of the kinaesthetic self is reached when it overlaps the self-image and there is no such division. At such a moment someone has incorporated his self-image. Self-images, as we will see in the following paragraphs, are usually to be found in the space in front of a person. The picture in space is subjectively tied to the kinaesthetic self and the two are connected by mental construction lines.

NO CONNECTION BETWEEN THE SELF-IMAGE AND THE KINAESTHETIC SELF

If there is no connection between the self-image and the kinaesthetic self, then the self-image will seem like the image of a stranger. Such an unconnected image is actually an 'image of oneself', and not a self-image. If someone wants to make such an image into a self-image, the solution is to make that connection.

'Can you connect that image with your feeling of self? (The therapist points to the client's stomach). By making such a connection a person 'becomes' the image in question. The question of whether or not a person can 'be' this image is usually answered at once – if it doesn't fit then the very suggestion will trigger all sorts of objections. If the image does fit, a person can strengthen it by thinking, 'I am…', and reinforcing this with his breathing.

WARMTH, RADIATION AND FLOW
The quality of the kinaesthetic self seems to improve when it takes up a greater area, feels warmer, radiates and flows. The inverse of this also seems to be a universal pattern.

3.4.1.2 *Emotions arising from self-evaluation*
Many people speak of 'positive' or 'negative' self-images. The positive or negative quality of a self-image reflects the feelings it

causes in its owner. Someone with a negative self-image looks at that image, consciously or otherwise, and evaluates it as negative. The emotions caused by this self-judgement cause the complaints (Hall, 1996). It is not always possible to tell the difference between the emotions arising from self-image evaluation and the kinaes-thetic self; for many clients there is a correlation.

If someone's self-image is difficult to find it can be because of its negative contents; a part of the client would rather not look at it and unconsciously keeps it out of sight, far away or very small. In this case it is useful to work with the part of the personality that is responsible for this censorship; Bandler and Grinder's (1979) 'six-step reframing' is the technique to use. I also often use Technique 13 (see page 115) to replace a negative self-image with a positive one.

Negative self-images can be discovered when the therapist suggests that the client brings his image closer and makes it bigger – with a positive self-image this will cause positive emotions, with a negative one self-image enlargement will cause an unpleasant sensation.

3.4.1.3   *The familiar sensations of self*

Beside the emotions arising from self-evaluation and the kinaes-thetic self, we find what is most clearly called the 'familiar sensations of self'. We need to be aware that the inner senses that take care of posture – muscle tone, breathing and circulation – continually supply the brain with information. Within certain limits these sensations can be called 'normal'. They are usually constant or they occur in a standard sequence. Only if our heart starts to beat faster than normal, our stomach is particularly full or empty, we adopt an unusual position or breathe in an unusual way do we become conscious of them. We are so used to these inner stimuli that we only notice them when something changes. It's just like the taste of your own tongue; you are only aware of it if your attention is drawn to it, (if you are ill or have just read this sentence.)

The familiar sensations of self are involved when someone says that he 'is not feeling his usual self'.

Many therapists have noticed that clients hold on to these familiar feelings even when they are negative – 'give me my good old depression back' – and a therapeutic change can be hindered by fear of the unknown. Wessler (1990) speaks of the 'emotional set point' – the threshold of emotional overreaction. If a change forces someone to abandon this point he will becomes scared and resistant.

3.4.2   *Visual patterns in the awareness of self*

As already described in the introduction, the speed at which the human brain can process pictures is greater than we are con- sciously able to comprehend. From clinical and other observations it is possible to deduce that in this stream of pictures there are also pictures which have to do with the person themself. Herein will be mental 'snapshots' as well as more generalised visual self-con- structions. These last mental creations determine the more perma- nent self-concept, the part that has to do with relationships and with 'being'. The awareness of self is the meaning-construction that lets you know who you are – which is why we are thinking of generalised visualisations when we speak of 'self-images'.

Many psychologists assume that the 'self-image' is an abstraction that is not specially related to any particular visual construction. It is relatively rare among social scientists to take the concept 'self- image' literally to mean a visual image.

Self-images in this literal sense are used in the so-called 'swish- technique' (Bandler, 1985; Andreas, Faulkner and McDonald, 1994; McDonald, 1997) This technique also illustrates the great thera- peutic influence a positive self-image can have, particularly when directly connected to problem behaviour (Derks and Hollander, 1996a).

The difficulty in becoming fully aware of spontaneous self-images is an obstacle for experimenters and therapists alike. It makes the scientist suspicious – do these images really exist? The therapist or counsellor needs to take it on trust. In order to be able to work with it in practice the therapist has to believe that all people make such visual constructions. This belief allows the therapist to remain open for all the variations that clients can demonstrate. Therapists who doubt the existence of self-images, will be unable to help a doubtful client through their initial barriers. The scientific researcher, however, is caught (should be caught) within the dilemma of whether they have created the images with suggestion or made visible something which pre-existed. As far as I can see, this difficult situation is inherent in the exploration of unconscious cognition.

3.4.2.1 *Hunting for self-images*

Someone's visual activity will receive an extra impulse when we ask: 'Can you *see* a picture of yourself?' and it will start many people off on a frenetic search. Unfortunately this kind of question starts such a broad search that it is impossible to indicate which one of all the resulting images is *the* self-image. If, as a therapist, you know what you are looking for, then you ask leading questions which you support with body language. So ask yourself, what exactly are you looking for when you explore someone's self-image?

Within the framework of the social panorama techniques we seldom look for the *content* of self-images, but rather for their sensory qualities (sub-modalities) and, in particular, their location. In other words: we have found the self-image when we know *where* someone sees it, *how big* it is, at *what level the eyes are, in what direction it is looking* and, possibly, how light or dark it is. Sometimes we also need to know whether its content has a positive or a negative connotation.

When looking for someone's self-image I always assume the following:

1. Self-images show the person who they are and also what social role they have to play. They give constant subconscious information about someone's social position. (Metaphor: The self-image is a social compass that shows 'social north'.) A question to find a self-image: Which picture shows you who you are and what your role or position is? Where do you see that image? How big is it?

2. Self-images come into play in contexts in which knowledge of your own position and role is important. This is valid as much for imaginary as actual interaction. A metaphorical question to explore self-images: Is there a picture that shows what your part in that play is? A literal question: Can you see who you are in that situation with those people?

3. At any given moment there is always a 'leading' self-image that defines the awareness of self and the social role to be played. Question: Who do you choose to be?

4. The self-image can be absent when you think you are alone, 'turned inwards', 'on your own' or meditating. It can also be absent in interactions where you are 'completely open', 'completely, spontaneously yourself', or in a similar state. It can be very important information if all the signals, both verbal and non-verbal, point to the absence of a self-image. Usually a part of the client is censoring their self-image because it is emotionally negative and needs to be suppressed. Logically, a self-image can also be absent in people with very limited social skills or a very weak ego.

5. Self-images are unconscious until you are reminded of them. A question to make someone aware of an unconscious self-image: Just pretend that you can see your self-image. Where would you see it, if you could? How big would it be?

6. It is practical for a therapist to behave as if there is only one self-image possible, and also to realise that many unstable flashes of self-awareness can, if you're lucky, slowly turn into one clear visualisation. As trance deepens, the quality of the picture usually improves. Suggestion: Relax and wait and see if a self-image appears. Where do you see it?

7. Self-images are located in the space in front of you and are connected to the kinaesthetic self. Question: Imagine that there is a connecting line going forward from your feeling of self. Does it join to an image? How far away is it? (Support this question with gestures in the space in front of the client.)

8. The intensity and size of the kinaesthetic self increase as the self-image comes closer, becomes bigger, higher, lighter or more central.

9. As well as the location in front of you, there can be other 'self-locations'. These are often auditory – inner voices.
    Multiple self-images indicate either a multiple experience of self, multiple personalities, (Van der Hart, 1991) or a simultaneous awareness of multiple social contexts.

10. Self-images which are not 'front centre' indicate a conviction that 'I mustn't put myself in the centre', or 'I should not be the centre of attention'.
    Question: 'Why may you or can't you see yourself in the middle?' This should elicit the limiting belief (Hollander, Derks and Meijer, 1990).

3.4.3 *Finding transtemporal and transcontextual self-images*[40]

The self-images I work with in my practice can be divided into two categories:

1. *Transtemporal self-image*: This is the image of who you are, who you have always been and who you will continue to be. This is, as it were, the part that corresponds with what Lakoff and Johnson call the 'folk theory of essences' (1999). It is the unchangeable self that spans past, present and future. It may be philosophically or linguistically inaccurate, but it is meaningful from the point of view of therapy.

2. *Contextual self-image:* This is a picture of who you are within a certain (social) situation. This link with the situation ties in with the Gergen's post-modern concept of identity (1998). In therapeutic practice this type of self-image is useful when a client is searching for the right 'role' in difficult situations. 'How should I behave?', 'Who should I be for these people?'

---

[40] This connects to the so-called 'Identity as a resource pattern' which was developed by Jaap Hollander (IEP practitioner's handouts, 2004).

Technique 9: Finding the transtemporal self-image

Indication: When someone needs a general strengthening of the self

1. Take your time and look at your life as if it were a documentary film of your autobiography. (A film screen can be suggested to help this, or a look at the line of life (Derks, 1998c).
2. Ask yourself, 'Who have I always been, who am I now, and who shall I always be?'
3. Relax, and wait until a word or picture about YOU comes out of your subconscious. Accept any word or picture, however vague it may be, and trust that it is the right one. If you get a word, look for a picture. If you have a picture, try and find a word. (Expect to find metaphorical self-images.)
4. Where do you see the picture? How big is it?

Technique 10: Finding a contextual self-image

Indication: When someone needs more empowerment in situation

1. Choose a context (e.g. school).
2. Imagine you are back in the middle of that context. (Help the client to get right into the situation.)
3. Who do you feel you are in this situation? (e.g. Feel as if you were back at school.)
4. Concentrate on this feeling of self and make it stronger.
5. Holding on to the feeling look straight in front of you.
6. Look at the image of yourself that is connected (with a line, energy link, or cord) with the feeling of yourself in that context. (Look for the picture of yourself at school that belongs to the feeling of self and which tells you who you are or what your role is.)
7. Where do you see that image? How big is it?

You may find some self-images are completely inside the body. If so, neither the image nor the connection will be visible. This situation we can describe as complete association with the self-image. My research indicates that this complete association is experienced as being very positive. Most people, however, are not capable of meaningful interaction when they are completely integrated with their self-image. (see previous section, 3.4.2.1, point 4) Therapeutically we use the 'bringing inside of the self-image' as a method of optimising the awareness of self.

Technique 11: Experiment with a group in 'The narrow alley'

Indication: The need to understand more about personal power

The following exercise is suitable for trainers who would like to experiment with the self-image in a group. The trainer does Part I (steps 1 to 7) with the whole group in the form of a conducted fantasy. At the end of this part you can check how the self-image appears to each member of the group.

In Part II (steps 8 to 13) the trainer should first demonstrate with someone in front of the group, after which the group will practise in pairs for about 15 minutes.

Part I

1. Concentrate on your feeling of self as it is now.
2. Decide exactly where in your body you have this feeling.
3. Imagine a line running forward from that feeling.
4. Where, on that line, is your self-image, the picture that lets you know who you are?

5. Once you know where your self-image is, move it about 30 metres away and make it really small. We'll call that 'far off and small'.

6. Bring the image closer, to about half a metre away from you, make it slightly larger than life and imagine it's in bright sunlight. We'll call this 'close, big and bright'.
7. Now take that self-image into yourself. You will probably have to turn it round to do that. This we will call 'turned into yourself'.

Part II

8. Find a partner and stand opposite each other about seven metres apart. Put two seats in the middle in such a way that only one person at a time can pass between them. Imagine that you are in an alleyway.
9. Choose, without telling each other, one of the above-mentioned positions for your self-image – either 'far off and small', 'close, big and bright', or 'turned into yourself'.
10. Once you have chosen, make sure you are experiencing your self-image in that way.
11. When you are ready, walk slowly towards each other, passing between the seats.
12. Turn and face each other and repeat steps 9 to 12. (Choose a different position for your self-image.)
13. After doing this three times discuss with each other what it was like. One question to ask would be 'In what way were the meetings different?'

3.4.4   The perceptual positions of the self-image

As mentioned in Chapter 1, social cognitive development almost certainly begins with the personification of self. Thus a child first learns to think from his own point of view; the first perceptual position (Grinder and DeLozier, 1987). Later he will learn to appreciate other people's points of view.

This development continues in relation to the self-image, too. People learn to see their self-image from their own point of view (first position) but they can also look at themselves through the eyes of someone else (second position). In addition to this they can imagine how another person sees themself. Then they see the self-image of other-personification; in other words, they see what they believe to be the self-image of someone else.

A self-image seen from the first position is a complex phenomenon; the self is seen from two places at once. A person looks at it from the centre of his social panorama, but sees something that it is actually not possible to see, like a captain on a ship cannot see his ship on the horizon.

A self-image seen from the second position is an even more complex piece of mental gymnastics. This complicated cognitive construction implies that you observe yourself from the location of the personification of another and from their point of view. You see your image as you think someone else sees it.

We will see the importance of the second-position self-image when we come to 'authority' in Chapter 4. The second position seems to appear under the influence of a dominant figure – you think that the image the 'authority' has of you is more important than your own self-image.

3.5   *Voices of the will: The auditory self*

Words have the power to activate the experiences they refer to. If I say 'dog' then I call up my dog sub-programme, even if it remains subliminal (Fauconnier, 1997). Theoretically, when people speak of 'I', 'me' or 'myself' there is always some form of self-awareness. This can also be triggered by hearing one's name or nickname.

Another auditory aspect of the self is hearing one's own internal voice. Some people regard their internal voice as the centre of their self-awareness. If this voice is silenced (through meditation or aphasia) then this aspect of the experience of self is lost.

Though all personifications can have a voice, only the voices of the self-personifications contribute to self-awareness. Voices of the personifications of others seem to be outside a person's control. These 'strange' voices can be intimidating both for the client and the psychiatrist. If all personifications are parts of a person (see Chapter 1) it becomes logical to try and control their voices. Bandler has made a video where he shows an extraordinary example of working with a paranoid schizophrenic, Andy (NLP

Comprehensive tapes, 1986). He gets the client's hallucinated personages to sing songs on command.

If more than one personification is active at the same time, one 'me' speaks with its own voice to another 'me' who also has its own way of speaking. Auditory parts of oneself are often situated at the side or back of the social panorama, but very seldom at the front.

3.6   *Tasting and smelling oneself*

The olfactory and gustatory aspects must not be left out of an overview of self-awareness. Someone's repertoire of bodily smells can be an important part of the 'self'. Süskind, in his book *Perfume*, plays with the idea that someone without their own scent is a nonentity who will be ignored by other people. This novel opens our noses and describes how our own familiar scent can be an important part of ourselves. In this respect scent and taste are similar.

Apparently scent is much more important for women in their choice of partner than it is for men, who tend to be more interested in the way someone looks. Women choose men whose body scent is different from their own – this fosters genetic diversity (Walsh, 1996).

3.7   *The function of self-awareness*

Most psychologists of my acquaintance believe that the awareness of self is important, and, intuitively, most non-psychologists know it too. Even so, it is difficult to explain theoretically what generates that importance. What makes 'self' so essential? I will try and answer this question.

The concept of 'hierarchy' plays an increasing role in cognitive psychology (Kunda, 1999). Theoreticians are of the opinion that we defend ourselves from chaos by structuring our thoughts in a hierarchical fashion. This hierarchy arises from strong mental structures directing other, less dominant programmes. A hierarchy works optimally when a very few dominant mental constructions control a large number of weaker ones. In other words, our thinking works well when only a few, highly placed beliefs, neuronal networks or cognitive constructions rule all the others. Such 'aristocratic' programmes make decisions and remove internal uncertainties.

A part of our mental hierarchy is illustrated in the so-called (neuro)logical levels introduced by Dilts (1990) who got it from Bateson (1972), who in his turn was influenced by Wittgenstein and Carnap.[41] To keep it simple I would like to define the logical levels as follows:

At the top of the hierarchy is the level usually described as 'spirituality'; this consists of all sorts of unifying experiences which have to do with the relationship between the individual and the universe, nature, society or god. Spirituality is the category of experience that transcends the individual. These spiritual thoughts are expressed using extremely strong submodalities and overshadow all other thinking.

Bateson (1972) expresses this as follows: 'A high logical type (level) organises the information on all lower levels.' As we have already seen, this hierarchical structure of our mental software has some important purposes:

1. To prevent chaos.
2. To simplify choice.
3. To help resolve inner conflicts.

Choices between a higher or lower level will automatically be in favour of the higher. A choice between two alternatives of apparently identical worth can be made by using convictions and values belonging to a higher logical level – in the same way that a conflict between two army officers of equal rank (e.g. attack or retreat) can only be decided by someone of a higher rank.

In Dilts' (1990) view, spirituality is the highest rank, which is why an intense spiritual experience can direct the course of all thinking. One step lower in Dilts' hierarchy we find identity. Dilts defines this as "whatever one believes oneself to be". He also says: "That which one believes to be unchangeable."

The psychological reality of unconscious cognition certainly does not consist of six categories which are separate and discrete – spirituality, identity, belief, ability, behaviour and environment – as Dilts suggests in his model. However, these pigeonholes give us a way of dealing with something that is otherwise very difficult to comprehend. Some of my colleagues and I are of the opinion that it is the sensory quality of the constructions in those pigeonholes which determine their relative status. The strength of a thought is determined by its sensory quality (submodality) (Derks and Hollander, 1996a).

The sensory qualities of self-awareness seldom have the intensity of a spiritual experience, and those of lower levels even less. However, the human brain also seems to have a sort of top limit for intensity: the lightest, most central, hardest, clearest, highest, nearest experience. Astronomers who try and imagine the 'big bang' will hit this limit. It is impossible to comprehend any more. Although this maximum is often reserved for thoughts that transcend the individual, it can also be applied to the appreciation of self. Someone who does that will have an enormous awareness of self but will necessarily miss the spiritual level. It would seem 'flat out' in the brain is all there is – that if you have used that for yourself you can't give it any more when it comes to spirituality (Derks and Hollander, 1996b).

At times when the self-image is weak the spiritual level can keep chaos at bay. People who cannot rely on spirituality have, of necessity, to use their self-awareness to counter imminent disorder.

Using this perspective I suggest that self-awareness fulfils four important functions:

1. It helps to preserve the contours of the personality and influences all subordinate thought (cognitive hierarchy).

2. It enables people to see who they are and what their position is (self-image).

3. It helps to convey to others what position a person demands and into which category they wish to be put (the social self in assertive behaviour).

4. It makes it possible to reflect social relationships in the social panorama. If you work from a stable position it is possible to give the personifications of others stable positions as well.

3.8   *The social self*

There is more room in the modern Anglo-American culture for individuality than for collectivity (Hogg and Vaughan, 1995). In many other cultures people learn that the collective is more important than the individual. Many Hollywood films depict individual heroes competing against other individuals, whereas the film studios of Bollywood specialise more in tribal wars or family feuds. Most Westerners consider behaviour that is motivated by collectivity to be more or less irrational.

When we study the experience of identity we encounter the difference between the social self and the personal self. In other words, the 'us-side' and the 'me-side' of the self.

To find out which is dominant we ask someone, 'Which is more important to you, your opinion of yourself or others' opinion of you?'

If someone has a dominant social self he will think the opinion of others more important. Also, by listening to how often a person uses such words as 'group', 'clan', 'tribe', or 'society' we can ascertain whether they are more strongly influenced by their collective side or by their individuality. Clothes, tattoos and certain symbols can also give us clues.

Lakoff and Johnson (1997) found that the Japanese use the same conceptual metaphors (mentioned in the beginning of this chapter) as the Americans. The individual is present in cultures where the collective dominates; the difference lies in the priority that it is given. In Japan the social self is the boss. In a culture like that the social self will be higher than the personal self in the hierarchy of logical levels.

Logical levels in unconscious social cognition

Spirituality ··············	Individual spiritual connections Me – universe/god Collective spiritual connections Us – universe/god
Identity ····················	Transtemporal awareness of self: Me always. Personal self: Me as a unique creature Contextual self: Me at a specific moment. Tribal self: We are a family Social self: Together we are the same. Chosen groups: We are friends.
Beliefs ·····················	Beliefs about the social and spiritual world. Beliefs about the physical world Social skills
Capabilities ·············	All other skills Social behaviour: intercourse with own sort
Behaviour ···············	All other behaviour Social environment: social panorama on.
Environment ··········	

Non-social environment: social panorama off.

3.9   *Techniques for changing self-awareness*

In this chapter we will deal with various problems that have to do with dysfunction of self-awareness. There are two main guidelines for doing this:

1. First find the spatial cognitive structure of the problem by using the previously described assumptions – check the social panorama.

2. Discover from this structure where and how something needs to be changed in order to achieve an improvement.

For instance, if the structure consists of multiple self-images, then it will be clear that it would be better if there were fewer of them. If the structure is a small and far-away self-image, then an improvement would be to make it bigger and closer. If the structure is that of a dominant second position self-image, then it will need to be replaced with a first position one.

It is prudent, when carrying out interventions in the unconscious social cognition, to take into account the superior intelligence of the cognitive subconscious. Because of this great intelligence it is not necessary to induce a trance specifically in order to communicate with it (Lankton and Lankton, 1983) '...just close your eyes...' is usually enough. As Weitzenhoffer says in the foreword to Erickson, Rossi and Rossi (1976): "From the point of view of the subconscious there is no longer any difference between 'waking' and 'hypnotic' suggestions, or, if you like, between extra- and intra-hypnotic suggestions." (page xvii).

Assume that every suggestion that the client has understood has already been followed and has been translated into changed constructions of meaning. In short, the social unconscious can deal much faster with much more information than the therapist may expect, and it acts on it at once. Or as my old teacher Don Davis (1981) said: 'Name it and you make it happen.' In other words, if the therapist says, 'amalgamate all those self-images into one' and the client nods and says 'Yes' you can safely assume that the client has already created a picture of combined selves and that repetition of the suggestion will not be necessary.

You can see whether a suggestion has been followed in the verbal and particularly in the non-verbal reaction which follows it: 'Bring your self-image 10 metres nearer . .' will immediately be followed by a smile and a sigh that will tell you that it feels good. The client can usually also describe the effect. An immediate resistance to change, however, often overshadows the actual effect of the suggestion. This will consist of non-verbal reactions such as frowning, groaning, shaking the head – any signals that signify objections. The client will often put the obstacles into words, such as: 'No,

I can't keep the image so close, it keeps shooting away.' These obstacles are what the therapist needs to work on. 'What is stopping you?' or 'Try and get in touch with the part of you that is making the image shoot away.'

Following a suggestion doesn't need to happen consciously, but the effect of the suggestion is always conscious, and the corresponding changes in the awareness of self can be seen in immediate changes in the client's expression, breathing and posture.

Technique 12: Strengthening the transtemporal or contextual self

Indication: A weak self

This technique is a direct continuation of finding the transtemporal (Technique 9) and the contextual (Technique 10) self.

1. Ascertain the strength of the self-feeling on a scale of one to 10. Enlarge the self-image that goes with it. Make sure the eyes of the image are just above eye level and that it is in the middle and at the front. Bring it closer (to about one metre away) Make the connection stronger (light and about 10 centimetres thick) Make it clearer and lighter, as if it were bathed in sunlight.

2. Check the strength of the feeling, again on a scale of one to 10. If this gives an unpleasant feeling then the evaluation of the self-image is probably negative. (I saw myself as an idiot, now I see myself as a gigantic idiot.) If this happens use Technique 13.

3. Match this experience of self with the situation in which the client is going to need it.

4. Check if this change is ecological. Sometimes it is necessary to fine tune – the client should find the optimal size and location for his self-image.

Technique 13: Creating a positive self-image

Indication: A negative self-image

This approach is indicated when the enlargement and bringing closer of the self-image (as in Technique 12) causes negative emotional reactions.

This technique is based on the fact that every self-image is nothing more than a fantasy construction made by the client. A negative self-image is as imaginary as a positive one, so you are justified in asking the client to exchange their negative image for a positive one.

1. Ask the client to think of someone they love and respect. Help them to intensify the feeling by visualising the person close to them. Once the client is experiencing the feeling very intensely, the therapist should anchor it kinaesthetically.

2. Use this anchor to connect the feeling of love and respect with a self-image. 'Feel the love and respect and change the image of the other person into an image of yourself so you end up looking at yourself with those feelings.'

3. When the client has managed to follow these suggestions, you will often see a radiant expression, try and get them to hold on to it for at least five minutes.

4. Connect the newly created positive self-image with the situation in which the client had problems with a negative self-judgement

5. Check any possible objections to the new self-image. These can indicate limiting identity beliefs ('it's all wrong', 'mustn't', 'can't'), which are often the result of early negative judgements from parents.

This intervention has had a wonderfully positive effect on many clients: through it a person can experience, sometimes for the first time, what it is to like and respect yourself. However, a client can also become conscious of all sorts of objections. If this happens the client will spontaneously report which beliefs are cancelling out the connection between the loving feeling and the self-image. They will speak of traumatic experiences or the internalised voices of disapproving parents. Something must be done about these objections before a positive self-image can become permanent (Andreas, 2001).

Technique 14: Consolidation of a positive identity

Indication: To implement a better self-image

You do not need to hunt for limiting beliefs if a client can keep hold of an improved self-judgement for several minutes. It is worthwhile reinforcing the improvement by using the 'Change Personal History' procedure. (Bandler and Grinder, 1979) The most simple approach is as follows:

1. Ask the client to experience the improved self-image as strongly as possible.
2. Ask the client to see himself as a toddler.
3. Have the client teach himself as a toddler to feel and keep hold of the improved self-image.
4. Ask the client to step into himself as the toddler.
5. Have the client, as that small child, re-live the lesson about his improved self (step 3).
6. Once the lesson, together with the feeling, has been assimilated, let the client go slowly through their life imagining how it would have been if they had had this improved self-image.
7. Test the new self-image in the future.
8. Check if there are any objections.

3.10 The self panorama

When a client is asked where his self-image is, they will normally point to one location, but it could also be in two, three or more. If there are several, there will probably be one leading self, situated somewhere around 12 o'clock. A person can also have several observing selves who will usually be next to him, speaking and observing from there.

If the parts of the self are to be found in a complex arrangement in space then we can use the term 'self-panorama', a landscape of self-personifications. Over the last decade it has become normal for psychologists to speak of 'sub-personalities' or 'personality parts'. In fact all personality parts can be found around (and in) the subject. Studying these locations can teach us a lot about the personality. In Chapter 4, which is about social power, we will make the acquaintance of 'the law of the dominant personification.'

This law states which part of the personality has the lead in any given situation. This can be either a self-personification or an other-personification.

Technique 15: The fusing of self-personifications

Indication: Multiple selves need integration

Literature about multiple personalities is seldom about the ease with which the therapy progresses (Van der Hart, 1991). The specialists seem to want to convince us of the almost impossible task facing a therapist who works with a 'real' MPD (multiple personality disorder) patient (Boon and Draaijer, 1995).

I don't know if the following techniques worked because the clients weren't 'real' or because there were other factors involved. I will leave the reader to judge, as a lengthy discussion of the subject does not fall within the scope of this book.

The technique, 'negotiating between parts', as it was described by Bandler and Grinder in 1979, forms a base from which many internal conflicts can be solved. (This is dealt with at length in Derks and Hollander, 1996a). This approach is also suitable for the integration of personality parts on the logical level of identity. Since the invention of this technique it has been successfully applied several hundreds of thousands of times – at least 500 by me personally. In other words, if 'negotiating between parts' is skilfully used, it is a trustworthy manner of reconciling, bringing together and sometimes integrating personality parts. In the case of multiple personalities with more than one alternate personality state or 'alter', the technique needs a strategic sequence of work because only two parts can be dealt with at the same time.

The type of internal conflict that can often be resolved by negotiation between parts can, just as easily, be resolved with the help of 'a resource from the prologue' (Derks, 1998d), particularly if this is a resource from the highest level, a spiritual resource or 'core-state' (Andreas and Andreas, 1994). That means that the client and thera-pist search together for a capacity that would have prevented the client's internal conflicts if they had had it at the time.

The critical part of finding the right resources is questioning. The stan-dard 'core-state' procedure from Andreas and Andreas (1994) can also be used.

Before the right resource is called upon, the client should indicate at what stage of their life (where on their line of life) the conflict was absent. In other words, what was the prologue of the moment of separation. There is often a clearly noticeable moment at which the first personality part began to go off on its own.

As soon as the client has found this moment, the therapist can ask, 'what would you have needed to prevent that conflict?' or, 'What ability would have made the split unnecessary?'

If this capacity is adequately defined, then the resource can be found and activated. In order to do this the client needs intensively to relive a recent experience where they used this ability. 'What was it like when you were using that ability? Think about how it feels, what you notice, how you are breathing, what you say to yourself or to others...' Erickson's assumption that people (always) have access to the necessary resources is of critical importance here. Therapists who do not believe this often cannot motivate the client to look hard enough.

The resource is applied in the prologue to the moment of separation. This is done by getting the client, with the resource still active, to go back to the age they were in the prologue.

Technique 16: A resource in the prologue to the moment of splitting off

Indication: A multiple identity

We use the so-called 'line of life' technique (Derks, 1998d; James and Woodsmall, 1988).

1. Look back to the first moment of separation.
2. Observe from the sidelines and see what resources you were short of at that moment. What should you have been able to do to keep the unity in yourself?
3. Still as an observer, look for a time in your life that you did have those resources.
4. Go back to the moment that you had the resources and relive the experience as intensely as you can.
5. Go back, with the resources anchored in your body, along the line of life to a neutral moment before the moment of separation (the prologue).

6. From there, take the resources with you into the future. Go through the moment of separation with those resources and carry on into the here and now. Add those resources to all the relevant experiences, change everything you need to and continue on into the future.
7. Step back onto the sidelines and check if there are any objections to using those resources in the sort of situations where you have had an internal conflict or a problematical self-feeling.
8. Go back into the future and check if there is anything missing.

When using these procedures it is often necessary to fine tune according to the needs of the client. It is sometimes necessary to repeat steps 2 to 6 several times with different resources. If several moments of separation are found on the line of life, it is a good idea to mark them first, and then to check if the resources that have been found are adequate in each case or if something more is needed. The more dissociation there is, the more this procedure can be divided over several sessions.

Technique 17: Limiting beliefs about identity

Indication: Convictions that you are not good enough etc.

In this book I will only deal with one technique for the change of limiting social beliefs, this will be described in Chapter 5. You can easily transpose this from the context of social attitudes to that of limiting beliefs about identity.

3.11 Some comments about collective identity

Family life is the blueprint for a person's further social cognitive development. The family we come from is, for most of us, the first group-personification in our social panorama (Brown, 1988). We generalise our family members into one cognitive unit, and experience it as a social object with its own location, capabilities, feelings, motivations, identity, name and point of view. This family personification can dominate us: we can lose ourselves under the influence of the family even while feeling that we are a part of it.

The auditory experience of the family includes the names, the dialect and the language spoken by its members. Smell and taste also typify a family in terms of the food and drink it consumes and in the particular perfumes and body odours it has.

Just as with personal identity, we can subdivide the feelings of collective identity into three categories:

THE KINAESTHETIC 'US'
The feeling that belongs to the 'us' experience is often situated in a larger area of the body than the 'me-feeling' of the kinaesthetic self. Whereas the latter is just one point in the body and takes up only a few cubic centimetres, the former often reaches outside the body – usually at the sides and back, or round the shoulders. This feeling comes from the universal basic experiences of being close to other people, cuddling them, hanging on to one another and romping!

A sense of belonging can be accompanied by the feeling that the other members of the group are standing next to you or behind you. Most people use the word 'warmth' to describe the kinaesthetic quality of this feeling: e.g. 'I feel warmth and openness for my friends.'

The word 'attraction' describes one of the important kinaesthetic characteristics of social life. When you feel attracted to a group there is also a need to move physically towards it. In other cases you may feel that you are being pulled towards a group or pushed away from it.

The difference between 'them' and 'us' is paramount in the social self (Brown, 1988). The feeling of 'us' is often stronger in the presence of antagonistic others. 'Them' and 'us' can then be felt simultaneously.

One thing is certain, most people are familiar with feelings of belonging, and these feelings can spur them to enormous effort. For some people, being with their own group is often very important, and may sometimes cause them to cross whole continents to be with them.

THE JUDGMENTAL GROUP FEELING

What is your reaction to the words 'white slavers', 'odd-job men', 'mountaineers', 'paedophiles' or 'millionaires'? The name of a group activates a picture of that group somewhere in your social panorama. This is often followed by an evaluative emotion: a judgment about a group.

That feeling is a direct reaction to the visual or auditory image of that group. We can divide those feelings roughly into three types:

1. Appreciation (love, admiration, fellow-feeling).
2. Rejection (hate, aversion, xenophobia, alienation).
3. Neutrality.

THE FAMILIAR IN-THE-GROUP SENSATION

This is the feeling you get when in the middle of a familiar group. It is easy to experiment with the in-the-group sensation; you only need to imagine that you are together with the members of a familiar group and to remember how that feels. Imagine, for instance, that you are back with your playmates in nursery school or in the army again. Whenever you want to experience the in-group feeling all you have to do is remember a group, team or class and imagine yourself back among them.

What wouldn't you give to be back with your friends from the past? Is it physically impossible? Then do it in your imagination and you'll recapture that feeling of 'us'.

Chapter 4

The creation of power

4.1 *Making people important*

In Chapter 3 I described how a hierarchical organisation of thought helps to prevent mental chaos. This hierarchy develops automatically as a by-product of making choices. Human lives are full of choices: should I stay in with Mamma or should I go out with Papa? Should I have a cat or a dog? A Pizza Verde or a Quattro Stazione?' Shall I wear a skirt or a pair of trousers? In order to make a choice, one concept needs to prevail over the other. This is done by making it mentally more important. The concept that prevails will be more important because it is represented as such in the mind. In other words, it will be given more prominent sensory qualities (Bandler, 1985). It will be bigger, broader, lighter, heavier, etc. The level of its importance will be maintained within the memory image of that concept.

After a life of choice and decision-making there will eventually develop a cognitive structure whereby some concepts dominate others, which in their turn will dominate lesser concepts, together forming a solid hierarchical structure (Dilts, 1990). By fitting everything together in a pyramid, the person will have inner peace and outer certainty. The more a person has already assigned a rank order within an area of choice, the easier it will be to make a decision – and be immediately able to choose what is most important to them. If the differences in importance are still unclear they will first need to create the hierarchy and find reasons for making a certain image bigger, heavier, brighter or taller. Someone whose thinking is fully hierarchically organised will usually be able to make fast decisions. According to Dilts and his colleagues we must see leadership qualities largely as a result of such inner coherence.

When people apply this same cognitive principle to personifications, a social hierarchy will emerge in their thinking. They make one personification more important than another. From my research into social representation, I have concluded that beside all other influences, this hierarchy is primarily how social power is created in the mind. In this book we assume that the levels of importance at which people represent themselves and others determine their place on the social ladder. Authority, dominance, inequality, natural leadership and the tendency to follow others and be submissive to them, are all principally products of mental representation. Social hierarchy in its broadest form is the result of unconscious cognitive calculations where one personification is made more important than another. In other words, however superior a person's qualities may be, they will remain insignificant if other people see it that way.

4.2   *Metaphors about power*

Power is the prima donna of the social opera and the star on the stage of unconscious social cognition. Everyone knows that there is such a thing as inequality, every social psychologist or sociologist encounters it. But this is a poorly researched area because of the unconscious and implicit character of the cognitive principles that govern differences in power.

According to Lakoff and Johnson (1999) social power is generally based on the conceptual metaphor 'big is important'. This seems to be supported by a number of very clear basic experiences. For instance, large objects attract more attention than small ones; they are often heavy and difficult to manipulate. Children are small and powerless and are surrounded by people who are large and powerful. Big people can force you into a powerless position.

Big people can either punish little people or protect them. The oldest are usually the biggest. Because these experiences are common to all, everyone develops roughly the same cognitive linguistic patterns in relation to power and the lack of it. The powerful are represented as big.

World literature and history are inexhaustible resources for the study of powerful people. Robert Greene and Joost Elfers (1998) draw from Japanese, Chinese and European history in their amusing work, *The 48 Laws of Power*. They answer the question, 'what must you do to become powerful?' with a whole list of behavioural tips. Their implicit metaphor is 'Power is a skill that can be learnt', but they have nothing to say about how you should visualise yourself and others in your mind's eye in order to gain power.

The first person in social psychology to define different types of power was Raven (1965). He originated the categories 'reward power', 'coercive power', 'legitimate power', 'reference power' and 'expert power'. In 1970 he added 'information power' to the list. This classic division tells us that there are six reasons for putting someone in a prominent position in our social panorama. The implicit metaphor that Raven worked with is, 'power is property'. Power is something you 'own' and all power falls into either one or a combination of these categories.

Mulder (1977) formulated a set of mathematical rules to which social power conforms. His effort to express the relationship between the powerful and the less powerful in a formula is one of the most progressive approaches in social psychology. You could say that his rules describe patterns of behaviour that must be the result of unconscious cognitive processes at work. For instance, someone who has power does everything he can to keep it and to increase it. Mulder's own metaphor is 'power results from the laws of nature'. Without explicitly naming it, he is also very clear about the role of mental space since he always represents the powerful person, C, above the less powerful, P. In short, he agrees with the obvious fact that people place powerful figures higher in their social panoramas. The core concept in the work of Mulder, however, is called 'power distance' instead of 'power level'. In fact, his theory is about the laws that govern vertical distances.

Other research, however, puts this logical-mathematical approach into a different perspective. In it, power is represented as irrational because, among other things, power is the result of domination. And 'dominant' is something you are, not something you have or do. In this category of theories the implicit metaphor is, 'power is a personality trait'. Someone who is dominant can often have a lot of influence without any knowledge of the power game, without 'owning' any power sources or having anything to do with natural laws. The social panorama model can incorporate this research if we just take note of the fact that, in general, people place personifications of attractive people (Burgoon, 1991), aggressive people (Gunn, 1991), fast thinkers (Sinclair and Derks, 1990), rational and far-seeing people (Morris, 1992), big people (Gunn, 1991), men and celebrities in a prominent, high position in their social panorama. Kalma's research (1991) proves that this positioning is done by lightning-fast, unconscious processes. We assign status to someone within a few milliseconds of the first meeting even when we have no knowledge of their sources of power and even before they have spoken a single word. Women seem to be particularly good at instantaneously determining the pecking order within a group of men (see Johnstone, 1979:33–74). Once we have assigned a rank to someone, their personification usually stays in that position. He or she will be stored at that level in memory.

As well as status-defining factors that seem to be universal and genetically determined, like sex and size, the hierarchical position people assign to one another is also determined by culture. Whenever people see power as a product of culture they use the metaphor of 'power as a role'. People have to learn the importance, in their culture, of age, titles, priests, monks, soldiers, civil servants, aristocracy, income, sporting achievements or the possession of cattle, but once they know this the way in which they make personifications important is universal. In all cultures this is done by making the figure large and putting it in a high, central position.

A simple experiment which I have been doing since 1990 with hundreds of people in training groups gives me great confidence in the existence of a general pattern in the location of authority. I ask my trainees to think of someone who makes them uncomfortable and shy – a boss, an authority or an expert. Next I ask them to call up this feeling of uncertainty. As soon as they are experiencing this feeling I check in what direction they are looking. Then I ask them to point this out – at least 90% of the fingers point to a position high in the central area.

I have acquired much more detailed insight into this unconscious cognitive pattern while helping clients to change their feelings of subserviency into feelings of equality.

4.3   *Patterns of authority*[42]

Dominance and submission are constructed in the mind by representing the self-personification and the other-personification unequally. By making the self-personification small and far away and the image of the other large and close, the other-personification is made prominent and the self-personification subordinate.

These patterns only became visible by analysing social representations on the basis of their sensory characteristics, as this follows from the work that Bandler (1985) and Dilts and Epstein (1989) called 'submodalities'.

In unconscious social cognition, meaning arises from putting several personifications in the same mental space at the same time (Fauconnier, 1997). It is not enough to look only at the other-personification to understand its influence; we need to blend the personifications into the concept of a relationship (Fauconnier and Turner, 2002). We need to comprehend the relationship that results from the simultaneous experience of two personifications. In the case of authority it will be the comparison of the sensory characteristics of the image of the self-personification with those of the other-personification. If the social emotional meaning is one of authority, submission or social inequality then the images of the personifications will display a number of the following characteristics:

---

[42] The inter group subject can be elaborated on further than is done in this book. However, the essence is in Chapter 5.

DISTANCE

I will perceive the other as more powerful if their image is located closer than my self-image.

HEIGHT

I will perceive the other as more powerful if their eyes are situated higher than mine, seen from the first perceptual position (from my own point of view). In other words, if I have to look up to meet the other's eyes, then I perceive them to be stronger.

DISTANCE AND HEIGHT

The influence of a personification becomes less as the distance becomes greater, but the influence that is lost by distance can be regained by height. Therefore, distant personifications that are placed high can still have a great deal of influence, particularly if they are placed centrally.

FROM CENTRE FRONT TO DIRECTLY ABOVE THE HEAD

You perceive the other as being more powerful if their image is in front of you and more central than your own. The most influential personifications are situated on a line drawn from centre front to directly above the top of your head.

IN FRONT AND BEHIND

An important personification situated in front and outside the intimate circle is often perceived as an opponent, while the same personification, if it is behind and within the intimate circle, will be seen as a support.

BREADTH AND THICKNESS

Perceived mass (thickness, breadth, and weight) can serve to enhance the importance of a personification.

ON TOP, AROUND, INSIDE
In some special cases authorities are perceived directly above the self-personification and therefore outside the field of vision, where it is difficult to keep an eye on them. This makes such a personification especially influential because you can't control an invisible personification – they will have more influence on you than you on them. The same applies to other-personifications that are perceived around a person; they can exert an imperceptible influence on the self-personification. Personifications that are perceived on the inside of a person are not usually authorities, but they do have a subtle influence and are likely to engender a belief that there are 'stronger powers' at work.

SOCIAL SUPPORT
The power of a personification increases when it is visualised as being surrounded by supporting personifications, e.g. when you see a president with millions of voters behind them. Social support can also take the form of other sources of power, such as money, fans, access to the media or military might.

4.4 Problems with the highly placed

If we assume that authority is the consequence of the patterns described above, then that means that changes in status will be accompanied by changes in these patterns.

Dutch children believe in St. Nicholas who, to them, is a cross between Santa Claus and the Bogeyman: not only does he bring presents if you are good, but he puts you in a sack and takes you away if you are naughty. And he knows everything there is to know about you. St. Nicholas was the highest authority on earth for me when I was small; he was unbelievably high. I saw him straight in front and dead centre, supported by an army of helpers and with unlimited financial resources. He also had 'coercive' and 'information' power (Raven, 1965). This last was in the form of data, collected by spies, about all children and their behaviour. I believed that even the queen had to obey him, which is why I asked my mother, "Why didn't St. Nicholas put Hitler in his sack?"

Now I see it differently….

As hierarchy stops chaos in our heads, so it does in society. Differences in social power are not necessarily problematical; on the contrary, this principle of order is usually extremely useful (Hanson, 1995) but power can also cause problems. The two most important categories of problem are:

1. Being blocked by someone else's power.
2. Realising the disturbing effects of our own power.

In this book we examine both sides of the issue. Being blocked by the power of another is more common; many of my clients have this sort of problem. The second category is more or less limited to an elite: presidents, pop stars, aristocracy, magnates and actors. Nevertheless, this type of problem can still be serious; if I can't get on with my boss then it's my problem, but if a world leader gets tangled up in his own position of power then many will suffer.

4.4.1   Patterns in problems with authority

Problems make themselves known in consciousness which is why it is relatively easy to analyse patterns in problems. The conscious mind is a 'troubleshooting device' (Baars, 1983; Derks and Goldblatt, 1985); if there is a problem somewhere, then our attention goes straight to it. One of the reasons why diagnostics makes up such a large part of psychology is because problematical experiences are relatively accessible to introspection, interview or questionnaires.

A number of remarkable patterns emerge when my clients complain of problems with authority. As I tried to discover a structure in these patterns, most of my efforts were taken up by the very noticeable changes in the so-called perceptual positions (DeLozier and Grinder, 1987). Many characteristics of subordination seem to point to a compulsive shift from the first to the second perceptual position. Is this coincidence? What cognitive process hides behind such a complaint as, for instance, 'Whenever my boss comes in I just lose myself, and I can only think about what he thinks of me'? This question will be central in the following pages.[43]

WHAT ARE THE SYMPTOMS OF EXCESSIVE SUBSERVIENCE?

1. You move yourself into the position of the authority. In your mind you take the place of that personification by using the second perceptual position. Doing this you see your self-image from the second position, instead of the first. The kinaesthetic self is pushed to the background by the feelings that are ascribed to the other-personification. You focus on what you think are the authority's beliefs and values and try to fathom his motives and, if possible, to satisfy his needs. In short, you begin to see yourself as you think the authority sees you, and you think and feel what you imagine him to be thinking and feeling.

---

[43] Obedience and suggestibility point at hypnotic phenomena. The connection between submission, trance and hypnosis is superbly explored by Robert Temple (1989) in his book *Open to Suggestion*.

2. You become shy, start stammering, blush and you get palpitations. Your breathing falters, you cannot meet eye to eye and you get tunnel vision. You are in a state of 'submission trance'.

3. You cannot express yourself; you feel that your creativity and your freedom of action are blocked.

4. You have the tendency to obey the authority, sometimes even if you have resolved not to.

5. You only want to give the authority positive feedback; you compliment them, agree with them, praise them and try to please them.

6. You are afraid of being rejected or punished by the authority and you want to be praised and rewarded.

7. You ascribe your submissive behaviour to the qualities of the authority and so put power in their hands. You abdicate control of the interaction to the other.

As we have already remarked, these problems are only one side of the coin; it can also be difficult for the authority. Authorities suffer too. In the following summary of their problems we see distrust, power addiction and a lack of intimate contact with equals. The first of these problems is the opposite of that in our previous list; authorities are often stuck in the first perceptual position.

We should see perceptual position as being the central principle determining social power. Powerful people remain in the first perceptual position, while their followers shift easily into the second.

Chapter 1 suggests that the second perceptual position demands a higher level of development than the first, which is supported by the fact that many people are only able to use the first position. Should we conclude from this that people who have developed the ability to use the second position are the only ones to be susceptible to authority? Is that why men are so often the bosses? Can the dominant behaviour of men be ascribed to their inferior ability to identify with other people and not, after all, only to their greater average size? Are women the victims of their own superior social skills?

Complaints about authority from people in command are not often heard in the offices of psychotherapists, but if people in command do complain – and I have had the pleasure several times – then I have heard, for instance, "It seems that the whole thing depends on me. I don't see people any more, only 'yes, sir', 'no, sir' robots. I sometimes wonder what sort of bastard I really am."

WHAT ARE THE SYMPTOMS WHEN YOU HAVE PROBLEMS WITH YOUR OWN AUTHORITY?
1. You always feel a very strong kinaesthetic self and you see a big self-image, which may be inside you. You are always in the first perceptual position; either you are not able to take the second position or your subordinates continually push you back into the first. This they can do by continually asking about your opinions, feelings and ideas. Verbally and non-verbally they seem to focus on your values, beliefs, wishes and feelings. They respect, praise and admire you.

2. You have a (pleasant) feeling of power, respect and superiority. Addiction to this pleasant feeling can, however, lead to the exploitation of other people. In particular you can tend to regard other people as lesser beings and to de-personify them.

3. You have unlimited freedom to express yourself and to use your creativity; even your wildest, rudest or coarsest pronouncements are received with enthusiasm.

4. You receive continuous positive feedback in the form of smiles or presents; everyone is polite, submissive and helpful.

5. You never hear bad news; no one dares to give you negative feedback. If things are not going well you are the last to hear it.

6. You no longer have intimate relationships with equals. Patterns five and six often lead to social disorientation and isolation: 'it's lonely at the top'.

They find it difficult to ask for psychological help because the relationship with a therapist requires inverting the hierarchy. The only people who would be qualified to be a personal counsellor would be either an extremely expensive guru, someone like the Pope, or else a person with no power at all, such as a child or a prostitute.

7. You mistrust other people and are afraid to lose power (leader's paranoia). You fear the people closest to you the most – you are afraid that they are waiting for an opportunity to overthrow you. You need several secret services to check on one another.

8. You no longer know where your power comes from: are your followers forcing it on you or are your achievements, superior qualities and activities responsible? You try to believe the latter.

9. There is a conflict between your first position self-image and that from the second position; there is an enormous discrepancy between who you believe yourself to be and what your followers think you are.

As well as these problems – those that have to do directly with the people involved in an authority relationship – there can also be problems to do with the misuse of power by third parties. For instance, when a general sees that one of his officers is misusing his power over a subordinate. In a situation like that the general has a problem even though he is not directly involved.[44]

4.5   *The mystery of sudden submission*

The most dramatic power situation is acute subservience. This occurs in a confrontation between highly placed individuals and subordinates when all the above-mentioned problems with submission occur at once.

This situation is so generally evident that there was no scientific name for it. The experience of acute subservience is most like unexpectedly meeting someone with whom you are secretly in

---

[44] A similar pattern is seen in relation to spiritual authorities. This will be one of the main issues in Chapter 7.

love; the symptoms are possibly very similar in structure. In order to explain this type of sudden change in behaviour I asked questions about the interaction between physical social reality and the social panorama in someone's mind. I wanted to find out what went on that caused someone to become upset when they encountered someone whom they perceived as an authority.

4.5.1   Classical conditioning of submission

Mental constructions – as personifications are – create a stable image of objects that are of themselves mutable. The enormous changeability of things is made bearable by the fact that people can look at the world of tomorrow and the day after tomorrow with the eyes of today and yesterday. In the framework of this study we can translate Piaget's (1965) concept of 'object permanence' into 'person permanence'. People don't stay the same for a second, but in our mind we imagine them as relatively stable objects. The cognitive stabilisation of relationships forms a large part of the function of social cognition – you are always a child to your mother. We live in a relatively stable social world because people make relatively permanent images of one another.

In the animal world an alpha wolf doesn't have to prove his superiority every second of his reign. Once he is accepted as leader, the alpha only needs to lift his tail and the other wolves automatically manifest submission and follow him. The submission response in wolves seems to be based on classic conditioning – tail up by one wolf means head down by the other. The question is, what has been conditioned, and how? With wolves, one wolf comes out of a bitter struggle as the strongest. But there can also be a history: they may already have learned, in earlier wrestling matches, who was the strongest. The winner learns to code himself as superior and the others as inferior. Does this mean that wolves also use a visual social panorama? Or do they do it by scent? Or is it perhaps something they hear inside that tells them who's the boss?

CLASSICAL CONDITIONING AS STABILISATION OF RELATIONSHIPS
We could say that classic conditioning stabilises leadership for both people and animals. This saves energy – if the stimulus, the

'director', has an off day, he doesn't immediately get deposed by his second in command who is, at that moment, stronger.

But not only status differences are stabilised in this way. What is true for authority is also true for every type of relationship, though it is seldom as noticeable as by authority.

I assume that when someone creates a personification they put it in a particular location in their social panorama, and that this location defines the relationship. So when someone has made a personification that requires submission, then the factor 'location' is chiefly responsible. By an actual meeting between the maker of the personification and the flesh and blood authority the personification of the latter is awoken in the social panorama of the former. The real person is the stimulus, the personification the response.

CLASSICAL CONDITIONING OF SELF-AWARENESS
Using the first hypothesis I made in Chapter 2, 'relationship equals location', I worked on the assumption that the self-personification always stays the same. Only if the self-personification is constant can the location of the other-personification completely define the emotional meaning of the relationship. However, from Chapter 3, we know that self-awareness is not at all a constant factor. The experience of self is coupled to context. In other words, self-awareness is also subject to classic conditioning – the context is the stimulus for a particular self-awareness.

CLASSICAL CONDITIONING OF POWER
Even in nature the survival of the fittest does not work very well if all a survivor's energy is taken up with the struggle for power. Once social animals have accepted a leader – elections are over – they have to go back to collecting food, controlling their territory and bringing up their young.

Mulder (1977) emphasised in his mathematical approach how terrifyingly stable top positions can be. Wherever there is no democratic structure with regular elections, leaders often stay in power for long periods (Mobutu, Suharto, Stalin, Mao, Saddam).

Conclusion: an authority is a conditioned stimulus for submission. That doesn't, however, answer the question of why that stimulus causes such a strong response in cases of acute subservience.

4.5.2   *Subservience and the dynamics of personification*

AUTHORITY AND THE SELF-IMAGE

Your self-image shows you who you are and what your role is among other people. If all the others are more important, then you see yourself as smaller, and that self-image tells you automatically that you should play a less prominent part. A child who does not do this is usually corrected very quickly – it has to learn its place. Acute subservience is fostered by an upbringing in which a child has been taught to put itself at the back.

KEEPING AUTHORITY AT A DISTANCE

It seems to be a universal cognitive principle that the emotional influence of a mental representation is reduced if it is farther away. Personifications that are distant have less influence than a personification that is in the same direction but nearer.

For instance, Private Smith may represent his general as being five metres tall. In order to be able to interact with him every day he puts him 50 metres away in his social panorama. This distance is necessary to make it possible for Smith to keep his feelings of submission within bounds during his working day. It is more comfortable to keep an authority at a great distance, particularly if his power source is punishment and he provokes fear. Smith would suffer a constant feeling of fear[42] if he were to keep a five metres tall general close to him all the time.

Clients who have violent fathers and cruel mothers usually still have their parents close to them in their social panorama. That occasions constant emotional strain, which can eventually lead to all sorts of symptoms. The question is, why don't those clients just put their parents a couple of street lengths away? The reason is

---

[42] The inter group subject could be elaborated further. However, the essence is in Chapter 5.

that these clients often don't want to put their unpleasant parents too far away because they still hope to receive love and respect from them. Those positive feelings would be very weak from a great distance.

For the personifications of loved ones and idols, the need is usually the other way round. They act as a sort of authority in the social panorama. Many people place them very close so they receive a continuous subliminal positive feeling from their presence. That is idolisation.

The factor of distance can help us understand how acute subservience can occur when a distantly placed authority is suddenly put very close.

POTENTIAL FOR AUTHORITY

Even when you are not intimidated by it, you can usually assess the subjective 'potential for authority' of a distantly placed authority figure fairly accurately. Think about which is more important to you: the Queen, the doctor, the tax inspector, Sean Connery or the world champion of your favourite sport.

'REAL' AUTHORITY COMES TOO CLOSE

Some of my clients tell me, 'I see my boss a long way away, and right now I don't feel anything. But I know that he can dominate me enormously.' The same people usually tell me that, if the authority figure were suddenly to appear, they would be incapable of standing up to him.

Take the Queen for instance. Normally she has no influence on me, but believe me, if she were suddenly to materialise next to me I would be very flustered indeed!

So what role does physical (real) distance play in questions of authority? Because it seems as if a switch is pulled when the Queen stands next to me – all the symptoms of intimidation suddenly appear. In the direct neighbourhood of Her Majesty my self-awareness disappears and I lose myself. Does that mean that my mental construction, in which she is kept at a safe distance, temporarily falls apart? Does that mean that in the end the stimulus takes precedence over the response?

No, because an authority has no more influence than you have given to it in your social panorama. For example, if I am an American surgeon visiting this country and suddenly the Queen appears next to me, it doesn't affect me. Not at all, because I don't know the woman, she has no place in my social panorama. Even if she is in the coronation coach with outriders I might still think that it was some sort of marketing activity for Disney World. Would I feel overwhelmed? No way.

Conclusion: the stimulus cannot be more powerful than its potential for authority. The power of the queen is totally dependent on how I visualise her, and the potential for her dominance is locked into that. The question is, how does that work with acute subservience? Why does person A suddenly behave submissively as soon as the 'real' person B, whom they normally see high but distant, comes physically near?

4.5.3   Breaking through the neutral distance

If you do not want to be troubled by an unpleasant and powerful personification, then you must place it far away. In fact all unpleasant personifications are less disturbing if they are farther away. A number of social workers who attended a course of mine saw their clients – drug addicts and criminals – at a distance of more than 25 mental metres in their social panoramas. 'To be on the safe side,' they said, but their problem was that in practice it turned out to be very difficult to have a positive influence on someone who was so far away in their minds.

In this book I use the term 'neutral distance' for the distance outside which there is no feeling, either submissive (unpleasant) or positive. If you place an authority outside the neutral distance, you will be able to stay in the first perceptual position. If you put an authority closer than that, they will have a continuous subliminal emotional influence and the second position can start to dominate. If you put your St. Nicholas too close then you feel a continuous tension and you will keep wondering if you have been good enough.

But what happens when a flesh and blood authority comes within the neutral distance? Imagine that the neutral distance for St. Nicholas for you is 50 mental metres and you have to sit on his lap? Can you keep him a long way away in your mind when you are that close? No, it is hardly possible. But why is that? While searching for an answer to this I had to use my scientific imagination. After some years of research I arrived at three hypotheses.

HYPOTHESIS A: INVISIBLE SELF-IMAGE

Why does a person lose himself? That happens when their self-image is inadequate by being too small, too vague, too fragmentary or too far away. The person loses the stream of information that dictates their role. The question, "Who am I here?" is no longer answered by unconscious information from the self-image so the kinaesthetic self becomes weaker and can even temporarily disappear altogether.

A dominant image of the authority will overwhelm the self-image, particularly if the authority is visualised centre front, in the place where the self-image is normally located. In short, the other-image replaces the self-image. The result is a shift to the second position; you see yourself from the other person's point of view and begin to act submissively.

Here we can also use the concept 'foreground-background' from Gestalt psychology – the image of the other comes to the foreground and the self-image goes to the back. When people describe such relationships they often say things like, 'When Pete's there, I see myself taking second place...'

HYPOTHESIS B: PERSPECTIVE

We have learnt the rules of perception from toys and other objects and later we apply these cognitive laws to imaginary objects like personifications.

One of these laws of perception is that of perspective – used here in the same way as by painters in art school. The law of perspective is that the nearer an object is, the larger it appears.

The earth's surface is the most important reference point, and is the yardstick that people use to estimate the distance of objects. This is quite easy for most people as long as an object is on the ground but, as soon as the earth's surface can no longer be used as a reference point, estimating size becomes much more difficult – as happens in the mountains, in the air, under water or in space.

Natural objects are usually associated with the earth's surface. A mountain we observe from a distance of 1500 metres and whose top has an elevation of about 15 degrees has to be roughly 400 metres high. Our brain automatically uses distance and elevation to estimate height.

What happens when an authority infringes the neutral distance? What happens when the Queen suddenly comes close or when you are sitting on St. Nicholas' lap?

As soon as you see that the 'real' distance from an authority is less than the neutral distance, you temporarily adapt your mental image to this. This adaptation, which is totally unconscious and automatic, mainly involves the application of the law of perspective to the image. Although the authority is a long way away in the social panorama, they still can be seen to be very large. When the brain registers the physical stimulus – the real flesh and blood person – you adapt your mental image to be the same size. If the image of the authority, which is so far away, is such a long way above the horizon, then perspective says that it must be immense. The height the personification of the authority above the horizon indicates the potential for authority and this potential is realised when the stimulus comes too close. St. Nicholas becomes gigantic, even bigger than the Queen.

HYPOTHESIS C: THE KINAESTHETIC SELF IS PUSHED OUT
Elements of the social panorama are not restricted to the earth's surface. Personifications can easily be located somewhere high up in the air. Nothing happens when you place someone above

yourself as long as they are far away. However, if the personification comes closer, then the image in your mind is perceived – in the same way as hypothesis B – as unusually large and starts to cause powerful emotions.

The feelings engendered by a dominant other-image deprive a person of his kinaesthetic self. This comes from the human inability to experience multiple emotions simultaneously. While you can quickly flip between multiple images in your mind's eye, you can only experience one emotion at a time. 'Mixed feelings' are very difficult to manage.

When the other-personification causes stronger emotions than the kinaesthetic self, it immediately replaces the self-personification and you shoot into the second perceptual position.

These were my theoretical observations about acute subservience.

4.6   From the description of patterns to their application

The classic anarchistic slogan, 'No master, no slave', seeks the solution to inequality by challenging authority.[45] Many 'liberators' have, however, understood that oppression stems from the oppressed: 'no slave, no master'. This chapter gives some insight into the cognitive process with which someone makes themself subordinate and can also help to accomplish the reverse.

As well as descriptive models, there are also pragmatic models in social science: models that can be used in practice. The following assumptions, 4, 5 and 6, belong to my pragmatic model; they are not meant to be scientifically tested but to be used as support for the therapist.

---

[45] I learned this slogan in the 1970s from Jaap van der Laan, who was my landlord for 15 years, and also acted as the boss of all anarchists in the city.

4.6.1 Assumption 4: The law of the dominant personification

This law states that people are, at any given time, dominated by the strongest personification in their social panorama. If they perceive the other-personification as being more prominent, then they shift to the perceptual position of that other. Being dominated means that, in your mind, you move to the location of the other-personification.

So if the sensory elements of my image of the Queen are stronger than those of my self-awareness, I will be dominated by the Queen and I will go to the second position with her. Social influence, according to this law, is determined by the strength of the sensory image of social representations.

The law of the dominant personification explains several phenomena that are related to identity such as acting, a state of possession (Johnstone, 1979) and personality disorders. We can regard all forms of discontinuity in self-awareness and its accompanying behaviour as the effect of personifications that take over the existing self.

If a *self-personification* (part, alter, sub-personality) is dominant then we get role changes which, to the extent that the transtemporal self is absent, will lead to multiple personality disorders. In the most extreme form there will be parts that are ignorant of one another's existence and there will be no connecting self-awareness.

If an *other-personification* is dominant then, in general, one of two things will happen: role-play or authority. When actors get into role, they make the relevant personification dominant over their own. The depth of the role will be determined by the relationship between their self-awareness and their awareness of the role-personification. Actors, when doing this, sometimes place their self-image inside or behind themselves in order to realise a maximum depth of the role and still not lose themselves. Some actors actually do lose their self-awareness and become, as it were, 'possessed' by the part they are playing (Johnstone, 1979:143 et seq.).

If a *group-personification* is dominant, then individuals lose themselves in their family, tribe, race, gang or the mass. In this case the us-feeling is stronger than the kinaesthetic self. (See also Chapter 5.)

If the dominant personification is a *spiritual-personification* then it will be a question of inspiration or possession, depending on the strength of the self-awareness (see Chapter 7).

If a *metaphorical-personification* is dominant then someone may feel they are being hijacked by 'the project', 'the computer', 'liberal socialism' or their car.

4.6.2   *Assumption 5: Representation dictates interaction*

The fifth assumption of the social panorama helps us whenever we are concerned with the changing of social attitudes. This assumption is central to Chapter 5, which is about such change, but we can also use it when we speak of changing subservience into equality, as in this chapter.

If we want to use the social panorama as an instrument of change then we must assume that the interaction between people is governed by their own social image. In short, 'representation dictates interaction'.

The theory, 'representation governs behaviour' – a proposition much used by modern cognitive psychologists – is equivalent to this. Actually it means the same thing, although it is put more generally.

4.6.3   Assumption 6: The frivolous assumption

THE MAGIC EFFECT OF ONE-SIDED CHANGE

In order to be able to work effectively with the techniques in this book, both the therapist and the client must be able to believe that they can achieve results by working on only one side of a relationship. If you believe that a relationship is solely the result of the characteristics of the other, then there is no point in changing your own thinking. Instead, you must believe that your thinking is important. The danger is that if you exaggerate this you will end up in the world of magic trying to influence the other person by the 'power of your thoughts'.

Assumption 6 is meant to help both therapist and client not only correct a total lack of power but also avoid fantasies of magical omnipotence.

Assumption 6, the frivolous assumption, says that you can change the attitude of the other (real) person by changing your own social representations. This is achieved by unconscious non-verbal communication.

If you are in love with someone, it is extremely difficult to pretend that you are not. It usually only works if the other person pretends that he or she doesn't notice. The same thing is true when you are angry with someone and try to behave 'normally'. It will cost a great deal of effort to look, breathe, walk, gesture, etc. in a normal fashion. People notice these things subliminally and their social cognition processes the information.

If I have unilaterally buried the hatchet and created a congruent positive feeling about the other, then they will unconsciously pick up subtle non-verbal signals from me. I radiate my new attitude by my relaxed features, steady look, supple gestures, relaxed and purposeful gait, slower breathing and a deeper resonance in my voice. It is very likely that the other will automatically react differently to me.

Clients who have problems in relationships with authority can immediately change this by placing themselves higher or the authority lower, but they often need a therapist to give them the idea.

Mol (1998) reports how children who were bullied were left alone after they had unilaterally improved their relationship with the bullies. This work consists mainly of manipulating locations of the self-image and other-personifications in combination with the transference of resources (see Chapter 5) and the changing of social beliefs.

4.6.4 Assumption 3 again: Location and abilities are the prime personification factors[46]

To change social attitudes we must adjust personifications. Assumption 1, in Chapter 1, states that personifications should be regarded as parts of the person. As thoroughly discussed in Chapter 2, such parts cannot be erased. This limit forces us to adopt other tactics if we want to change personifications. It has proved effective to:

a. Move personifications to other locations.
b. Enrich personifications with abilities.

---

[46] This assumption 3 was mentioned on page 74 in a different wording.

In short, we can achieve most with the personification factors 'location' and 'abilities'; the other personification factors play a much smaller part.

4.7 *Applications*

In my work as therapist I often see people who have problems with authority. With them I make extensive use of the following techniques. I use a combination because they cannot usually be used in isolation.

Bandler and Grinder (1979) say that in order to achieve a permanent result you need to do three things:

1. 'Future Pacing' – coupling the changes to future situations in which the client will need them.
2. 'Test ecology' – finding all objections that a client can offer to the application of the changes.
3. 'Change personal history' – having the client mentally take the changes back through their life and apply them to all situations where they would have made a difference.

These three activities can, for instance, ensure that someone connects a changed image of his boss to a number of future encounters (future pace). Next they check what could go wrong if they really used the new image of their boss (ecology). To do this you ask the client, 'Can you think of any objections to seeing your boss in this new light?' All objections that come to the surface must be taken seriously and the client will have to find a solution to them all. For instance, 'You say that your boss would think you were being disrespectful. What could you do to keep the new image without his thinking that?' The client thinks of a solution. As soon as there are no further objections to the new image of the boss, the client can mentally take it back to the first meeting with the boss and see what would have happened if they had had this image then (change personal history).

I may not explicitly mention these three activities in the techniques that follow but I assume that you will use them as a component of effective therapy and coaching.

4.7.1 Solving problems with authority

One thing most of the complaints that are brought to a therapist or coach have in common is that they have been occurring for a long time and in several contexts, and that the client has given up hope of being able to solve them himself (Derks and Hollander, 1996a). If the problem has to do with being dominated by another it is often because that other person plays on a weak point that the client developed in his youth; the dominant other triggers a weak self-image. If the connection to the family is clear then it is preferable to work with the family panorama from Chapter 6. If the connection is not certain then the techniques in this chapter are recommended.

Technique 18: From subservience to equality

Indication: Problems with submissiveness

1. Find the most recent context in which you were subservient – get right back into the situation.
2. Check the location of the authority figure.
3. Check the location of your self-image.
4. Make yourself positive and strong (Technique 12)
5. Visualise a new experience where the self is bigger and nearer than the authority. Anchor this experience.[47]
6. Go back along your line of life to a moment in your history before you knew the authority figure.
7. Use the anchor and come forward along your line of life, from the moment before you knew the authority, and on into the future. Connect this new experience to future meetings with the authority.
8. Check if there are any objections and find a solution for any you find.

---

[47] By the expression 'anchor' or 'anchoring' we mean the association between some stimulus (often a touching of the skin, a word or a gesture) and an inner experience. This is classical conditioning – combining the stimulus and this inner experience for some time. See Bandler and Grinder (1979) and Derks and Hollander (1996).

Technique 19: Abilities for equality

Indication: Too much power ascribed to the authority

1. Call up the feeling of subservience that is giving you problems.
2. Observe the authority and ask yourself the question, 'What ability does this person need in order to be able to maintain an equal relationship?' Name this ability. Let go of the feeling of subservience.
3. Call up an example in which you yourself have this ability. Make the experience of it as intense as possible. Give it a colour and surround yourself with that colour as you push the ability to its maximum strength.
4. Transfer the ability, in the form of a colour, to the authority. By doing this you can enrich the personification of the authority figure with the missing capability.
5. Call up the feeling of subservience again.
   What has changed?
   What objections, if any, are there to this image of the authority?
   Can you meet him from now on with this image in your mind?

If a client regularly has problems with having too much authority over other people, it can indicate a general inability to take the second perceptual position. The following technique gives some guidelines for training in this. If the problems are sporadic, Technique 21 can be used.

Technique 20: Exercise in taking the second position

Indication: Difficulty in understanding other people

1. Check if the client can recognise all the personification factors in themself and others (see Chapter 1, section 9, p. 11). For instance, 'What is your point of view on a certain situation, and how can that be different for someone else?' 'What do you feel in that situation, and how could that be different for someone else?' 'What is your self-image in that situation, and how would someone else see themself?' etc.
2. Use yourself in the present as an example, and ask the client, factor by factor, to guess your point of view.

E.g. 'How do you think I see you?' 'What do you think I feel about you? 'How do you think I see myself?' 'What do you think my motive is towards you, towards myself?' etc.
3. Find out which personification factor is the most difficult for the client.
4. Practise by literally changing places (actual location) when you have the client guessing abilities, feelings, motives, self-awareness, perspective, etc.
5. As the instant feedback begins to teach the client to do it with you (the therapist), try it with other people from the client's life. Do this in the imagination or, if possible, in reality.
6. Check the effect of the increased ability to empathise on the authority relationship as this is represented in the client's social panorama.

Technique 21: From domination to equality

Indication: Others act too shy for productive cooperation

1. Find the context in which you are dominant.
2. Check the location of the subservient other.
3. Check the location of your self-image.
4. Create a positive, strong image of the other; activate in yourself the capacities that he needs, and send them to him.
5. Create a new experience in which the other is close and on the same level. Anchor this experience.
6. Find a time in your own history before you knew the subordinate person.
7. Use the anchor and follow your line of life from the time before you knew each other on into the future.
8. Check whether there are any objections, and, if there are, solve them.

4.7.2 Power sources: wealth, beauty and the ability to punish

Imagine that you are at a party where there are beautiful people, good music and plenty to eat and drink. The fragrance of perfume mixes with the scent of the barbecue in the garden. How would you feel if you knew that you were completely broke? Would it make a difference if you knew that you had £250,000 in the bank?

It is plain that material wealth is the most important source of power in our society, so let us take a look at the role money, or the lack of it, plays in our social life. Though a lot of people think that there should be no difference, there are very few for whom rich or poor really counts for nothing. We often see a difference between the way someone reacts to money and how they think they ought to react. The question is, do you want money to play as important a part in your social life as it does in society as a whole?

Many people's self-respect depends on how much money they have. Their self-image is, to a large extent, determined by their finances. To have is to be. In a way that is justified – the more money you have, the more exceptional you are; you belong to the very exclusive club of the very rich.

Technique 22: Exercises for dealing with wealth

Part One: The rich other

Dealing with wealth means changing its critical sensory qualities in your social panorama. If you are thrown by rich people, try the following approach.

1. Think of a few rich people and call up your feelings about them.

2. Check the critical sensory qualities of wealth (Bandler, 1985). In other words, find the sensory quality in your image of a rich person which makes the feeling worse. What changes in the image if you imagine that the person is much richer or poorer? What do the images of rich people in general have in common? Are they in the same place? Are they perhaps the same colour or the same size? An example: rich people may seem bigger; in that case the critical sensory qualities will be 'size'.

3. Change the image of a rich person until you feel comfortable with it. This can be as simple as making the image of the person smaller or darker. Change that sensory aspect until the person no longer looks as if they are rich.

4. If that is difficult it can mean that there is a part of you that dis-agrees; make contact with that part and find its positive intention. Involve the part in the process and try again.

Such a change in the sensory attributes of wealth does not neces-sarily need to be permanent to be effective. Some people use it just before and during an interaction with a rich person; that can be enough. So next time you want something from a millionaire, shrink them a bit when you offer them a drink. (That is, if your critical sen-sory channel for wealth is 'size'.)

Technique 23: Exercises for dealing with wealth

Part Two: The poor self

1. Imagine that you possess 10 times as much money as you actu-ally have. How does your self-image change? What is the critical sensory channel involved?

2. Experiment with the critical sensory channel by imagining that you are as rich as you would like to be. It can be useful to use the image of someone who is that rich; visualise yourself with the same sensory values and connect that image to your kinaes-thetic self.

3. Make any changes that are necessary in that context. Keep an eye on the ecology, otherwise this experiment might get to be expensive! Work with an experienced therapist to avoid negative consequences.

Changing the sensory attributes of wealth is nothing new. You have probably heard someone say, "Now that I know her better, I no longer see her as a rich woman, just as a nice person." Someone who says something like that has gone through a similar process without the intervention of a therapist. Those who say 'riches are in your heart' probably know the principle too.

Jim, a share analyst, once told me that for him rich people were actually smaller. Why? He explained it as follows, 'In order to get rich, people have to use rigid materialistic principles. If you do that it is not so difficult to earn a lot of money on the stock exchange. Whenever I see someone who is rich I always think, "OK, you've won the game, but does anything else exist for you?"' This way it is easier for Jim to deal with rich people however broke he may sometimes be.

It is easy to see that this method is applicable to every social dimension. Once the critical sensory quality of a particular characteristic has been found it is possible to change your perception of the people who have it. Of course you will meet many objections on the path to permanent change, but Bandler and Grinder (1979) taught us to see internal resistance as self-defence. As has already been said, this method can lead to self-deception, so be careful. Remember that rich people are used to being treated in a special way and they may become irritated if you, like Jim, treat them differently. Try looking at the situation from the third perceptual position: see your own social panorama *and* that of the rich person. If you damage one of their most important dimensions the two will no longer match. Ask yourself if you are ready for this.

4.7.3   *Reward, punishment and withholding approval*

Reward and punishment shape our behaviour and they always involve social inequality (Raven, 1965). A relationship is, by definition, dominated by the person who rewards or punishes. Reward and punishment are so widespread that we must mention them as aspects of social power. First come parents, then teachers, military commanders, policemen, tax inspectors, bosses, leaders, partners and many others who can punish or reward you.

People with the power to punish must be represented in a threatening way in the social panorama. Look up to the left; this is often where people who can punish you are situated. Here, too, are the people whose approval and respect you desperately want to receive and by whom you feel punished when that approval doesn't materialise. The withholding of approval is a very powerful way of building authority.

Technique 24: Getting approval anyway

Indication: Still waiting for approval to come from someone

1. Visualise the authority who is refusing to give you respect, recognition or approval.
2. What ability is missing which causes them to be unable to give their approval? Name this ability.
3. Think of an example in your own life when you had this ability. Get inside the situation and feel how it was to have it.
4. Take a bird's eye view of the authority's line of life. Find a suitable moment to teach the authority that ability.
5. Give the authority that ability in any way you think is suitable. You could put it in a drink, for instance, shine it on him like a ray of light or just tell them about it.
6. Look again at the authority's line of life and see how it changes as a result of them having that ability.
7. Imagine that the authority now gives you their approval, all that you deserve and preferably a little more. Finally, in your mind, clone the authority; fill a football stadium with countless duplicates. Stand in the middle of them and receive approval from them all. Soak the feeling of appreciation into your bones.

Tests on animals have shown that an unpredictable pattern of reward and punishment has an enormous effect. Parents who punish and reward their children in a random fashion create a very strong dependence. Their authority is much stronger than that of parents who are predictable and reasonable.[48] The pattern, 'getting approval anyway' is useful in such situations.

In Chapter 6 you will see a similar approach, which is specifically aimed at the parent–child relationship.

4.8   Political power

The social panorama model gained a place in politics thanks to the Austrian professor of economy, Walter Ötsch, in particular

---

[48] I estimate this to apply to 70% of human beings.

through his study of the 'demagogic communication patterns' of the populist politician, Jörg Haider (Ötsch, 2000).

Politicians often understand very well to what extent power is made by social cognitive constructions. They create personifications in the minds of other people and they influence what those personifications look like. In their own social panorama they often have large numbers of interconnected personifications in shifting patterns that cause their power to increase and decrease.

Democratic power is in the hands of voters. A democratically elected leader must have an important sensory code in his mind for the image of the support of the electorate.

When two leaders meet, they each visualise the power of the other in their social panorama. In this way the images of both the first and the second perceptual position of all the personifications involved contribute to the way in which someone's power is experienced in such a meeting. What does the connection of the other to his followers look like? How many subversive elements are there in the image of that group? And, more importantly, in what juxtaposition does each leader see themself and the other? Are they opposite or next to each other?

In my seminars on the social panorama I ask chosen representatives of groups to negotiate. In this way both the participants and I can study a phenomenon that I have called, 'the negotiation panorama' (Derks, 1998c, 2000a). How do negotiators experience themselves, the people they represent, their negotiating partners and their group?

Technique 25 can help to coach or prepare someone who has to take part in a negotiation.

4.8.1 *Optimising the negotiation panorama*

Whenever a negotiation is about a conflict of interests between groups there are two social units that take the leading part: the personification of the negotiator and the personification of the people they represent. From the point of view of the followers it might seem that it is all the responsibility of the negotiator, but the negotiator's status, effectiveness, authority and mandate are completely dependent on the people they represent.

In a negotiation between groups this image is doubled because there are at least two negotiators and two represented groups involved. Because of this we can say that there is a social panorama from four viewpoints. We can create an image from the point of view of both negotiators and both groups. And we can also stand on the sidelines (third perceptual position) to look for solutions to difficult situations.

Technique 25: Determining a negotiation panorama

Indication: Preparing for difficult talks

You (negotiator A) are in the process of a negotiation. You need to find out how you experience the social power field that is involved. First, place four chairs in a space. Put the two negotiators' chairs opposite each other and the two chairs for the groups to be represented behind them. Move the chairs until they are in the right place in the negotiation panorama. Explore the panorama by going from chair to chair.

1. Take, successively, the following perceptual positions:
   - your own (first position, negotiator A)
   - that of your opposite number (second position, negotiator B)
   - that of your own group (second position, group A)
   - that of the other group (second position, group B)

2. Check your own feeling of self and your self-image within the negotiation.

3. Check the connection between you and the people you are representing.

4. Check how you see your opposite number, their people and the connection between them.

5. Check how you think your opposite number sees you and your group.

6. Check how you experience the spatial position of all four.

7. Check the whole negotiation panorama for 'heavyweights' – authorities and supporting or opposing coalitions.

By using the social panorama to map large power structures you can adapt them to the needs of politicians. This principle has already proved to have great potential in business communication, too.

Chapter 5

Relationships with groups

5.1 Patterns in unconscious 'pigeonhole' thinking

In the last decades cognitive psychologists have tacitly agreed on one thing: that our thinking is ruled by classification and hierarchy, which people use to give shape to their mental maps of the world. Social cognition psychologists, too, use this as a theoretical starting point into how people categorise and assign ranks to themselves and others (Kunda, 1999) when they create their blueprint of social reality.

In Chapter 4, I described the mechanism by which people create hierarchical relationships, big fish and little fish – the relative status aspect of the social panorama. The processes used in categorisation will be the central subject of this chapter. This is obviously important as problems between groups are caused by social maps in which some personifications are put in wrong, negative or inimical pigeonholes. The key to the social cartography of peace would seem to lie in the answer to the question, 'How do people classify one another?' (Derks and Hollander, 1996a).

Social psychological research into this question looks at individual and cultural patterns within social classifications. What are the types into which people are divided within a particular culture or subculture? Which groups engender positive feelings, and which negative? Who is seen as being powerful, intelligent, rich, aggressive or submissive? Augoustinos and Innes (1990) found a way to cluster this sort of data so that it could be represented schematically. Their two dimensional graphs show a population's 'average' map of social reality. In such an integrated social representation model you can see which group is rated positive, which negative and which groups are considered the most important.

When we translate this area of research into the three-dimensional space of the social panorama it appears that there is a specific location behind every pigeonhole. Using Technique 2: "Finding the location among all mankind" (Chapter 2) we can see what categories a person uses and where they are located in his social panorama. If you ask a hundred people, 'Where do you see skippers, Bedouins or the royal family?' and then combine the

160

answers, the result will be an average 'three-dimensional social reality'.

The data that has been collated in this chapter emerged from a large number of therapy sessions that dealt with problematical relationships between groups. Many insights came also from demonstrations and exercises in more than 50 workshops in which groups were formed and made to feel hostile to one another by means of competition and gossip. The subsequent resolution of those negative attitudes yielded much insight into the cognitive mechanism.

5.1.1 Group-personifications

Group-personifications are the result of people putting one another into categories. They consist of multiple individuals who function as a single 'person-like cognitive construction'. Or, in lay terms, group-personifications come into existence when different individuals are all 'tarred with the same brush' on the basis of one characteristic. Expressions such as 'social scientists', 'Germans', or 'tourists', all betray such cognitive constructions. We can recognise particularly strong group-personifications by the word 'the' – for instance *'the* Belgians', *'the* methodologists', *'the* fishermen' or, even more clearly, by making the noun singular as well; 'the Spaniard', 'the Frenchman', 'the Boche', 'the Jap', 'the Geordie'. Such group-personifications are also furnished with abilities, feelings, motives, self-awareness, perspective, spiritual connections and their own location in a person's social panorama.

The necessary cognitive processes for the formation of group-personifications are often referred to by the words 'generalisation' and 'stereotype'. If the group-personification is coupled with the formation of negative attitudes then we can speak of 'discrimination', 'racism', 'prejudice', 'ethnocentricity', 'inter-group polarisation' or 'in-group/out-group thinking'. If a large number of people within a society use this social pigeonhole thinking in a similar way, it can result in uncontrollable forces. Here I think it will be enough to say that throughout human history pigeonhole thinking has formed the social-cognitive fuel for an endless series of bloody confrontations. Wars like those in the Balkans, Afghanistan,

Rwanda, Northern Ireland and Israel prove that the processes are easily called into existence, but once started, are very difficult to check. The need for more insight into the psychological mechanism that is at the base of these conflicts has occupied many a psychologist, among whom Allport (1954) and Sherif and Hovland (1961). A large part of social psychology has developed from these studies.

To stay within the framework of my research into the patterns in unconscious social cognition and their applications we will restrict ourselves here to the following questions:

1. What is the spatial structure of social attitudes?
2. How can we use the knowledge of this spatial structure to improve problematical relationships with group-personifications?

5.2   Social attitudes in the social panorama

Simply put, a social attitude is nothing more than the feeling elicited by thinking about particular people (Heider, 1958). In other words, you think about a personification and that gives you either a good, neutral or bad feeling. If you want to understand where that comes from and ask yourself, 'Why do I feel slightly sick when I think about butchers?' you may sometimes discover a really solid reason, but much more often you will find nothing tangible. The unpleasant feeling in your stomach is there and that's it. You 'just don't like' butchers, it doesn't 'click' between you, or butchers are 'not your type'. In short, the lack of introspective access makes it very clear that there are unconscious processes at work.

As already mentioned in Chapter 3 with regard to the feeling of self, we have to assume that the prominent role of gut feelings in social life has an ontogenetic basis. In other words, we need to be aware of the fact that in the human embryo the development of the digestive system precedes that of the brain (Gershon, 1998). Long before the brain takes over control of the body, the intestines are intelligently turning milk into more baby. Gershon calls the enormous number of nerve cells surrounding the intestines the 'second brain'. His hypothesis is that people in their first months of life think more with their stomach than with their head.

The importance of gut feelings in social interaction can probably be reduced to a combination of two very early, physically based conceptual metaphors:

1. I am my stomach
2. Mother is food

These conceptual metaphors, which are transformed from basic experiences, later become the automatic thought processes that form the building blocks of the cognitive unconscious.

'I am my stomach' and the effect that mother's feeding has on me (nice, satisfied, full) may later be generalised into another conceptual metaphor, 'Nice people give me a good feeling in my stomach'. Gershon indicates that gut feelings influence our decision-making in an unconscious, autonomous way. The gut supplies positive or negative feelings that are probably variations on the basic experience of 'good food' and 'bad food'. Social attitudes, looked at like that, have an unconscious undertone that tells us whether or not someone 'tastes' good.[49]

5.2.1 Social attitudes function unconsciously

There has also been some experimental social-psychological research done into the degree to which social classification processes are unconscious and automatic. Devine (1989) was of the opinion that everyone used unconscious stereotyping. In particular, her experiments with subliminal word display showed that a connection between the words 'African-American' and 'aggression' was elicited in almost all test subjects. In other words, prejudice against a particular group within a culture functions unconsciously and it would appear that everyone belonging to that culture is susceptible to it. After a number of experiments that followed on from this, Kunda and Sinclair (1999) came to the

---

[49] This gives Freud's oral and anal phase a new meaning.

rather more optimistic conclusion that people differ in the degree to which they allow their behaviour to be dictated by these unconscious prejudices. Kunda and Sinclair imply that the difference between a racist and a non-racist is that the latter control their unconscious racist associations and do not act on them.

Research by Chen and Bargh (1997) has shown that unconscious stereotyping also has an effect on those who are being stereotyped. They discovered that black applicants before a selection committee were unconsciously treated differently from white applicants, which had the effect that the black applicants were more awkward in their interview. This, of course, reinforced the prejudice the committee already had about their incompetence. This research supports Assumption 5 in this book that a person's social representation governs the interactions they have. Chen and Bragh also add foundation to Assumption 6, the frivolous assumption – the image you have of someone has an actual effect on their behaviour. I use this unconscious interaction as the underlying assumption when I speak in this book of unilateral improvement of human relationships. If A changes their attitude to B, then that has an effect on B's attitude to A: I attribute this effect to unconscious non-verbal communication.

5.2.2 Us and them

Lakoff and Johnson (1999:341) describe what they call the 'container metaphor'. As already mentioned in Chapter 1, this has to do with a universal abstract concept, the essence of which is the difference between 'inside' and 'outside'. A container is a thing you can put things into and take them out again. A womb is a 'container', even a baby is something you put something into and out of which something comes. A cradle, a room, a house and a car are all examples of containers. The conceptual metaphor of something which things can be put into or taken out of is probably also unconsciously applied to the family and other social entities: within the family and outside it, within the tribe and outside it, within the nation and outside it.

The universal character of inside-outside thinking leads to thinking in terms of in-groups and out-groups. The most extreme form of this, idealising one's own group and rejecting and hating the other, has certainly been the cause of a great deal of bloodshed. The container metaphor is universal, so the distinction between 'them' and 'us' would seem to be anchored in the genes. But in spite of this, in this book I work on the assumption that the social application of the container metaphor is learnt. I shall also assume that the extent and the manner of such thinking is variable and susceptible to influence.

Thinking in terms of in-groups and out-groups is not necessarily a bad thing. It is most noticeable when it has destructive consequences. But 'us and them' thinking can also be cultivated, in the form of competition, to get the best out of people. Sport, art, the economy, science and technology all flourish under controlled rivalry. Most people I know would love to live in a world in which competition served progress but there was still peace. In short, there is more than one side to unconscious social pigeonhole thinking and knowledge of the inherent patterns may help to prevent deadly excesses.

5.2.3 Belonging

One of the most basic patterns in someone's unconscious social cognition is the difference between the groups to which they feel that they do or do not belong. In social psychology (Brown, 1988) these phenomena are broadly grouped under the name 'social identity'. What I will add in this book is some examination of the sensory qualities of the cognitive constructions involved. How is 'social identity' placed within mental space and what is its sensory form?

From my research it would appear that in the first instance the difference between belonging and not belonging is made by the internal sense of feeling. 'The feeling of belonging' consists of a combination of two essential components, the kinaesthetic self and the kinaesthetic image of the group.

The critical reader will understand that defining such vague patterns is an art in itself. Words are often not enough to describe the answer to the question, 'How do you know that you belong to this group?'

When you ask people this question you will immediately notice that they indicate areas of feeling in space and in their bodies by means of gestures. If you ask test subjects to describe the relationship between themselves and the group with their hands, a fairly coherent image will emerge. My working hypothesis is that in the experience of 'belonging' the kinaesthetic self is surrounded by a feeling of the group. An 'us-feeling' arises when the 'me-feeling' is surrounded by feelings that are connected to and blend with the group.

The location of the 'us-feeling' takes up a larger area of the body than the kinaesthetic self and is often also partly felt outside the body in the air around it. This form of feeling in empty space outside the limits of the body, where there are no physical sensors, indicates cognitive abilities that have received very little attention within academic psychology, but which are described in detail in the typically Dutch discipline, 'Haptonomy' (Veldman, 1987). The basic experience of actual bodily contact with warm-blooded others is possibly the origin of the development of such social feeling constructions outside the body.

By 'not belonging', the feeling of self and the feeling of the group stay separate; there is no connection between the 'me-feeling' and the kinaesthetic representation of the group. 'I don't belong' is a synonym for 'I'm not part of it', 'I am not in', or 'I'm outside'. These expressions mirror the application of the container metaphor to the kinaesthetic self; the representation of the group is the container and the feeling of self can be inside or outside it. Because this pattern is so self-evident, I probably do not need to support it with any more examples.

The image or images that someone has of a group to which they belong will dictate not only their role within the group but also affect their self-image. Someone's self-image is often literally a part of the group image; they see themselves as a group member among other members, and so know what their role should be. The close relationship between the phenomenon 'self-image' and 'image of a group you belong to' is easily explained on the basis of the hypotheses in Chapters 1 and 3. There I said that the development of an image of others precedes that of the self-image. We see others first, and construct an image of ourselves among others in a later phase of development. This self-image allows us to see ourselves in the same way that we see others. In the (individual) self-image we usually leave the others out, but in the image of a group to which we belong we often see ourselves in their midst. It is more like a mental 'group photograph' in which we recognise ourselves and is often a snapshot of a moment that illustrates membership of the group; the time someone received a degree, when the whole family was at a funeral or the first time someone went to a football match.

The awareness of self changes with the context (Gergen, 1998). A well-chosen self-image will ensure that a person plays an appropriate role in any given situation. In the same way, people can base their role behaviour, appropriately or not, on the fact that they belong to a certain group. Though you may be inordinately proud of being a marine, you will probably discover that it does not provide the most appropriate role for every situation.

Just as the self-image changes with context, so will membership of one group play a more important part in certain situations than membership of another. What Brown (1988) calls 'social identity' is the sum total of the groups to which a person belongs. That is a nice definition, but how does someone know, in any given social environment, what is the best choice for his group identification? This probably works in the same way that self-awareness is linked to a particular context, by classic conditioning. If you are a marine, then the stimulus 'barracks' will elicit the image of 'the marine', which will tell you how to play the role.

PERCEPTUAL POSITIONS AND 'BELONGING'
People can experience the feelings they ascribe to their own group in the first perceptual position. 'I am a marine and I feel as a marine. We marines feel ourselves to be superior saviours in hopeless situations ....'

For people who are not part of a group, they can only experience the feelings of that group in the second position. If you are not a marine, then you can answer the question, 'How would a marine feel?' by imagining that you are one, by putting yourself in his place, by stepping into a marine's shoes or by placing your kinaesthetic self inside what you (possibly unconsciously) imagine to be 'the marines'. Doing this you might discover, to your surprise, that, 'Actually, they feel like puppets in the hands of fat politicians with over-large cigars ....'

The experience of second position group feelings can be a helpful stage in the transition from outsider to group member. In short, you meet a good bunch of people, think about them, put yourself in their place and then start to want to belong. 'Belonging' implies that it is possible to experience the 'us-feeling' in the first position. 'When I was drinking with the marines every week, I thought, … Hey! I'd like to be one of them. I bought a uniform and a cap in the army surplus and now I really belong! Don't I?'

No, you don't.

LOYALTY
The way in which people become members of a group is, on its own, a whole area for research. The question here is, what is the process of transition from outsider to group member? For instance, it is not enough to buy the uniform to become a marine; you must first undergo several months of very hard training and only when you have survived all the ordeals do you receive the coveted beret. Then you are proud to belong. The procedure of acceptance is like a painful initiation ritual. That is very different from becoming a member of an average cricket club, where paying your dues and buying the clothes is enough to become fully accepted as a member. Playing well helps to raise your status.

A person can be 'born into …' or 'married into …' a family, tribe, country or aristocracy. To become a member of yet other groups you may have to buy your way in, be approved, be elected or achieve something special. How does someone become a member of a crime syndicate? Not by filling in an application form! It may be a birthright, as in the Mafia – in which case family membership is linked to syndicate membership. In some African black magic circles you have to poison a family member before you can join[50] and, just as with the Neapolitan Camorra, the only way you can leave is by way of the undertaker.

The way someone becomes a member of a group is very important in determining the degree of loyalty. Most people are more loyal to their family than to their colleagues, but some of them will be more loyal to their football club than to the company they work for. Usually, the more difficult the initiation, the greater the loyalty; the murder of a relation forces members of that African secret society to develop a much stronger loyalty to the syndicate than to their family.

We can discover the hierarchy of the groups to which someone belongs on the basis of loyalty. This can be done simply by asking, 'If you had to choose between the marines and your family, which would you choose?' One group will be chosen, and that group will often be higher and closer in the person's social panorama.

In cultures with a great tradition of family loyalty (e.g. Africa), this loyalty can be experienced as a hindrance to personal development. To get on in a material or social sense people first need to escape their family, but disloyalty to the family is often a taboo for which the penalty is death.[51] Such secret societies help people to get away from their families. Members support one another, afford protection against the revenge of the family and give one another privileges that are usually worth more than anything the family can offer.

5.2.4   *Patterns in group-personifications*

The notion of a group consists of a number of visual, auditory and kinaesthetic components. If you draw someone's attention to these sensory characteristics, they will usually be able to tell you fairly precisely exactly where they see, hear and feel something.

---

[50] With thanks to Peter van Abspoel who told me about his very close encounter with an African black magical secret syndicate.
[51] It is difficult to accumulate money, because all income is shared with all family members. To safeguard a starting capital for a business is very difficult.

In the following summary I will describe the patterns I have come across in connection with 'us and them' thinking and 'belonging'.

PERSONIFICATION FACTORS

In Chapter 1 I described a group-personification as multiple individuals functioning as a single concept in someone's thinking. I assume that the same personification factors are ascribed to it as to all other personification types. First, people give a group a specific location. Then the group is assigned abilities, feelings, motives, self-awareness, spiritual connections, its own view of the world, physical existence and a name.

We certainly ascribe all nine personification factors to our 'own' group, and we have filled them in for 'ourself' so we know where we are, what we can do, what we feel, what we want, how we see ourselves, how we fit into the universe and what our perspective on the world is. We know, too, what we look like, how we sound and feel and we know our name.

I also explained how the omission of personification factors can lead to the experience of 'otherness'. A personification cannot exist without a location; if you do not give a group a location in your social panorama you deny its existence. If you omit abilities, you see the group as incompetent and powerless. Without motives they have no will of their own. If you leave out feelings then the group becomes an insensitive object. If you omit their self-awareness they become faceless numbers who are not aware of what they do. If you leave out their spiritual connection they become soulless heathens. Even if you do ascribe all nine personification factors to an unfriendly group these factors may have too little content or negative values – wrong place, disgusting abilities, asocial motives, inferior feelings, a stupid idea of the world and a spiritual connection with the devil.

The development of a strong negative attitude to out-groups is often accompanied by the omissions of several personification factors with the result that the group appears not to be human.

DISTANCE

Distance plays a crucial role in the distinction between 'them' and 'us'; the in-group is close and the out-group far away. In general, personifications of groups to which you do not belong are placed far away. Usually, the larger the group of 'others' is, the farther away it is.

What happens if such a large group of others comes very close? It will cause extreme tension, particularly if it consists of highly placed individuals. If the personification of a group to which you do not belong is dominant, then the 'law of the dominant person-ification' (see paragraph 4.6.1) sees to it that you will feel obliged to be assimilated by that group. If the attitude to the group is positive, then you will be 'sucked in' and experience 'us'. If the attitude is negative then it will be a mental struggle to stay out of it.

The situation of a toddler in its family is that of a confrontation with a dominant group and the child will usually be assimilated by its family. Identification with the other family members and the family as a whole ensures the necessary development of the 'us-feeling'. The family, as a dominant group-personification, plays an essential role in human socialisation; it ensures that people become acquainted with feelings of solidarity that they can later apply to other groups. Many adults continue to personify their family as a unit (see Chapter 6).

The importance of the family within a culture will be a factor in determining the family's place in someone's social panorama and how loyal he will be to that family. People from cultures in which the family is central seem usually to have their family-personification all round them, a few feet away.[52]

BREADTH
Group-personifications are usually wider than individual other-personifications and can surround a person. If the group-personification completely encircles someone, then they will automatically feel themselves to be a member of that group.

HEIGHT
The height of the eyes of a group-personification is usually more difficult to ascertain than by individual other-personifications, but height is just as important for groups as for individuals. The significance of height in dominance and subordination seems to be a universal pattern with very few exceptions. An 'own' group will feel stronger if it is seen as being higher.

Ötsch (2000, 2001), in his study of the demagogic communication of the populist politician, Jörg Haider, found that if his out-groups were high then they were dangerous enemies (Korruptionisten), but if they were low then they were weak trash (Sozialschmarotzer). Ötsch uses the concept 'demagogic

---

[52] On the initiative of Benny Gelenbrecht, we saw a special social panorama course devoted to cross-cultural psychotherapy in June 2002.

panorama' for the social construction in which the 'us' is autocratically led against 'them' by a 'super-us' (the leader).

LEFT OR RIGHT

In many people's social panorama the distinction between left and right corresponds with the social dimension that, for them, comes next in importance to power (height) and intimacy (distance). A person can, for instance, choose to put friends on the right and enemies on the left, or women on the right and men on the left.

More often than not the 'own' group is visualised straight in front. As in-group and out-group thinking begin to dominate, then a radical left-right division can come into being, as happened in the Netherlands in the 1970s.

DARK AND LIGHT

Most people associate light and dark with positive or negative attitudes. Making a personification lighter almost always makes it appear more positive.

COLOUR

Colour varies with light and dark. More light, together with more warm colours (yellow, orange or red), will almost always improve the attitude to a group.

It is difficult to say whether dark colours are universally connected with a negative attitude. The generally accepted preference for a dark skin colour as an ideal of beauty for Northern Europeans would seem to contradict this universality.[53]

MOVEMENT

Group-personifications can seem to be moving in a particular direction. It usually has a strong emotional influence if they are approaching from the front. Then, of course, the question is, are they friends or foes?

---

[53] Because of cultural taboos, I will leave this subject alone.

SOUND

A personification's auditory part is a voice that speaks of its feelings, motives and beliefs. In the case of a group-personification people generally say that they hear these voices from wherever the group is located. Auditory signals usually get clearer if one takes the second perceptual position.

The voice of the in-group automatically comes from close by, while that of an out-group seems to come from afar. The qualities of these voices can differ radically, too. It is interesting to listen to the voices people use to quote one another. If someone puts into words what they think is the opinion of an out-group, they will usually do it in an unpleasant, grating voice.

INTERPERSONAL BONDS WITH GROUPS

When people think about a particular group they usually have – in addition to judgmental feelings, which are usually experienced in the gut – sensations on the side of the body on which the group is situated in the social panorama. If the group is on their left, then the feeling is also on that side. The feeling is connected to the image of the group. Interpersonal bonds can also exist between the person and the group. These bonds become stronger and warmer the more positive the attitude to the group becomes. A person will then speak of a 'connection' with the group.

5.2.5 *Patterns in peace loving*

Extremely negative 'them-thinking' is usually associated with de-personification of an out-group. For instance, people can describe an out-group as; 'They are animals without any feelings.' Enemy out-groups are very often dismissed with a wealth of creative scatological metaphors.

When a person organises his social reality around two extremes – friends and enemies – we speak of polarisation. Adorno (Adorno, Frenkel-Brunswick, Levinson and Sanford, 1950) is of the opinion that the tendency to polarise is associated with authoritarian personalities. People with such personalities are less tolerant of complexity, ambiguity and uncertainty and polarisation gives them security and clarity. The toleration, or even appreciation, of ambivalent social situations seems to be a prerequisite for peace-ability. A tolerant person will actually enjoy the excitement that can be caused by cultural misunderstandings, unexpected behaviour and incomprehension. Polarisers exaggerate the differences in their social panorama, non-polarisers level out the inequalities in their map of social reality.

A pacifist I once met manifested a number of remarkable patterns, which I later came across again in the stories of other non-polarisers. One of these was that the individual is central in the social experience of peace-loving people such as Gandhi, Mandela and Nathan. One person will be in the foreground while their group membership will be way off in the background; for that reason they have very few group-personifications. They will often speak lovingly about the beauty and uniqueness of individual people, but never about the invincibility of their football team, the superiority of their company, the supremacy of their nation or claim that their church is the chosen one.

Their most important in-group is humanity, as we can infer from such pronouncements as, 'I feel a part of humanity and see myself in the first place as a human being.' They see humanity all the way round them in their social panorama. One drawback is that these people have a relatively weak bond with their own social units; they don't really feel a part of any club, family or tribe. The pacifist I spoke to actually told me that her relationship with good friends was more important to her than that with her direct family.

Love of humanity and the world as a whole is an important value in many systems of belief; the ancient Greeks had a word for it, *'sympateia ton holon'* (Pannekoek, 1983).

Another thing that is noticeable is that peace-lovers make use of unity-creating sensory qualities, like a golden glow that encircles everyone – both in-groups and out-groups. Sometimes this unifying, all-encompassing imagery is behind religious, philosophical or other ideological expressions such as, for instance; 'We all reflect the light of the love of god'.

Andreas and Andreas (1994) speak of 'core states' to describe what people describe as 'total connection', 'total harmony', 'all-encompassing love', 'connection with the god that is present in us all', 'being a part of nature', 'cosmic unity', and 'being at peace with everything'. These inner states consist of unifying experiences that usually accompany transpersonal consciousness. Apparently the need to polarise and think in pigeonholes diminishes if a person has contact with the feeling of being one with everyone and everything. Connecting personifications by thinking in this way fosters reconciliation,[54] forgiveness[55] and inner peace.

As we will also cover in Chapter 7, this type of experience often causes a merging of disconnected inner parts. Dilts' highest logical level, spirituality, offers the possibility to resolve inner conflict. Inner unity created by these concepts will have a direct reflection in the peace-loving manner in which a person subsequently experiences the world.

5.3   *Changing social attitudes*

We learn most of our social attitudes from parents, friends and teachers. If we identify with someone we almost automatically adopt some of their social attitudes (Heider, 1958). What we call 'culture' consists partly of social attitudes that are shared by many people and the easy transfer of those attitudes from one person to another results in a society that is relatively difficult to change. However, a change in social attitudes is exactly what is necessary if cultural progress is to be achieved. If we want to have any birds left in our country we will have to start regarding environmentalists as heroes, and not as 'nature freaks'. In the tragic example of the Cultural Revolution in Mao's China, such a change became the degradation of 'intellectual' to 'reactionary'. Another example,

---

[54] Tim Hallbom and Suzy Smith use spiritual resources within their forgiveness techniques.

[55] Glaudemans (2002) presents a practical application in seven steps of forgiveness. He discriminates what he calls 'forgiveness towards the other' (by saying: 'I forgive you' from 'forgiveness towards the inside'. The latter is forgiving the internalized other, the personification. Forgiveness towards the inside is forgiving oneself. Spiritual notions play a major role in Glaudemans' work.

current in the Netherlands, is the use of the term 'multi-cultural society'. This has an anti-xenophobic effect, changing immigrants from a threat into an asset. It helps the Dutch to feel like the best multicultural nation in Europe.[56]

As they are transferred from one person to another, social maps are automatically simplified (Ötsch, 2000). Nuances disappear and the image becomes more black and white. The use of simplistic social maps is encouraged and rewarded in many societies: pigeonhole thinking gives security; if an opinion is repeated often enough and shared by all, then it must be true!

Although a group as a whole can distinguish another group as a whole, it is still the individuals who program this into their social panorama. Can we not use our knowledge of how this works to help form positive social attitudes?

The 'natural swings' of social attitudes show that, in spite of their robustness, they can be changed. Polarisation is usually followed by de-polarisation. In the course of time, opinions shift from one end of the spectrum to the other. For instance, 20 years ago biological psychologists were considered to be neo-fascists, while now they are greatly respected in scientific circles. Though changes in social attitudes do happen spontaneously, we can hasten the process by special interventions.

People who consult a therapist because they want to change their attitude to a particular group are relatively easy to help. It is often enough just to move the group-personification to a better location. It is a totally different situation when the social sciences are consulted by someone who wants to modify the social attitudes of people who are not motivated to change, such as a politician who wants to influence the attitudes of citizens or a manager who would like to make some specific change in the attitude of their staff.

---

[56] The view of the Dutch on themselves as being very tolerant and open to foreigners is probably not accurate in comparison to other nationalities. It might be that the Dutch are in fact doing poorly in this respect, but see themselves as outstanding in accepting other cultures. Finding pride in that will help improve on what is there.

Here I will first deal with techniques for working with clients who are intrinsically motivated to change. At the end of the chapter I will briefly speak of changing social attitudes in groups that are not motivated. (For anyone who is specifically interested in this, I recommend Derks, 1998c, 2000d and Ötsch, 2000)

5.3.1   Three examples of change through coaching

JANET

The organisation which Janet worked for had fused with another company the year before. Janet was not very happy with this, particularly now that the employees of both companies were working in the same office. She always used the words 'they' and 'them' when speaking of colleagues from the other company and 'we' when she spoke of her old colleagues.

It had been pointed out to her during a performance assessment that she would never be able to work well with 'them' if she continued to feel such a strong demarcation.

For Janet, the distinction between familiar and unfamiliar colleagues was crucial. Of course there were other important distinctions – manager/non-manager, male/female, and (very important to her) people with pets and those without – but these other dimensions were less significant.

The critical sensory qualities (sub-modalities) that Janet used to code the difference between 'us' and 'them' were colour, location and size. 'They' were blue, far away, usually on the left and small. 'We' in her social panorama were reddish-brown, all around her and life-size.

In this case I asked Janet directly to change the sensory attributes; 'What would happen if you gave them warmer colours, brought them closer and made them life-size?' (Technique 26) She thought for a moment and then answered, 'That feels funny.' After a moment she added, 'And I don't know who 'we' are any more.' Then, surprised, 'How can we keep things under control if they come so close?'

It is normal that internal objections arise almost immediately when you are working with sensory attributes, particularly if you are changing them. So I asked Janet, 'What could you do to stop being bothered by the thought that you no longer know who 'we' are?' In that way I fed 'knowing who we are' back to her. I helped her look for ways to achieve this by using six-step reframing (Bandler and Grinder, 1979). Janet, who was now in a hypnotic trance, nodded that she had managed it. Then I checked if there were any more objections using her words, 'under control'. 'What could go wrong if you no longer have things under control?' Janet started to think about that.

After a few more short interventions the distinction between 'us' and 'them' appeared to have disappeared. Janet felt much more free, but also somewhat emotional. The feelings that came to the surface were worthy of note; she described 'solidarity with humanity'. Janet realised just how small-minded she had been and was happy to be free of it.

JANE

Jane, an Indonesian woman, lives in Holland. Her story is characteristic of many members of minorities who run the risk of developing a weak social identity because the surrounding majority dominates their social world. Living in the middle of a dominant majority, they often underestimate the worth of their own group. The law of the dominant personification will often drive them into the second perceptual position with the dominant out-group and they will easily assimilate that group's standards and values. For instance, Afro-Americans complain that they have been brainwashed into believing that they are inferior to European Americans. Sometimes this self-discrimination is only a part of the picture; many people who belong to a minority have two different locations for their own group in their social panorama. These double locations for the in-group will inevitably lead to conflicts within the social awareness.

Jane was troubled by the conviction that she couldn't function optimally in her work because of her Indonesian origin. She believed that 'Indos' were meek and subservient, but she often had to chair important political meetings. She always did this adequately, but the stress was affecting her physically; she felt she had to prepare more and more carefully – more than anyone else would have to because she was an 'Indo'. She suffered a lot of stomach-ache.

In her social panorama the double location was expressed by Indos (1) being on her right and lower than the horizon, with Indos (2) next to her. The Dutch were on the left and higher – they were her dominant out-group.

When I suggested that she move the group Indos (1) to the left, it was immediately obvious that this was not a good solution for Jane. If she did that the Indos would be directly under the Dutch and that was not an encouraging thought. I asked her what ability the Indos (1) and (2) would have needed to be end up in a better location (Technique 27). Though this was a complex question Jane had no difficulty with it. 'Assertiveness', she answered, decidedly. Then I asked her to think back to a moment when she herself had felt really assertive. That was not a problem for her and she had no trouble making contact with such a moment. Then I asked her to send the assertiveness as a bundle of light to both groups of Indos in the time that they formed only one group. Jane told me that she sent the assertiveness to the year 1930 – the 'good old days'. When she indicated that she had created a much more assertive group, I asked her to watch how they developed, in the ensuing years, into a single unit in her social panorama. She told me that she had to stop from time to time to give them some more assertiveness, but finally she saw the Indos as a single, more assertive group. It had taken several minutes and some encouragement from me, but the result made her smile.

I then enquired if she was aware of a 'we-Indos' feeling. Yes, she was. Could she also feel the 'we-Dutch'? Yes, she could feel that, too. I then asked her to blend the visual images of the Indos and Dutch into a homogeneous mixture (Technique 29). It took her some time, but she managed it. The way she sighed when she did it spoke volumes about the impact of the intervention. Now she could no longer visually distinguish the two groups. I asked her to do the same thing with her feelings about the two groups. Once the Indos and the Dutch were indistinguishable by feel, too, I asked her to connect what she saw with what she felt. In this way

I encouraged her to restore the unity in this part of her new awareness of self. Further questioning elicited no apparent objections to this change. As a test I asked provocatively, 'Are you just doing as you're told because I am Dutch and you are just an Indo?'

'NO!' She was very emphatic.

Altogether this took about 25 minutes. The next day she told me that she had chaired a meeting in a much more relaxed state and had done well in it. She could still see no difference between Indos and Dutch.

PETRA

As arranged, at exactly six o'clock, Petra came into the restaurant where we were going to talk about 'apartheid' and the social panorama. She came originally from the neighbourhood of Johannesburg and had lived in Holland for three years.

In Petra's social panorama the Dutch were at the front and to the right. Germans were on the right, too, but farther back (Petra's father, who had emigrated to South Africa in the 1950s, had spent the war years in Holland). White South Africans were at the front to the left and were connected with black South Africans. 'Trusted blacks' occupied a grey area between the blacks and the whites.

The whites and the blacks were at more or less the same height. Petra's whole social panorama was, in fact, at roughly the same height. For her, distance seemed to be a much more important parameter than height. After having thought about it for a minute, Petra said that there was a difference between 'good' blacks and 'bad' ones, who were violent and criminal. She found it difficult to focus on them; they kept sliding away behind her to the left. Extremist white racists were behind the 'good' whites so they were not visible to Petra.

After we had mapped out the situation, I asked Petra if she wanted to change anything in her attitudes. She said she did, she would like to have less 'apartheid' in her thinking.

So I asked her to mix the blacks and the whites to such an extent that there was no more difference (Technique 29). I gave her five minutes to do this and watched her carefully while she did it. Then I asked her what had happened. She said, 'We need more room for ourselves.'

Petra had already told me that she saw more blacks than whites, (which is actually the case in South Africa). This I worked into the process: I asked her to make sure that there was also more 'room for ourselves'. She then re-sorted blacks and whites until there was more variety and with more whites around and next to her. 'That feels right', she said.

Then I asked her to test what this would mean in reality, 'Imagine that you are back in South Africa and feel the changes you have just made.' Petra was now convinced that her already mild attitude to race had become much milder.

5.4   *Techniques for voluntary change*

Here follows a series of descriptions of procedures for guiding clients from one social attitude to another. The reader may recognise some of the techniques from Chapter 2, where they were used for individual other-personifications. These are for group-personifications, though the method is often identical. In short, the following techniques can, in most cases, be used for changing attitudes to any sort of personification.

Technique 26: Improving a social attitude by moving a group personification

Indication: Limiting attitude towards a group

1.   Bring the client into contact with their social panorama.

2.   Find the location of the problematical group-personification.

3.   Find the location of a reference personification – a personification with which the client has a relationship that can be used as

an example; the sort of relationship the client would like to have with the problematical group-personification.

4. Move the problematical group-personification to the location of the reference personification. It is important to remember that the exact reference location is seldom achieved but, if the problematical personification can come somewhere near it, the relationship will usually be sufficiently improved. 'Click' the personification into place in the new location.

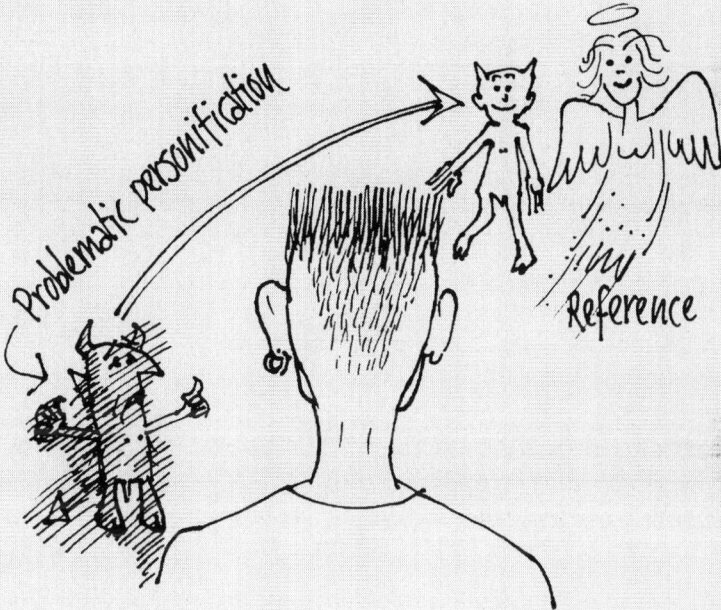

5. Clean up the old location; make sure that all traces of the image of the problematical group-personification have been removed.

6. Check for any possible objections; look for non-verbal as well as verbal signs of resistance or doubt. The simplest way to deal with objections is working with parts, as described by Bandler and Grinder (1979).

Technique 27: Kinaesthetic depolarisation of the out-group

Method one: Dance

1. Think about the best party you ever went to. Look at the people and listen to the sounds. Smell, taste and feel that party again. Enjoy it for a moment and then come back to the here and now.

2. Visualise the problematical out-group.

3. Imagine them coming closer to you.

4. Imagine that the members of the group are encircling you: feel them, smell them and touch them.
    (If you feel fear or hatred, then first use Technique 31 or 32)

5. Imagine that you are at a party with the members of the out-group. Use your memory of the best party you ever went to. Imagine you are dancing with the out-group (a real dance with the eyes closed works better; best of all is a real dance with the real out-group).

6. Check for objections.

Technique 28: Depolarisation of the out-group

Method two: Mix them!

1. Visualise the out-group.

2. Visualise and feel a familiar in-group.

3. Put the members of the out-group round the in-group; make them the same size and the same colour.

4. Mix the in-group and the out-group until you can't tell the difference between them. (Take plenty of time for this.)

5. Check for objections.

Technique 29: Solving bi-locations in group personification

Indication: A group is multiply represented

A bi-location is the representation of the same personification in two different locations in someone's social panorama.

1. Find both locations for the doubly represented group-personification.

2. See if there was ever a time when this group-personification was a single unit.

3. Find out what ability the group-personification lacked that caused the split. Name it.
   (Or look for the ability that the client would have needed to continue to see the group-personification as one whole)

4. Call up that ability in the present, using experiences in which the client had that ability.

5. Take the ability back in time to a moment when the group-personification was still a single unit. Transfer the ability to the group-personification.

6. Watch the group-personification grow up as a single unit into the present.

7. Check if the group-personification is now seen in only one location.

8. Check for objections.

(Note: 'Negotiating between parts' (Bandler and Grinder, 1979; Derks and Hollander, 1996a) is also suitable for this. There we define 'putting the personification in its place' as the behaviour of separate parts, so the person has one part that puts the group in one spot and another part which places it somewhere else.)

5.4.1 Techniques for hate and fear

When people hate a group intensely it often takes more than the above techniques to affect a change. We can reliably deal with this problem by using a technique from classic hypnotherapy ('silent abreaction', Wolberg, 1948) as a preparatory step. With this technique clients let go of their anger before starting to change their social representations. This method, which I refer to as 'Shoot' in this book, has in past decades almost never failed me (Hollander, Derks and Meijer, 1990). The process goes much more smoothly when the therapist connects with the hostile feelings of the client instead of asking them to forgive the other, as is done in some other methods (Dilts, Hallbom and Smith, 1990).

'Figure eight', the technique which follows 'shoot', comes from a procedure that was originally called 'Eye Movement De-sensitisation Reprocessing' (EMDR) by Shapiro (1995). The variant presented here was originally developed by Tim Hallbom and has been supplemented with some ideas from Henk Hoenderdos (1994). In general, therapists choose this approach for the reduction of fear. Here we deal with feared group-personifications.

Technique 30: Shoot! Neutralising hate for a group-personification by silent abreaction and the transference of abilities

Indication: Strong negative emotions in connection to a group

1. *Silent venting of emotions.*
   Imagine that you are in a cinema looking at the screen. They are showing the film, 'The Great Revenge'. See yourself and your group as the heroes; make yourselves as strong as possible and use anything you need to settle the score with the hated group. Now the hated group-personification appears. Watch the film, in which everything happens that your angry feelings can demand. Stay in the role of observer and watch how your group takes revenge and communicates with the hated group. Go on till you have had enough of it.

---

2. *Find the missing ability.*
    Ask yourself, 'What ability is this group lacking that makes it so unpleasant?' (There may be more than one missing ability)

3. *Activate this ability in yourself.*
    Find an example in your own life when you had the ability that the hated group is lacking. Put yourself into the memory and relive it as intensely as possible. Look, listen and feel. Notice your breathing and your voice. It is best to exaggerate the experience a little. Choose a colour that suits the ability. Stay with the feeling of the ability and imagine that you are surrounded by a cloud of this colour.

4. *Transfer the ability.*
    Think about the hated group and send the ability to them. Watch the coloured cloud of ability reach the hated group-personification. If you find it difficult, imagine using a laser gun or some other imaginary weapon to shoot the ability to them. Go on until you see that it is enough.

5. If there are more abilities to transfer, go back to step 3. You have transferred enough abilities when the group-personification elicits a neutral feeling.

6. Check if there is any objection to approaching the group with the new feelings in the future.

Technique 31: Figure of eight!

Indication: Fear for a group

Notice in which direction the client looks while they are calling up and feeling their fear for a group-personification.

1. With your hands, create for the client a visual anchor for this location.

2. Ask the client to keep their head still and to follow your finger with their eyes.

3. Trace a figure of eight on its side in the air with your finger about 70 centimetres in front of the client, with the middle of the eight in the same place as the focus of the visual anchor. Do not do this too fast. Every time you pass the visual anchor reinforce the activation of the thought of the fear-inspiring group-personification by saying its name. Do this about 10 times and test the intensity of the remaining fear (you can use a scale of one to 10).

4. Continue with this movement, and variations of it, until the client tells you he feels less fear.

5. Check for objections.

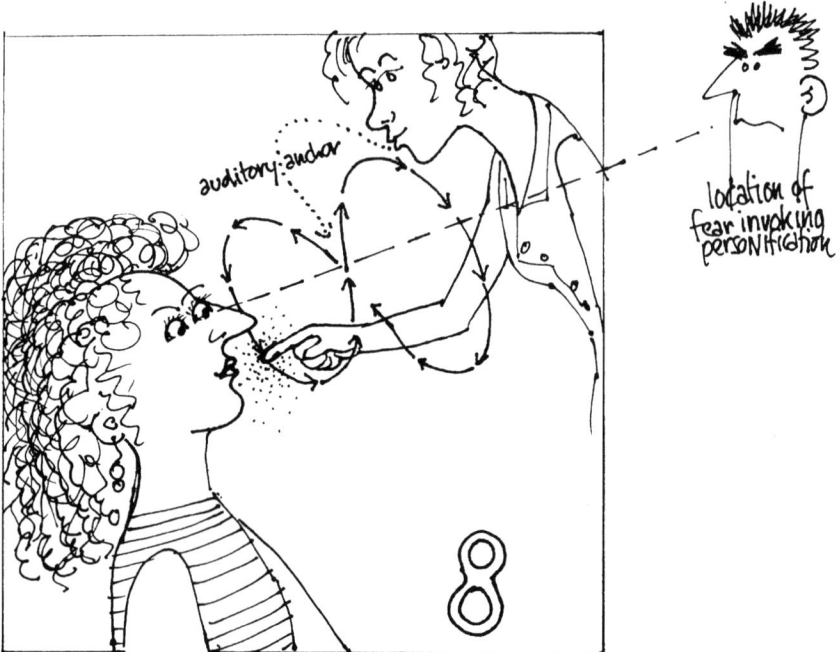

5.4.2 Bringing an image forward from the other side of the brain

Al and Marylin Sargent devised a method of putting cognitive elements from the dominant side of the brain in the background and bringing images from the other side to the foreground. They give a number of procedures in their book, *The Other Mind's Eye* (Sargent, 1999). René Duba (2000) experimented in Holland with the same process. Here is a short version that can be a useful supplement to the other techniques in this book.

Technique 32: Showing the other side

Indication: Problematic feelings in relation to a group

1. Call up the feeling that you get from the problem personification. What is the location of that personification?

2. Imagine that your head is a car. From which side are you seeing the problem personification, the driver's or the passenger's side? (This is a metaphor which helps switch hemispheres.)

3. Move your point of view to the other side of the car.

4. What does the problem-personification look like from there? What is its location when you see it from this side?

5. Reinforce this last image and let the first one fade into the background.

6. What effect does this have on the feeling that belongs to the problem-personification?

7. Check for objections.

5.5 Checking for objections

All the above techniques finish with 'check for objections'. This is a very important element in all these techniques, and is critical to their success.

Most objections can be made visible by ascribing them to parts of the personality.

The thought process is as follows:

1. There is some form of resistance to the change.

2. This happens when a part anticipates that the change will cause a 'dangerous' situation. 'Danger' is anything that threatens the private objectives of the personality part.

3. When such a part notices that the change brings risk, it tries to tighten its grip and reverse the change. As soon as a part starts doing this it changes the way the personification is represented in the social panorama.

4. For instance, when moving a personification to another location you will find that some personifications can reach the target locations while others will only be able to move a very small distance in the right direction. If you try to move them any further, they shoot back as if they were on elastic. The client will immediately notice how much 'give' there is for change.

5. As soon as you encounter resistance you try to get in touch with the recalcitrant part. By suggestion, you personify the part and make it visible, audible and tangible (Bandler and Grinder, 1979).

6. As soon as you have established communication with the personified part you try to discover what the positive intention was behind its resistance. What is it trying to achieve or avoid for the client?

In our efforts to change ethnocentric attitudes in our clients, my colleagues and I have discovered that the parts responsible for the polarisation often have a number of characteristic positive intentions in common in the same way that we have found a number of recurring positive intentions in clients who smoke. Many 'smoking parts' want to supply the client with diversion, relaxation, a good taste, a warm feeling, concentration and social interactions.

Although smoking is unhealthy, these positive intentions are quite normal and there is nothing intrinsically wrong with them.

In the same way ethnocentric parts are trying to achieve a number of normal, useful goals.

5.5.1   Three types of parts and their positive intentions

In Assumption 1 (Chapter 1) I posited that all personifications are actually part of the person. This vision has some practical implications. With it we can, among other things, mould the mechanics of changing social attitudes into a workable form. The result is the following overview of parts involved in the changing of a negative attitude towards an out-group. I define three types:

1.   The out-group-personification.
2.   The parts that are *in favour of* a change of attitude.
3.   The parts that are *against* such a change.

1.   The Out-Group-Personification

What a person sees in his social panorama is the visual projection of the out-group-personification. If someone hates Germans he sees his own inner hated Germans. In other words, they see the German part that they created themselves.

When we work with out-groups, we are confronted with the fact that the human brain does not see 'real' people, but only personifications. I don't know any actual Germans; I only know my ideas about them. When I look for the positive intentions (motives) of Germans I am looking for the content of the motives of my German-personification. The question, 'What is the Germans' positive intention? What do they want to achieve or to avoid?' therefore means, 'What is the positive intention of this part of me?' By putting myself in the second perceptual position with my out-group-personification, putting myself in the place of my inner German, I can usually quickly get an insight into its motives.

A therapist working with the social panorama should be very clear about the distinction between 'real people in the outside world' and the 'image of these people in your head'. Many clients, however, find this view too complex; it is not easy to prevent a client confusing 'real people' with 'personifications'. Experience has taught that it is only necessary to explain the difference to clients if you get stuck at this point, for instance, when a client, from pure hate, refuses to transfer abilities to an out-group-personification. In that case, if clients can be made to see that they are actually transferring abilities to themselves, to a self-made inner image and not the real out-group, then they will do it.

A lack of understanding on the part of the client does not need to get in the way of the therapy. The therapist can always stop looking for positive intentions and concentrate on the transference of abilities. They can usually continue with 'Shoot!' (Technique 31), which is a method that does not ask for positive intentions. By doing this, the question changes from, 'What is the positive intention of the Mongol hordes?' to 'What ability do the Mongol hordes lack?' The transference of abilities is one of the most effective interventions in changing social attitudes.

2. Parts that are in favour of changing social attitudes
These are the parts that have brought the client to the therapist. Before trying to change anything, it is a good idea for the therapist to understand the motives of these parts. What does the client want to achieve with an attitude change? An example: What becomes possible in the life of a client who hates the Irish if he starts thinking more positively about them? Answer: 'I would be able to enjoy a pint of Guinness in Murphy's pub ....'

POSSIBLE POSITIVE INTENTIONS
The positive intentions of parts that want a change in social attitudes can be very diverse. Some examples:

a. Finding peace.
b. Being able to communicate freely with a group that one distrusts, hates or even admires too much.
c. Solving moral conflicts (sometimes with religious or ethical aspects).
d. Improvement of the health by resolving (post-traumatic) stress caused by confrontation with the out-group. Victims of violence would be a case in point.

3. Parts that are against changing social attitudes
As usually happens when change is being attempted, the parties that fight it get the most attention. We give these reactionary parts the attention they demand because we need them if we are to get anywhere. Change is only possible when these parts agree to it. Otherwise they will just sabotage the change and then we will be much worse off.

RAPPORT
Before we start on any intervention, we must first establish a good contact with the parts we want to influence. This can be achieved by matching their choice of key words, criteria, values and maybe even their racist[57] convictions. This can be difficult for therapists with opposing beliefs, but if they challenge the beliefs of the racist

---

[57] Racist and ethnocentric are used as synonymous here.

part they will lose rapport and achieve nothing. If we approach racist parts in a way that is too negative, they will distrust us, resist and keep quiet. Remember that these are the parts that need to change; they need to be motivated to co-operate.

To be able to do anything at all about changing a social attitude, we have to motivate these often hypocritical, sexist, racist, ethnocentric, scared, colonial, fascist, power-mad, territorial and small-minded sides of the client whether we like them or not.

In particular, we have to persuade the client to call a cease-fire in the war between these racist parts. We need to try to help the client to understand their apparently ugly shadow side, which, whether they like it or not, does control a part of their behaviour.

Making contact helps us to realise that we therapists can also be hosting such parts. Often the more we are troubled by them, the more energy we will put into suppressing them. As soon as someone in the outside world wakes our suppressed racist feelings by, for instance, a racist statement, we overreact because of the conflict within ourselves. Anneke Meyer based a technique on this structure, which she called the 'Inside-out Model' (Derks and Hollander, 1996a).

The ice can be quickly broken with the racist part of a client if we admit that we, too, harbour such feelings. Therapists who dismiss this as 'manipulative' have much less chance of guiding their clients to positive attitudes.

DIFFERENTIATING BETWEEN INTENTION AND BEHAVIOUR

The best way to get to know the positive intentions of ethnocentric parts is to create rapport with them. Once we know their positive intentions, both our opinion and that of other parts of the client, we change almost immediately. We no longer see the racist behaviour as irrational and aggressively evil, but as the behaviour of someone who knows no better. In short, though someone's behaviour can be aggressive, the intentions behind it are never 'evil'. This point, postulated by Bandler and Grinder in 1979, always meets a lot of resistance, but in 25 years their belief that 'Every behaviour has a positive intention and was once someone's best available option' has proved pragmatically to be enormously useful.

A classic example: What could possibly be the positive intentions of serial killers? We may come across 'righting a wrong', 'livelihood', 'sexual satisfaction', 'changing a feeling of powerlessness into a feeling of power' and 'raising oneself out of the mediocre'. Most readers will have to admit that they have been known to seek justice, income, sexual satisfaction and power and glory. Most of us, however, do it in a more acceptable manner.

Once we know the objectives of racist clients we can help them obtain the abilities they need in order to change the ethnocentric behaviour and to achieve goals in a more acceptable way. This could be by getting justice through the courts, income from a normal job, sexual satisfaction within a reciprocal relationship, gaining power by the 'position game', or seeking glory by extraordinary sporting, aesthetic or economic prowess.

AVOIDING AND ACHIEVING

Bandler and Grinder (1979) demonstrated how important it can be to reframe 'avoidance' into 'achievement'. We can transform a positive intention, which is to avoid something unpleasant, into the achievement of something by asking the client 'What do you want?' or 'want instead?'. A positive intention translated in this way gives more direction to possible alternative behaviour. In the list that follows, the positive intentions are in brackets, expressed in terms of 'achievement'.

If person A (Israeli) hates group B (Palestinians) we can ask, 'What does hate for this group achieve for you? What end does it serve?' The answer will probably be one or more of the following possibilities:

1. To prevent me or my family and friends being hurt, damaged or killed.
    (To obtain safety, health and prosperity for myself and my family and friends.)

2. To prevent my tribe and my genes disappearing.
   (To reproduce my own genes.)

3. To protect scarce resources.
   (To have enough to live on.)

4. To prevent me from losing my territory, my home and resources.
   (To have enough room to bring up my children, grow crops, work and build a house.)

5. To prevent the loss of my cultural heritage.
   (To be able to practise my religion, celebrate feast days and speak my native tongue.)

6. To prevent strangers frightening me and making me uncertain.
   (To be able to relax and enjoy myself with strangers.)

7. To avoid losing my social self.
   (To maintain a strong bond with my community and to keep our social identity.)

8. To prevent myself from feeling lonely and alienated.
   (To enjoy strong social ties.)

9. To prevent social disintegration.
   (To become stronger and feel stimulated by competition.)

10. To stop myself feeling powerless and inferior.
    (To feel strong and full of self-confidence.)

11. To stop being jealous.
    (To be satisfied with my lifestyle.)

12. To stop myself feeling out of control.
    (To be able to deal with chaotic situations with a feeling of control.)

To repeat, knowing positive intentions makes it possible to look for more effective behaviour. Hating an enemy and fighting them is usually only effective if you can eliminate that enemy completely in one go. Because this is not usually possible in intergroup conflicts, the only choice that remains is to continue a conflict that can drag on for decades. The question then is, what is the most effective manner of reaching your positive intentions: years of bombing and terror or peaceful co-existence?

5.6   *Changing limiting social beliefs*

Yoriko, a Japanese woman, wanted to change her negative attitude to Africans. At my suggestion she moved the Africans from left to right and from low to high in her social panorama. After she had done the latter she looked straight at me and said, 'Yes, but what did they do to deserve such a high position?' Yoriko told me that she believed that 'high' hierarchical positions had to be earned. She did say that she had no objection to moving the Africans from left to right – 'right means favourable to me', she said – but moving them higher was a problem.

'Europeans, Japanese and Americans have all achieved something, Africans have not', she told me. This meant that Yoriko had a *social belief* that made it impossible for her to change her attitude.

This example of resistance points in the direction of the concept of 'limiting beliefs' (Dilts, 1990). Yoriko believed that a hierarchical position (expressed in the vertical dimension) was dependent on performance.

Some further questioning made it clear that some achievements were worth more than others in Yoriko's image of the world. For instance, sporting achievements were worth less to her than achievements in literature, art, economy or technology.

Yoriko believed hierarchy to be very important; her social panorama was unusually vertical and she could distinguish between the smallest differences in status. She was motivated by an inherent desire to climb the social ladder by means of achievements. This belief got in the way of changing her negative attitude to Africans.

The following technique is the easiest I know for changing beliefs. The therapist need not be concerned with the content of the belief, but the steps must be followed very accurately. The many practical applications of this technique make it worth learning by heart.

Technique 33: Tabula rasa! Convincing the younger self – a short pattern for changing limiting social beliefs

Indication: A conviction blocks change

1. What does the client want to be able to do? (Yorika wanted to think more positively about Africans.)

2. Why can she not do it? What belief is stopping her? (That a high position is dependent on achievements which, according to Yorika's criteria, the Africans had not produced.)

3. Ask the client to repeat the belief in her mind and at the same time to go back to a time before she had this belief. (Yorika did not yet believe this when she was two years old.)

4. Find out what advantages this belief has achieved up to now – safety, security, social identity and behaviour. In other words, 'What was positive about having this attitude?' or, 'What did you get out of believing this?' (This belief has ensured that Yorika has done her best throughout her life and achieved a great deal.)

5. Send the adult client back along the timeline to a moment well before the belief started, when she was still a clean sheet, *tabula rasa*. You can ask the client to travel back in a time machine in the role of aunt (or uncle). Once she has arrived she should contact her younger self. (Yoriko spoke in her mind to herself when she was 18 months old.)

6. Ask the client to present her younger self with an alternative vision that conforms to two conditions:

   a) *The new vision must supply the same advantages as the old one.* (Yoriko must go on doing her best and achieving.)
   b) *The new vision must lead to acceptable social behaviour.* (Yoriko has to see Africans in a more positive light.)

Note: it is almost never necessary to do this out loud. Many clients are perfectly capable of giving a new point of view to their younger self without the therapist knowing anything about it. They just start to convince their younger self and find their own words in the process. (It remains a mystery what Yoriko told her younger self, but it must have been something very convincing.)

7. Check if the client's younger self has completely accepted the new attitude. (Yoriko could see that her younger self believed it utterly.)

8. Ask the client to step into her younger self and to listen to and remember well what her adult self has to say. (Yoriko said that she believed it and would never forget it.)

9. Now the client can grow up into the present with her new belief. (Yoriko took a few minutes to go through her life imagining the changes brought about by the new belief. When she was back in the present she looked at me.)

10. Check whether the client's opinion has changed by asking a provocative question about the old belief. 'But still, the Africans don't really deserve it, do they, Yoriko?' (They're very good in their own way,' said Yoriko, smiling.)
    A new attitude will only be kept if it engenders no objections, and only then will the client have access to the desired social behaviour.)

5.7   *Demagogy, war and peace*

Until now we have been looking at changing the social attitudes of individual clients who have come to our practice of their own accord, but sometimes politicians, managers or socially motivated leaders will want to change certain attitudes in people who are not themselves motivated to change. They come to you and beg, 'Mr Communications Expert, how can I change these racists' minds?' I was once approached by someone from the United Nations who was involved in trying to heal the mental scars in Rwanda. The bloodbath there was the result of systematic ethno-centric indoctrination by radio Mille Collines. Would other communication techniques be able to reverse the process?

In my book, *Das Spiel Sozialer Beziehungen* (Derks, 2000b) I deal at more length with the possibilities of changing social attitudes through speeches and the media. That book was actually a practical extension to Allport's *The Nature of Prejudice* (1954). Continuing from this, Koomen (1992) gives a number of practical guidelines for reducing tension between groups. He mentions successively: (a) Make sure that the groups have the same status. (b) Contradict the stereotypes that are commonly used and give examples of exceptions and deviations. (c) Make sure that the groups have common goals. (d) Create situations in which the members of the two groups can have intimate relationships with one another and the members have to approach one another as individuals. (e) Introduce standards for contact that will ensure equality.

An interesting application of the social panorama model to ethno-centric communication is the previously mentioned work by Ötsch (2000, 2001). He studied the part played by location in demagogic communication patterns such as those of Jörg Haider and Adolf Hitler. This study gives plenty of ideas for communication tech-niques aimed at the formation of the opposite attitudes: the mov-ing of the out-group to an equal height and to a co-operative (left or right) position.

The personification theory from Chapter 1 also offers a clear refer-ence. When speaking to a group of people who have a negative attitude to an out-group, you can systematically go through all the personification factors. You mention the name of a person from the out-group, discuss his appearance and suggest (non-verbally) a better location. You also describe this person's abilities and his motives, feelings, self-awareness, perspective and spiritual con-nection. By adding second position suggestions you make it easy for your audience to construct a complete personification. For instance, Omar is a good-humoured man who always wears a white shirt and blue jeans. He usually comes and sits by me and we watch the strolling passers-by together. He is a poet and singer who wants to get his work known. He is often sad about the situ-ation in our country. He believes in himself and his work, but he sees how his artistic career, and not only his, is frustrated by poli-tics. Fortunately he has a strong connection with god and nature, 'That helps me to bear it', he says. When I imagine myself in his shoes I admire his humour and his friendliness.

Chapter 6
The family panorama

6.1   *The invisible family that surrounds you*

This chapter introduces the application of the social panorama that will probably have greatest impact on the field of psychotherapy. To orient ourselves we will start with a look into history.

In the 1950s the American therapist, Carl Whitaker, unsatisfied with the results he was getting with individual clients, started to treat families as a whole and so started family therapy (Walker, 1996). This was followed by the development of many different streams of family therapy (Lange, 2000). As well as influences from psychoanalysis, Gestalt psychology, and behavioural psychology, we also come across incidental ideas from applied cognitive linguistics (Bandler, Grinder and Satir, 1976). Typical of all these streams is that the therapist works with several family members at the same time.

System and family therapists have, after Bateson (1972), Satir (1972), Watzlawick, Beavin and Jackson (1967) – the so-called Palo Alto tradition – concentrated on pattern recognition. In this they are primarily interested in patterns of interaction – repeating series of communicative behaviour. For example, every time father snaps at mother, mother smiles at daughter. From an analysis of such a pattern, system therapists aim at starting an improvement in the way in which one sends and receives messages within the family (Bandler, Grinder and Satir, 1976). These patterns of interaction are usually considered by family therapists to be the behaviour of the family as a unit. In other words, the family members are all sharing these patterns of communication – they do it together – and, if the patterns are a problem, they will have to change them together. System therapists regard families as functional units.

The system therapists derive their world of concepts from the general system theory of Bertalanffy (1968). A system is a collection of parts that are interconnected in such a way, that when one part changes the others will change along. Bertalanffy, as mathematician/biologist, makes use of a number of very abstract concepts that are far removed from the way people really think and act (see also O'Connor and McDermott, 1997). A system therapist is a bit like a car mechanic who has learnt to think in terms of 'traffic flow'. If he has a broken-down car in his garage, then all he considers is how it is connected to a reduced necessity of spreading the times of the rush hour. Everything he thinks is inarguably correct and the concepts are aesthetically satisfying. It may be right and it may be elegant, but it doesn't help him replace the piston rings. System therapists believe that you cannot cure a family by treating only one individual family member. The system theory concept of 'homeostasis' supports this idea; any system has to find an internal balance. The 'madness' of a family member who has been designated as the patient is said to be the result of this search for a homeostatic equilibrium. If only one family member is cured it will throw the system out of balance. Once that patient is sane, another child in the family will probably go mad to restore the balance again. A wonderful idea … but does it really work like that in the real world? On how many examples is this view based?

In De Shazer's foundations for solution-focused therapy (Cladder, 2000) this restrictive idea of 'homeostasis' is contradicted. De Shazer (1989) is of the opinion that you *can* cure a family by working with just one family member. He also says that you have to work with whoever is willing and avoid forcing reluctant family members to go into a therapy that would be useless anyway. He also says that therapists should not hide behind homeostasis, for instance they should not blame their failures on the fact that other members of a client's family may have refused therapy.

The family panorama, as described in this book, is an extension of this criticism of the system therapy and is a very useful instrument in helping to restore harmony in a family through just one of its members.

6.1.1 *From system to cognitive construction*

Family therapists are not the only ones who consider families to be units, most 'normal' people do that too, as can be deduced from such expressions as 'the family' and 'your family', which sound as if they refer to physical objects. 'My family took a hard line', 'I grew up in a family that had a thing for machines'. These linguistic constructions point to the existence of family group-personifications as described in the previous chapter.

People have social relationships with such group-personifications in the same way as they do with individuals. 'My relationship with my family is not very good'. 'I would like to get closer to my family'. Family-personifications are an application of the conceptual container metaphor spoken of by Lakoff and Johnson (1999). Families are social-cognitive constructions, and they are 'hollow'. A person is born 'into' a family and grows up 'within' it. If everything is as it should be, it is also 'warm' inside.

6.2 Assumption 5 again: Representation governs interaction

In this chapter I will be almost completely ignoring the previously mentioned Palo-Alto tradition of systems, interaction patterns and communication patterns. In this book I am interested in finding patterns in social cognition, seen in mental space as constructions of thought. I do not see the family as a particular system of senders and receivers that is governed by rules of interaction, but rather as a collection of personifications that function according to the assumptions of this book. Assumptions such as, for instance, Assumption 1, in which the family group-personification and the family member *personifications* are seen as *parts of the individual* who is thinking about them (Schwarz, 1997).[58] Because both the total family group-personification and the individual family member personifications are experienced in particular locations, we can also apply Assumption 2, *'relationship is location'*.

Though communication is very important in the development and formation of this collection of family-personifications, in the final analysis I see interaction as being less important than social constructions. Assumption 5, *'representation governs interaction'* is the critical factor in this. At the risk of appearing immodest, I would claim that this book fits within a new family therapeutic paradigm, in which interaction patterns are seen as the result of how people give 'pictorial' shape to one another in their thinking (Steens, 1995).

---

[58] R.C. Schwarz (1997) developed an entire method of therapy on the basis of this assumption, called 'Internal Family Systems Therapy'. The spatial organization of the internalized family members plays no significant role in Schwarz's work.

System therapists distinguish 'subsystems' and 'system levels' (Lange, 2000). They look at the 'sections' of social reality that are relevant to their work, such as the individual family member, pair relationships within the family, the family-of-origin as a whole, the extended family, the family history for some generations back and the smaller or greater social environment around the family, with children's homes, child protection, youth services and society as a whole on the highest level. From the point of view of cognitive linguistics we may say that every distinction people make in their language relates to a conceptual difference. All these subsystems and levels can, in theory, also function as (group or metaphoric) personifications.

If we want to make sense out of the concept of 'systems' within the framework of the social panorama, then we can say that there are three levels of social cognitive system within a family. All three levels are systems of interconnected social representations that influence each other.

Personifications: System level 1. A personification constitutes a system with the personification factors as its elements (parts). A change in one factor will affect the other personification factors. If we change 'self-concept' or 'feelings' as factors in a personification, this may influence other personification factors like for instance 'location' or 'spiritual connection'. This influence must be ascribed to unconscious calculations: The client's unconscious operating system infers what the change in one personification factor implies for the others. Most interventions in this book are changes in the factors 'location' or 'abilities' with the aim of improving the personification as a whole. In other words: give mother's personification a better location and more honesty and it will automatically start to feel better, have a nicer perspective on the world, more self awareness, more motivation and a more intense spiritual life.

Social panoramas: System level 2. This system has the personified family members as its elements, as these function subjectively within the mind of the individual client. The spatial representation of this is what we call here the client's family panorama. The parts of this system are interconnected in such a way that change within one of the personifications usually influences all the other personifications within someone's family panorama. So if a person starts seeing his mother in a different light, their unconscious will 'work out' what influence this will have on the personifications of the other family members. The most remarkable effect of these calculations is that after a change in one of them the other personifications may change location 'spontaneously'. In other words, the family member personifications are interconnected as the elements of a system.

Social reality: System 3. This consists of the system of real family members. These members all carry family panoramas in their minds and interact with one another and think about one another on the basis of these images. The family panorama of the client is one such panorama in which a change has taken place. In other words, when the client, in whatever way, communicates his changed views on his mother to the other family members, they will influence their family panoramas.

Changes within the first system level have consequences for the second level; what happens in the client's family panorama affects the lives of the other real family members. If Pete starts seeing his father differently, then that will affect how the rest of the family sees Dad. This result can be explained by the effect of conscious, but more particularly unconscious, verbal and non-verbal communication – the 'frivolous' assumption, Assumption 6, which says that we can change the attitude of the other (real) person by changing our own social representations.

So, again, my view in this is that the manner in which family members see, hear and feel their relatives in their minds defines the communication between them. If mother, for instance, is seen by the whole family as being strong and dominant, they will all automatically adopt a subordinate position to her. But if little Frank looks down on her because he caught her with the postman, then, with that image in his mind, he will probably be extremely rude to her.

Families usually expend a lot of energy on convincing one another of how they 'should' see one another. This social 'norming' usually uses all four channels of relational communication (already described in Chapter 2):

1. Naming relationships. (He is my brother)
2. Speaking of locations. (You are above your sister)
3. Showing locations. (Gestures and pointing to locations)
4. The use of metaphors. (We come from a warm nest)

It is more the relational content of this communication and not so much the patterns within it that creates the image of the family. It is what family members suggest to one another that they should see and feel – even if it is only done once – that determines their images of one another. In this way a mother might say to her children, 'Daddy is my lovely little pig' and at the same time smile at something (the image of a piglet?) in her arms. By that, she is using all four of the above channels at the same time and she will only need to do it once to affect the image the children form of their father.

In therapy situations it becomes obvious how family panoramas can be interwoven. In particular, the way parents see their own family of origin seeps imperceptibly into the social world of their children. From what we observe in therapy we must conclude that parents, sometimes by the most minimal of hints, can radically influence the social life of their children. Children will create images of deceased uncles and aunts, great-grandparents and other dead relatives they have never ever encountered in real life. Putting them in dominant locations and identifying and counter-identifying with these unmet ancestors can have far-reaching and sometimes uncanny effects. In working with the family panorama this subject may well stretch your imagination to its limits.

6.3   Therapeutic applications of the family panorama

What are the possibilities for therapeutic application of the family panorama?

First of all, family relationships that have become stranded can easily be pulled off the rocks. The methods for changing social attitudes described in the previous chapter are applicable in exactly the same way to problematical family relationships.

Secondly, deep-rooted limiting social behaviour patterns can be unearthed and changed. For instance, I had a client who could not deal with rude colleagues, friends or children, and had never been able to. He told me that in his early childhood he had always been rather alone in the family and so had learnt to put himself 'above' potential playmates. He felt that his grandfather should have given him more the feeling that he was special and criticised him less. Using these apparently unconnected facts – for me as an outsider – I could use the techniques described further on in this chapter to teach him to feel 'equal' to these playmates. On the basis of this imaginary experience he is now confident that he can deal with rude people by setting his own limits for them. In this way he could get rid of a deep-rooted limiting social behaviour pattern.

The techniques presented in this chapter gain scope when we put someone's family panorama in a developmental perspective and see it as the result of several generations of family history. The inter-generational aspect (Boszormenyi-Nagy, 1987) will also be given a place in this work, and make the essential 'loyalty patterns' and 'identification patterns' visible in the family panorama. For instance, a grandfather who sees the brother who was killed in the war in his grandson (identification) will put his grandson in a very special place in his social panorama. As a reaction to this the grandson will put his grandfather in an intimate place (loyalty), but he will now go through life as, at least in part, his grandfather's dead brother. The question then is, 'What effect will this have on his social development? Will he become a soldier because he unconsciously copies his grandfather's brother?'

The general starting point when working with the family panorama is that people build on the very first experiences in their family when constructing their model of social reality (Koch, 1955). This means that many present-day problems are a direct continuation of the early situation at home (Koch, 1958).

Toman (1961) saw the composition of the nuclear family, the number of children, their sex and relative ages, as a very trustworthy prognosis of its members' personalities. In his book *Family Constellations* he tried to express this in mathematical terms. The emphasis put by Koch and Toman on the composition of the family has taken root with many psychotherapists, but nowadays there are few who believe that you can really infer a person's character from the composition of the family he comes from.

Studying the family panorama helps us to explain how connections between the composition of the family and social behaviour can develop. In other words, if you are the youngest in a family with five older sisters, the youngest of whom is six years older than you, then the image you will make of your parents and your sisters all around you will be the result of each one's age and sex, and will almost automatically be very like the image that other people from similar families make. This means that you grow up with a social panorama that will dictate social behaviour patterns very like those of other people with a similar family image.

If we assume that someone's family panorama forms the foundation for his social development, then the constituents of the family will be a very strong factor in determining that development. For instance, if John places his father large and central as child, then he may do the same with his employer when he is an adult. His colleagues will probably say, 'John has an authority complex'.

Lakoff and Johnson's (1999) work implies that the family in early youth affords basic experiences from which a person will distil his conceptual metaphors for social life and that these conceptual metaphors control the unconscious social operating system, which constitutes the social part of personality.

The question that arises for therapists is, 'How far can we retroactively restructure the foundation of someone's social panorama and be sure that the new construction we place on it will actually stay put?' Or, in other words, is it possible to make permanent changes in someone's social operating system?

The procedures in this chapter aim at changing these social foundations. Clinical practice has shown that, with them, we can change problematical social behaviour patterns that at first sight appear to be inherent (Derks, 1996, 2000d; Walker, 2004).

6.4 A family consists of all types of personifications

If we define the mental representation of a family as a collection of personifications, then the question arises, 'What types of personifications?' Until now I have found the most practical answer to be that families can be built up of all five personification types, group-personifications, other-personifications, self-personifications, spiritual-personifications and metaphorical-personifications, but they do not all need to have equal importance.

The importance of the family group-personification seems to vary with the culture. In Southern Europe or Africa, for instance, the 'family' will often be the most important factor in all choices. The head of the family embodies the family spirit and primary loyalty is to the family as a whole. Family feuds imply that group-personifications of friendly and hostile clans are also a part of the family panoramas. In large families with, for instance, more than 20 children, there can also be a group-personification such as, 'my older brothers'.

In addition to this in all cultures that I know of, family members personify one another as individuals. These family member other-personifications generally play a major part.

Because a person thinks of himself as being inside the 'container' of the family, his own self-personification will also be part of that family. If someone has multiple selves, they will all have a place within the family. In extreme forms of multiple personality disorder the family will be enriched with as many self-personifications as there are 'alters'. This can be awkward for the remaining family members; they may create multiple other-personifications for the split person.

The collection of personifications which makes up a family includes spiritual personifications as well as the representation of living relatives – personifications of dead people, ancestors, gods and spirits. If someone is brought up as a Christian or a Muslim, God or Allah will also belong in the family, even if that deity is shared with the neighbours. The spiritual family panorama is described very explicitly in some cultures. On the Indonesian island of Flores, for instance, each family has its own family gods and the whole family worships the spirits of their common ancestors.

Metaphoric personifications, too, can have an important place within families. Think of 'the car', 'the business', 'the antique collection', 'the church', 'the farm', 'the boat', 'the dog', 'the caravan', 'the political party' or 'the political ideal'. I once had the pleasure of working with people in whose family 'the orchestra' was personified in a very dominant way – the word of the orchestra was law.

The family panoramas within a family usually have personifications of the same flesh and blood people in common and they do not create those personifications in isolation; family members influence one another very strongly in the design of their social panorama.

6.5   Support for the family panorama model

One of the greatest supports for the family panorama paradigm is the way in which non-psychologists react when I tell them about it. To my frustration they do not seem to find it at all new. People often say that it is 'ordinary', 'regular' or 'natural'; the recognition is a sort of intuitive understanding. As I have already mentioned, use of these words indicates automatic information processing that goes on outside the consciousness, and this supports my theory that everyone unconsciously has a family panorama, complete with the relevant 'software'.

At the risk of labouring the point, I would like to refer again to everyday language. In conversations about family life you will often hear such words and expression as, 'proximity', 'distance', 'next to each other', 'My father was out of reach', 'My ex-wife was coming between us', 'There is no room in my life for another man'. As well as this linguistic evidence, non-verbal behaviour such as glances, nodding and gestures also point to the spatial organisation of family-personifications.

Other evidence of the crucial role of location in family life comes from interventions used in various schools of family therapy.

Satir worked with location in her so-called sculpture technique (1972). In this technique family members were given the instruction to make a living sculpture of their family. Such a living group of statues turned out to be a good diagnostic tool. Satir discovered that by changing the positions in the sculpture she could help to solve relational problems.

Minuchin changed relationships within a family by asking its members to move from one chair to another, or to swap chairs with another family member. Minuchin developed these 'topographical' interventions, as he called them, after he had seen the great influence of changing places (Minuchin and Fishman, 1981).

Family panoramas were already recorded in the 1960s, when they were called 'sociograms' by therapists who were inspired by the social field theory of Lewin (1951).

Moreno (1991) in his psychodrama and Pesso (Souget, 1985) in his psychomotor therapy worked with interventions in which spatial positioning played a part. None of these methods, however, is based on the assumption that location is the primary or most basic form in which people represent relationships. Is the social panorama unique in this?

My Austrian colleague, Walter Ötsch, gave me great pleasure by telling me about the existence of a therapy that also uses changing locations as its primary intervention technique. He wrote to me in 1995, 'Is Bert Hellinger's "systemic therapy" not based on the same social phenomenon as the social panorama? After all, moving family members is Hellinger's most important intervention.'

Hellinger? I had never heard of him. But since then, now in 2004, Hellinger's work and that of his colleagues, Weber (1998, 2000, 2001), Hellinger and Beaumont (1998), Varga von Kibet (Varga von Kibet and Sparrer, 1998; Varga von Kibet, 2001) and many others have gained a lot of ground. I will dedicate the last part of this chapter to their 'constellation' method. Here people (therapy group members) are used as substitutes that are placed in the space and so make the social panorama of the client visible. Hellinger developed this way of working partly from Satir's 'family sculptures' and partly from his own experience in South Africa, where the Zulus use constellation-like rituals with their ancestors.

The 'constellation' method is a particularly attractive method that, as well as causing an almost addictive fascination, also raises a number of questions. Because my thinking was already firmly anchored in the social panorama model I was able to use that as a frame of reference to explore Hellinger's method (Derks, 1996; Derks and Hollander, 1998). This has contributed enormously in validating the concepts of the social panorama model and to its further development.

6.6 Techniques for the exploration of family panoramas

A family panorama consists of a three-dimensional cognitive construction that is built up from family-personifications. The degree to which these personifications are uniformly represented can differ greatly. Some personifications may lack personification factors, or those factors may be lacking content. As well as this, the personifications in a family panorama can also move, or be combined, multiple, blocked or all-embracing. These various characteristics mean that the researcher must be prepared for all sorts of answer to the question, 'Where do you experience your family?'

A flexible and purposeful approach is necessary in order to achieve useful results. Fortunately, in my seminars, one demonstration is usually enough to enable most people to map one another's family panoramas.

The complexity of most family panoramas makes it imperative to record in some way the locations that are found. Drawing a plan is the most obvious solution but people can also use dolls, coins, shoes or pieces of paper.

The aforementioned 'constellation method', in which substitutes play the part of personifications, was developed in Germany. Many therapists there became enamoured of the palpable and sometimes dramatic character of the constellations. However, personifications that floated high in the air, were mixed together, inside the client's body, double or very small were, from a practical point of view, impossible to represent accurately with substitutes. And how many therapists have a group of substitutes handy when they need them?

When I work with clients, drawing a sketch of the positions is almost always enough. If I need to make it more concrete I put a piece of paper on the floor for each personification. The client can then stand on them and so put himself in the role of other family members. Since the personification is a part of the client, the exclusive identification with that part will be most reliable; substitutes lack this level reliability.

As already described in Chapter 2, it is important to make sure that the client is working on the right level of abstraction when finding the locations of personifications. By saying, 'Think about all the people in the world in the way they surround you...' we can usually get most clients quickly to a suitable state to start from. From there we can ask about the locations of very familiar personifications such as the parents or the partner. As soon as one location has been found the others usually follow quite easily.

When exploring the family panorama, we want to find the locations that have developed over a longer period, a general image that is representative for a whole episode of the clients' life. What we do not want are so-called 'geographic' locations or 'snapshots'.

We cannot use the seating arrangements at Christmas, 1991, or the situation in the living room on the 8th July 1978. I gave some hints about how to avoid this in Chapter 2.

Someone's family panorama can be either that of the present-day family structure or the family as it was in an earlier time of life. In my practice I make a lot of use of family panoramas from early youth. But whether we are exploring a current or an earlier panorama has very little influence on the way we go to work. This always starts by deciding from which period and context one needs to know the family panorama.

In the following technique I will add, in parenthesis, concrete instructions for the situation in which the family panorama you are looking for is one from early youth.

Technique 34: Exploring the family panorama

Indication: To diagnose problematic family relationships

1. Find an emotionally neutral memory from the period you want to use for the family panorama. Any reasonably clear memory will do (holiday, playing outside, a birthday, staying with someone, Christmas).

2. Step completely into this memory. Move yourself, complete with feelings, to that age.

3. Once you are there (in your imagination) look for a nearby quiet place where you can sit alone and think. Keep your eyes closed and look around you and think about all the people in the world, as you know them (neighbours, acquaintances, friends and family). (Here we are starting to draw the map.)

4. (Optional) Look for the location of the family as a whole among all those other people. Where do you see, hear or feel them?

5. Find the location, eye height and direction of gaze of your mother (father or partner).
    Once you have found that, find, one by one, the locations of your other family members.

6. Find the location, eye height and direction of gaze of other people who have influence in your family (grandfathers, grandmothers, aunts and uncles).

7. Find the location, eye height and direction of gaze of important people who have died, been banned, aborted or miscarried, gods, spirits and any metaphoric personifications there might be.

6.7 Family patterns on three levels: Human, family and individual

In my research I look for three different categories of patterns in family panoramas. My first focus is the general, human patterns. Here there are tendencies that are to be found by everyone. We call them: *(1) Universal family panorama patterns.*

We can also look to see what members of the same culture, tribe, extended or nuclear family have in common. For instance, where do people usually place their maternal grandmother? Then we are looking at: *(2) Collective family panorama patterns.*

Usually, however, we will be looking at the patterns in family panoramas on the individual level. For instance, how did Peter see his family when he was five years old? This is: *(3) Personal family panorama patterns.*

I shall now discuss my data within these three categories.

6.7.1 Universal family panorama patterns

At the beginning of this book I interpreted Piaget's (1965) classic concept of 'object permanence' into the social domain as 'person permanence'. A personification is the result of making the representation of external phenomena that we call 'people' permanent. Logically, the nearest family members – in particular the mother or twin – are the first to be personified. Once a baby has arrived at this 'family member permanence', it no longer needs to miss its mother when she is absent for a moment. By looking at and listening to its mental image of her, and by feeling her in its mind, it knows that she still exists.

A forty-year-old client complained of attacks of terrible loneliness. She called it 'existential loneliness.' It soon became apparent that she could not retain social images; she had never developed the strong notion of family member permanence that most of us have. When she went back to the time when she was five years old, she saw, after much searching, a few flashes of her parents, together, far away and totally wrapped up in each other. They were too far away to offer any warmth. In her present life when she did not see friends for some weeks it gave her the feeling that she was going to have to build the relationship again from scratch.

Another client complained of being afraid of being deserted. How did she do that? She did by thinking of her partner as being very close and the rest of humanity a long way away. If the partner were to disappear, then she would be left totally alone.

By most people the constant awareness of family ties forms the background to their social life. Their family is always there, somewhere under the surface, 'stationary' in their thinking. That continuous unconscious presence is most noticeable when an important member of the family is lost. This can cause the complete disorder in a person's social awareness.

But what characteristics do all family panoramas have in common? From my own experience I know that most adults represent their children and partner much closer than anyone else. The nuclear family forms the circle of intimacy. If family members are put at a distance it almost always indicates problems. Nearness is normal. Children, parents and partners are sometimes even put under the skin. The meaning of these close locations seems to be universal. A statement like, 'I love my daughter very much and I see her low on the left-hand side at a distance of 20 metres' will sound extremely strange to most people. If you love someone, then you see his or her personification close to you.

In the family panoramas of children who are happy in their family the child is often right in the centre, with all eyes on the child, who has everyone's attention. Parents who are close together indicate a stable family situation. 'Expansion' of the family panorama accompanies puberty. Once a child stands on its own feet, its parents often move from the front to the back (Weber, 1994).

Because the family panorama precedes the development of the social panorama in its more general form, a large part of the universal patterns in the family panorama overlap with the patterns we find in every form of social cognition.

Some fairly obvious patterns are:

1. The intensity of feelings decreases as the distance of the personification increases.
2. Personifications that are close together belong together.
3. A personification opposite the person, but outside the intimate circle, usually indicates a conflict. Within the intimate circle this position usually denotes affection.
4. Personifications that are looking away from each other have lost contact.
5. Personifications that are looking in the same direction are in harmony.
6. Personifications that are looking at someone's back are often 'on the same side'.
7. Size is equivalent to status.

6.7.2 *Collective family panoramas*

People from the same culture or subculture should, in theory, have similar patterns in their family panoramas. For instance, in cultures where children are usually brought up by their grandparents, we can expect the parents to be less prominent. If the infant mortality is high, then the babies will probably have a less central place in the family panorama than would otherwise be the case.

In my opinion, the social panorama could be a useful research tool for cultural anthropologists. Collective patterns in family panoramas can illustrate differences in culture. This application is an extension of the research into similarity of structure in the social panoramas of colleagues on the same team (Derks, 1996) or the same organisation (Stam, 1998; Weber, 2000).

Quantitative research into the similarity of patterns in the family panoramas of members of the same family is also important. It helps us to determine the influence of the family panoramas of the existing members of the family on the panoramas of those born later. It provides answers to the questions, 'To what extent is a family image transferred from generation to generation?' and 'To what extent do children take over the social reality of their parents and older siblings?'

We should see the automatic process of unconscious copying of the social panorama of significant others as one of the most important forces within a society.[59] This is how social relationships are transferred and perpetuated.

If a child copies his family panorama from the one already existing in the family, then we should expect a great similarity between the family panoramas of children in the same family. If that is so, then we can deduce the family images of the other children from the family panorama of one child. In short, the family panorama of one member can give us a great deal of information about a family's common social experience.

---

[59] Besides the automatic assimilation of values and beliefs from people to whom a strong positive emotional tie does exist, their social panorama will also partly be copied from them.

One day in May 1997, my sister who is two years older than me, was sitting quietly in my garden. I had once explored the family panorama that I had when I was five years old, so I asked her to remember hers from when she was seven. My sister did not know my work, and allowed herself easily to be taken back to 1955. The following illustrations show our respective family panoramas.

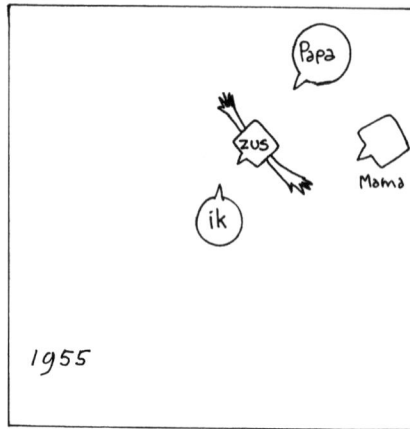

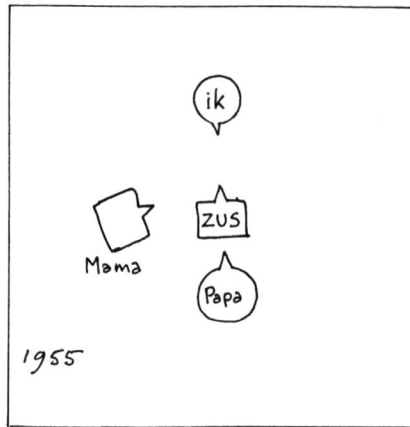

The similarities are obvious. What impressed me was the different way we interpreted the similar configurations. I asked her, 'What does it mean to you that you are between me and Dad?' My sister answered, 'That I was protecting you from him.' That view was very different from mine; I felt that she was denying me access to my father!

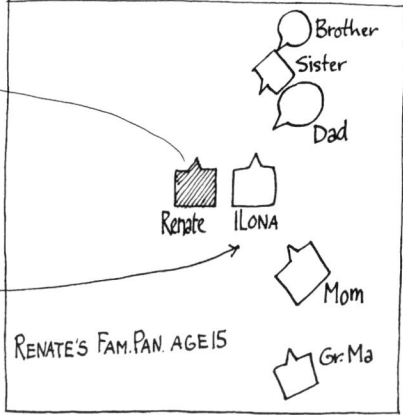

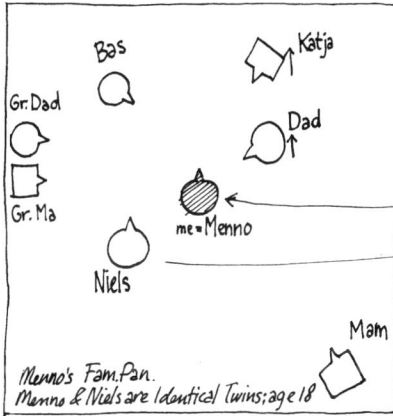

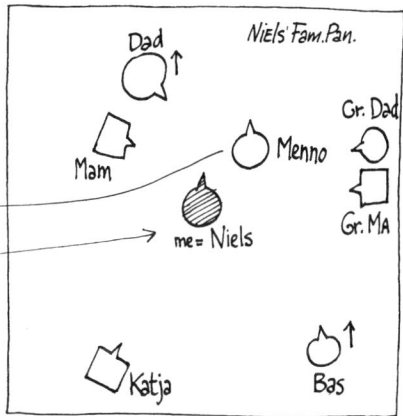

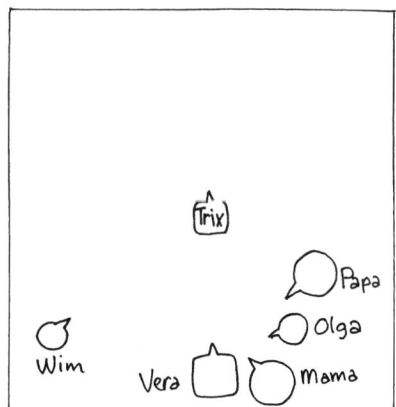

The ideal quantitative research into the extent of isomorphism in family panoramas can be done by comparing the panoramas of identical twins.[60] At the moment I have results from three pairs of identical twins (see previous page). Two I have thanks to Jan Snoek, a student with great interest in the social panorama. The other is from Henriëtte Mol, who managed to snare another set on a campsite.

I cannot draw any serious conclusions from these three instances, but one thing is evident; there are as many differences as there are similarities. At any rate no one family panorama can be said to be representative for the whole family. Therefore I must reject the tendency of many Family Constellation therapists to behave as if someone's family constellation is a fact that is above the individual, subjective experience. I prefer the view of Hellinger and Beaumont (1998), who say that they do not know how, psychologically speaking, the family constellation comes into being and doubt whether it is the only possible representation of the historical reality of a family. In short, children from the same family can grow up with very different family panoramas.

6.7.3 *Personal family panorama patterns*

The patterns that I introduced in Chapter 2 for the social panorama in general are all applicable to family panoramas. The configurations that we add here are typical for the family and are predominantly for diagnostic purposes by showing where change would be desirable. They are all deviations from what I call here the *universal ideal image* of a family. This ideal image is what we usually see when someone experiences their family as being harmonious, balanced and happy.

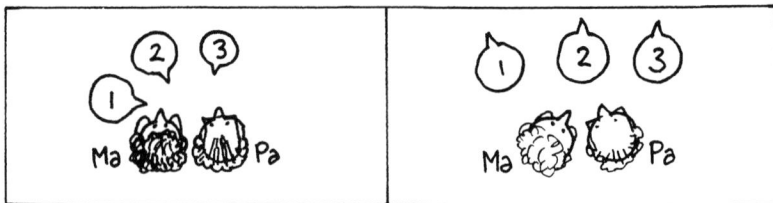

---

[60] Twins experienced an identical family composition. The impact of the composition of the family on development can be found out from comparing the social panoramas of twins.

THE UNIVERSAL IDEAL IMAGE OF A FAMILY

In his book, *Family Constellations*, Toman (1961:170) also sketches an image of what he calls the 'ideal family' construction. He would like to see all parents having first a son, then a daughter, then a son and then another daughter. In his opinion this would give the least psychopathology.

The universal ideal image of a family as a three-dimensional spatial cognitive construction becomes visible when we collate the final results of a great number of family panorama sessions. We get optimised family panoramas for which the clients say, 'Yes, that would be fantastic!'

In many of such situations the following patterns are recognisable (Weber, 1994; Hellinger, 1995; Derks, 1997a): The man is next to the woman and the children in an arc, with, counting clockwise, the oldest first and the youngest last. There are several possible variations to this that all fit within the ideal image. For instance, the parents can be reversed left to right (as in a 'castling' move in chess) and children under the age of two are often very near (in front of) the mother. Half-brothers and sisters can also be in different locations. The maternal grandparents are usually closer to their grandchildren that the paternal grandparents.

In a paternalistic culture the eye-level of the father will be higher than that of the mother, and an older child will be higher than a younger one. The grandparents will be behind their own child. Uncles and aunts and all dead relations are outside the intimate circle with the exception that children who have died can be inside it.

In the ideal family panorama of children who have left home, the parents are behind their children, with the parents tending to face each other while the children look out into open space.

Ideally, divorced parents have their children between them and their new partner with the children born of that marriage on the outside. In such a situation the panorama will be more like a circle with a large opening.[61] Whatever the arrangement in the ideal

---

[61] In Hellinger's constellation therapy as well in spontaneous recreations of families without the involvement of a therapist, the same patterns of 'ideal families' do surface in a very systematic manner.

family panorama, it will be dominated by acceptance, peace, respect, love and harmony. Changing a person's family panorama in the direction of this ideal will improve its members' emotional experience of it.

6.8   Deviations from the universal ideal image of a family

The following patterns can be used as diagnostic aids. The categories *a)* to *m)* indicate problems that can be helped by the transfer of abilities and the changing of locations.

a.   Negative attitudes
If someone has personifications in their family panorama that they hate, fear, reject, do not take seriously, despise or do not respect, then these should be changed into personifications that can be more positively experienced. This can be done by using the techniques for changing social attitudes already described in Chapter 5.

b.   The 12 o'clock location
Who is found straight in front of the client? Problematic personifications at this central spot (authoritarian fathers, bullies, ex-lovers) produce a continuous stream of unconscious information. Counter-identification with a personification on this location will make someone's self-image insecure (see also Chapter 8).

c.   Empty spaces
Everyone who is biologically a member of the family should be represented in the family panorama. A nuclear family should contain both biological parents, every sibling (living and dead) and the grandparents on both sides. If one of these is missing then the client may remark that the missing person is 'nowhere'. If several family members are looking at an empty space it can mean that there is a child who was given up for adoption or aborted, but it could also be a suicide, criminal, ex-partner, family enemy number one or a family member who is in prison or exiled. People from outside the intimate circle who died early in someone's life can have a great influence (Toman, 1961). Personifications who are looking at the ground (Hellinger, 1995) or staring at empty spots

can also be a clue. Find out who is missing and give them a place. Missing family members sometimes need to be given extra resources before they can be included in the family panorama.

d. Double locations

Seeing a member of the family in more than one location suggests an inner conflict. In this case, as Bandler and Grinder (1979) suggest, there are two parts of the personality at work, each of whom put the personification in a different location. So if there are two images of the same 'real' person, this is due to the fact that two different parts of the client in combination are making a distorted picture of social reality. If this causes problems, then it is important to get these parts of the client to communicate with each other and, if possible, combine them. That usually helps in achieving a single representation.

If a client speaks of 'restlessness' in the weeks after a change in his social panorama, you need to check if there is such a double image. Therapeutic changes in the location of personifications can lead to unwanted double locations when the old locations remain occupied. Such unintentional double locations must be cleared up.

When you use the constellation method to explore someone's social panorama it is very difficult to find double locations. After all, the client only has one substitute to use for each person to be represented. Hesitation when finding the right place for a substitute can suggest a double location.

e. Shared locations

If several 'real' people are represented in the same location, this can suggest generalisation. If the same place is shared by a living and a dead relative then the therapist should be especially alert – this is a sign of posthumous identification. In this way a child can take the place of a dead child. People can also be in the same place as someone from another generation, or another sex. When several family members share a location it often results in the confusion of their names.

Where necessary, differentiate the various personifications and send the dead to the kingdom of the dead (see Chapter 7). It is not possible to put two substitutes in the same place, and shared locations are not always at the same height, so if you are using the constellation method it will be difficult for the client to put them in the right place. Another problem with that method is that some clients have their social panorama inside their body. Family members who are experienced internally are very difficult to represent in a constellation using substitutes. When the kinaesthetic self falls inside the location of an other-personification, the client may not know their own identity anymore.

f. Immature positions
If adult clients still represent themselves within their intimate circle among sisters, brothers and parents it can make it difficult for them to find a partner or start their own family. You can check whether the client's family panorama is immature or the result of a 'small scale' social panorama by comparing their current panorama with the one they had as a child.

g. Non-specific personifications
A client can also have personifications that are difficult to classify. Are they group-personifications, other-personifications, self-personifications or spiritual personifications? The client must be helped to differentiate between individuals and groups, self and other, and the living and the dead. In some cases the sex of a personification is not clear. That is quite usual for self-personifications. For instance when a female client calls a personality part 'him'. If the sex of an other-personification is unclear then it is worth giving this some attention.

h. A too weak or split self
Some clients have an invisible, small, vague or far off self-image in the context of their family. In such a case the clients may complain of losing themselves when they are with their families. Here it can be useful to lower the family group-personification, make it smaller and put it further away at the same time as enlarging and bringing the self-image nearer. Multiple self-images within the same family context (self-image double locations) can suggest internal conflicts.

i. Withdrawn family members
If a family member is facing away from the others in a client's family panorama, it can mean that they no longer wants to belong to the family. The personification will have a reason for this

dissatisfaction, which can sometimes be found in the (rejecting, hateful, indifferent, authoritative, sick) behaviour of other family members. Adding resources to those family members can often solve this. If we work with the constellation method this tendency to withdraw will be apparent from exceptionally aloof positions.

j.   Problems with partners

Partners are usually within arm's length. If a partner is farther away it is usually a sign of a lack of intimacy. Partners who are large and immediately in front of someone are sometimes too dominant and need to be put to one side and a bit lower. Bi-locations of partner-personifications can cause innumerable problems, as well as ex-partners who are within the intimate circle or inside the body of the client. Ex-partners who are in front in the middle (even if they are far away) demand a lot of attention. If there are personifications between the self and the current partner that also signals difficulties. In short, the intimate circle should only comprise current partners, young children and parents.

k.   Isolation

If the client represents particular family members at a great distance from the others it will probably be necessary to bring them closer. In general, more distant relatives such as cousins, uncles and aunts have a place outside the intimate circle but they must still be palpable over that distance. The own side of the family is usually closer than the in-laws.

l.   Authority problems within the family

If there are family members who are experienced by the client as being much bigger than they are and/or right in front of them then their position should be changed. Usually these family members have too much influence and they must be lowered and put to one side. If a high-placed family member (alive or dead) is behind them, then that gives support.

m.   Fatal examples

Family members who have died young can be used as a role model and shorten the life of a client. Completely unconsciously the client has internalised the mental software that is connected to the cause of death: the lack of resources, negative feelings or self-destructive perspective of the personification of the dead person.

a) negative attitudes — hated, disrespected, feared

b) twelve o'clock — 12

c) empty spaces — Who is missing?

d) double locations — ① Daddy, ② Dad

e) shared locations — mom & daughter

f) immature positions — Dad, Mom, Child 40 years

g) non-specific — God, Mom, Granny, me

h) too weak or split self — Family Spirit, self images

i) Withdrawn members

j) problems with partners — Partner

k) isolation

l) authority in the family — me, dad, mom

m) fatal examples — criminal, disease suicide accident

ideal III — 2nd marriage, new kids, ex, ex, 1st marriage kids

ideal I — Children, Mom, Dad

ideal II — world, children left home, Mom, Dad

Hellinger (1995) emphasises a very strong tendency to want to follow a family member who has died young. If you work within the framework of the social panorama you will obviously want to give the dead person the resources which could have prevented his death. 'What resources did Jack need in order to stay healthy or not to become suicidal?' For this the client will return to an early time in the life of the dead relative in order to give them those resources. If family members have died in wars, disasters or accidents there can also be unconscious bands of loyalty that limit the development of survivors and their children.

6.8.1 Interpreting family panoramas

In the following sketch we see the family panorama of 26-year-old Petra. At the start of our conversation she told me that she wanted to make her own choices. Later it turned out that she was afraid of starting relationships with men because she was afraid of intense isolation if they left her.

When I asked her to remember a pleasant experience in her youth she came up with her fifth birthday. With no trouble she travelled back in time to re-experience that happy day. While she was there she could explore her family as it was in her childhood. As Petra, with her eyes closed, described what she saw I made a drawing of her family. When she opened her eyes she agreed that this was, indeed, how her family had looked.

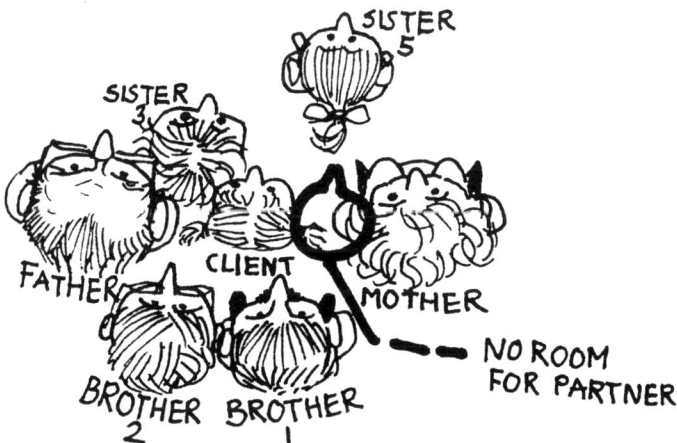

The question that immediately arises when one sees this picture is, 'What are these people looking at?'

One of things that is noticeable about Petra's family is that it is a close-knit whole surrounding her, and in which she says she feels safe. She also enjoyed being the 'little queen', surrounded by love and care. However, in her present-day social panorama she still felt surrounded by her parents and siblings; she was still in an immature position. In the last 21 years nothing much had changed in her image of her family; there was simply no room for a husband and family of her own.

I want to look at a few crucial questions around the interpretation of family panoramas in the light of this example. To start with, family panoramas that function well at a particular moment can be limiting at a later stage. (After all, Petra said that she had had a wonderful childhood.)

It often amazes me that clients always seem to benefit from changing their family panorama, whatever their problem. Is this a professional foible? Are we therapists too keen to push our technique onto everyone whether it is necessary or not? Perhaps, but in my opinion it is only partly true; and I obviously prefer a different explanation.

A person's family panorama is formed during childhood. It is a person's social blueprint and forms the basis for their patterns of social behaviour. They learn to use certain social behaviour patterns and to avoid others. So whatever the blueprint is like, it will always limit a person's repertoire of possibilities for social behaviour. Some people will reach one of these limits somewhere in middle life. By changing the childhood family panorama and therefore the social blueprint, we offer the client the chance to try other behaviour possibilities.

6.9   *Changing family panoramas*

Someone who has seen a lot of beautiful living rooms, leafs through lifestyle magazines every day and visits all the furniture shops is guaranteed to have a lot of ideas about how to arrange a living room. They will recognise the different styles, know exactly what they want and will be able to design their own room down to every detail. They will be completely certain about what should go where.

If another person has spent their life in a primitive culture where the huts all look more or less alike on the inside, they may never have thought about decoration and arrange their hut the way it has always been done. If someone were to ask them if there was a better way to arrange the chairs, cupboards and tables, they might probably become confused; they would have no idea....

Everyone starts life knowing only one example of the family panorama, their own.

This limited notion of alternative possibilities does not, however, mean that people cannot change the location of personifications in their family panorama. They can. However they don't very often come up with the idea of doing so deliberately. Only people who read this book or similar literature will try to give their family members new locations. Although other 'normal' people seem to change their family panorama a lot, they do it unconsciously and completely according to the rules of their own unconscious social operating system, which is programmed to manipulate personifications within the limits of a particular framework.

What you see of the social operating system in therapy is probably only the tip of the iceberg. Sometimes it seems that these same unconscious abilities are constantly updating the social panorama; whenever something changes in human relationships, it will be accompanied by a corresponding change in the locations of the personifications involved. In short, a person's social panorama is always on the move. When a son, for instance, gets good marks at school he goes up a notch in his father's family panorama. Or when a daughter gets mixed up with someone her mother thinks is a criminal, the mother will perhaps move her, according to the rules of her social operating system, to the left and far away.

This automatic, unconscious character is probably the reason that the answer to the question, 'Which location do you think would be better for your mother?' is often, 'I haven't the faintest idea...'

6.10 *The stimulus for change*

Dionne said, 'I don't have enough room' when she studied her family panorama with her eyes closed, upon which her therapist answered, 'Make some room.' Dionne managed to do it straight away and was very pleased.

John said to his therapist, 'My brother is in my way.' The therapist said, 'Move him out of the way.' Because there is nothing actually stopping John from doing this, he can immediately free himself from the negative influence of his brother.

Simple instructions like 'make room' and 'move' allow a client to steer his own unconsciously chosen course. Where exactly he puts his family members as a result of such an instruction depends on the way his social operating system is programmed. The clinical fact that this sort of intervention often works satisfactorily tells us something about the great human ability to adapt one's social panorama. In the tradition of the hypnotherapist Milton Erickson (Erickson and Rossi, 1983) both 'solution-focused therapy' (Cladder, 2000) and 'neuro-linguistic programming' (Bandler and Grinder, 1979; Derks and Hollander, 1996a) assume that clients already possess the abilities needed to solve their problems using so-called 'resources'. The social operating system is a part of the unconscious and contains the resources needed to solve problems with relationships.

In some cases, however, people need help in using these resources. Certain personifications seem to be in such a logical place that the idea of moving them would never arise without some external stimulus. The existence of such rigid personifications is justification for the therapeutic techniques in this book. When the client does not spontaneously change their panorama, the therapist must provide the impulse.

We see the most spectacular evidence for the ability to find, with the help of a therapist, better locations for family members in the technique called 'reimprinting' (Dilts, 1990). This technique is used on limiting beliefs that have their origins in traumatic experiences – often incidents that involved members of the family. By exploring the family panorama before and after the reimprinting,

one can see how the family members have moved. This before and after measurement demonstrates that personifications are moved spontaneously after reimprinting. Clients may describe it, for instance, as 'Now I have parents who belong together', or, 'I see him now more as an equal'. This discovery was of crucial importance to the development of the social panorama model.

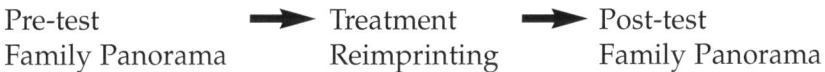

Pre-test ➡ Treatment ➡ Post-test
Family Panorama　　Reimprinting　　Family Panorama

Because reimprinting endows family-personifications with one or more abilities, it shows the importance of finding abilities as a way of getting personifications to change locations. When I first began to study this, I was amazed at the complexity of the 'spontaneous' movements of personifications during reimprinting. In many cases all family members had changed location – usually towards the earlier mentioned 'ideal' arrangement – once the trauma was removed.

In Dilts' (1990) original reimprinting no suggestions are made about changing locations. The difference in location before and after the intervention is therefore entirely due to the client's unconscious capabilities and, within the conceptual framework of this book, we can say that the improved social relationships were designed by the client's unconscious social operating system. It is as if the client's operating system works out exactly what the consequences of the new abilities of one personification will be for the others. We discussed these effects under the heading 'system level 2' at the beginning of this chapter.

In Germany and Austria various therapists, led by Ulf Pithan, have made the connection between reimprinting and system therapy (Grochowiak, 1996), in which the therapist does instigate location changes.

Once they have been given the idea, clients can often move family member personifications to better places without having first given them new abilities.

Take Jenny for instance. As soon as I suggested that she move her father to the left she started to smile as if a world had opened for her. She immediately assigned new places to her grandmother, her younger brother and her mother, whom she moved closer to her father. This she did with no further intervention on my part.

6.11 *Techniques for changing family panoramas*

Once a client has formulated therapeutic goals, we can find out what is blocking their realisation. Is it relationship problems within the family? Or does it involve deep-rooted social behaviour patterns?

In the first case we would need to help change the current family panorama. In the second case, particularly if the client has had this behaviour for a long time, working with the client's original family panorama would be indicated.

Eighteen-year-old Winnie had a lot of problems with her father. She was considering a complete break with her family but did not want to abandon her mother. Her doubt was an obstacle: 'But that man is such a swine…'

In order to help Winnie, we needed to work on her current family panorama. When we explored the panorama (Technique 34) we discovered that Winnie's father was in the middle, in front and one and a half meters above her. But she also found a small father diagonally behind her. The rest of the family was grouped rather haphazardly round them.

The best solution to her negative attitude to her father would be to add resources to his personification, but it was still too early for that. First we gave Winnie the chance to reduce her anger through venting (Techniques 7 and 30). After that she judged that her father was lacking compassion, openness and honesty. These three abilities were transferred to him from Winnie herself (Technique 36, which is more or less the same as Techniques 6 and 7). With another few adjustments we could take a look at her father-personification's double location. This was solved by transferring a binding ability to Winnie's line of life (Technique 37, which is analogous to Technique 16).

When working with the current family panorama, as we did with Winnie, then the following three techniques are very useful.

Technique 35: Moving the personification of a family member

Indication: Inadequate family ties

1. Find the location of the family-personification.

2. Use the family panorama patterns (see paragraph 6.7) to find a more suitable location for this member of the family.

3. Move the family member and clean the old location.

4. Make adjustments until there are no more objections to the new location.

Technique 36: Transferring abilities from the self-personification to the personification of a family member

Indication: Inadequate family ties

(If the attitude is very negative, first use Technique 7, venting)

1. What ability would give the family member personification a better location?

2. Identify and activate this ability in yourself.

3. Send this ability (in the form of a colour or as energy) to the family member personification and then check if the relationship is good enough and if the personification is now in a better location.

4. Make adjustments until there are no more objections.

Technique 37: Unifying double representations on the line of life

Indication: Problems with bi-locations

1. Find both locations for the personification.

2. Ask the client when, in the past, this personification only had one location. Take the client back to a moment before the split.

3. Now there are two equally valid options:

   a) To work with the self-personification
   b) To work with the other-personification

   For option a) (self-personification) ask the client something like, 'What ability would have enabled you to continue to see that personification in only one place?'

For option b) (other-personification) ask the client something like, 'What missing ability was responsible for the other ending up in two different places?'

4. Call up the relevant ability in the client in the present and ask them to take it back to the moment before the split.

5. Now there are also two versions, which continue from step 3. After option a) (self-personification) ask the client to grow up again, with that ability, into the present.
    After option b) (other-personification), first ask the client to give the ability to the other-personification. As soon as the ability is transferred the client should watch the other-personification grow up, with the ability, into the present.

6. Check if this procedure has changed the double location into a single representation.

6.11.1 A prototype case history

In the following paragraphs we take a look at changing deep-rooted social behaviour patterns. First, a case history as a kind of preview.[62]

SHARON
Sharon was a 45-year-old Caribbean woman. She complained that she could never say 'no', that she had problems with relationships and 'wrestled' with feelings of inferiority to her sister, who was two years older than her. These are all examples of deep-rooted social behaviour patterns. In short, an indication (Technique 38) for working with the childhood family panorama. Sharon was very motivated because she had suffered from these problems for as long as she could remember and had now reached a point where she could go no further.

---

[62] This case was edited to clarify the structure of the working process, which is why it differs in detail from Derks (1998, 2000).

Sharon came to therapy on a particularly hot day. We decided to work in some nearby woods. Sitting in the shadow she could concentrate optimally on formulating her objectives (Technique 39).

What Sharon wanted to achieve was to be able to 'follow her own feelings and intuition when her partner or family expected something else of her'.

I asked Sharon to think of a good test case (Technique 40), one we could use at the end to check the success of our work. 'If I imagine that I want to arrange something with my sister for my mother's birthday'. I first got her to imagine the situation. She told me that she immediately became confused. I asked her to give a mark (on a scale of one to 10) for the intensity of the accompanying bad feeling. She gave it eight and a half.

That finished the preparatory work. I thought it would be useful to study her family as it was when she was seven (Technique 34). After a journey through time back to a Caribbean island we made a model of her family on the ground with the help of twigs, leaves and beech mast.

Not only the beautiful surroundings, but also the complexity of Sharon's family at that age made working with her an interesting experience. She gave me a lively description of the meaning of all the things she had arranged on the ground. The description was not necessary for the therapy, but my personal curiosity about it improved our relationship.

Sharon's father, an army officer, was in front of the family as if he were leading a squad of men (see illustration). Sharon told me that he was insecure about his work, and also jealous of his oldest son, whom he regularly bullied and humiliated – maybe he doubted whether he was really the boy's father? This caused Sharon's mother to be extra protective of her son, and the grandmother played a large part in it, too. She supported her daughter and protected her grandson against his bullying father. As a result of all this the other children received too little parental attention. Sharon and her older sister compensated for this by supporting each other, but that made Sharon lean on her sister too much. Necessary or not, it was a fascinating story.

I copied the patterns in the wood onto a piece of paper and this is the result.

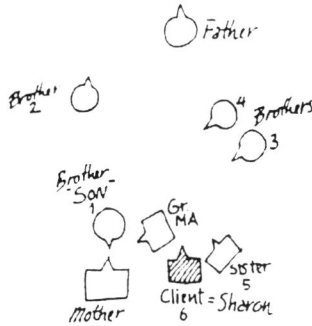

○ *Father*

Brother ○   ○⁴ *Brothers*
2   ◡ 3

Brother-
Son
1
  ○   ◇ *Gr*
          MA
  ▢   ▨   ◇ *Sister*
                   5
Mother   *Client = Sharon*
                6

When we had looked at this sketch (Patterns, paragraph 6.7; Technique 41) I asked Sharon, 'What was your father lacking that made him act like that?' (Technique 42).

She had to think about that one. Finally she said, 'Being able to give love. Yes, because he never had any. He lacked mother-love because his mother brought him up without loving him.'

After this I thought of moving the focus to her grandmother and looking for abilities that would have helped this lady to be a loving mother. But the energy with which Sharon had described the faults of her father stopped me. I thought, 'If it doesn't work with father we can always go back to his mother.' (Who, incidentally, was not in the picture because Sharon told me that she had never known her grandmother. Theoretically this would be no reason for not adding her to the panorama but, anyway, we didn't).

Sharon had no difficulty going back in her mind to the time when her father was still a baby. Calling up mother-love was easy, too – she was, after all, the mother of two sons. It didn't take her long to give that little boy (her father as a baby) the mother-love that he had missed. She did it in the form of a dark purple powder that she shook over him.

When Sharon said that it was enough I asked her to go and look – as if she were an aunt who visited regularly – how her father, with the help of the mother-love, grew up into a different man, one who was able to give love. She was to do it until the moment he met Sharon's mother. Would they still have got married if he had had that mother-love? She thought they would. After that she looked further at how her older brothers and sisters were born and grew up in a family with a father who had known mother-love. Sharon went on until I suggested that she was already in her mother's womb and could feel her father's love – the dark purple – all around her. 'That is much nicer, warmer and lighter...' she told me. I encouraged her to enjoy the feeling for a while and then told her that it was time for her to be born.

From her birth she grew up in a family with a father who himself had known a mother's love. She obviously enjoyed it. Then I told her to go on growing up until she was seven. She nodded to show that she had understood, but then she went into such a deep trance that she didn't even notice the noise of a group of children who were passing. She didn't react when one of them called, 'Why has that lady got her eyes shut?'

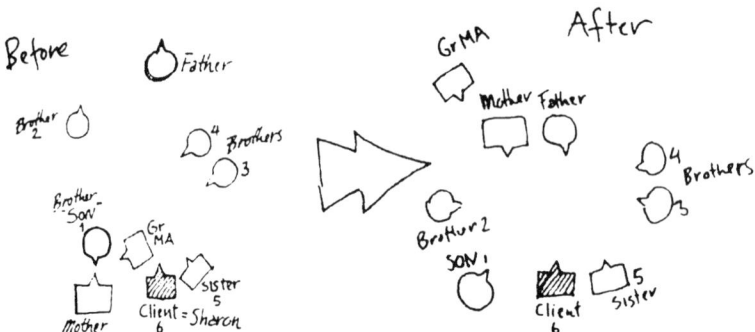

When, after about 15 minutes, she spontaneously came back to me as a seven-year-old, we had another look at the locations of her family. Everything was very much changed for the better (end of Technique 42).

After that I asked her to take the positions of each family member, one by one (Technique 43). To do this we made a number of clear marks on the ground for her to stand on; in my office I usually use pieces of paper to do this. We did this to check, by 'standing in the other person's shoes', whether all the personifications were satis-fied with their new positions.

After some adjustment for her brothers everyone seemed to be happy, so I asked Sharon to assimilate the new image of her fam-ily when she was seven years old (Technique 44). When she told me that she had memorised it I asked her to come with me on a school outing and to think about her improved family image in that context. After that we went shopping, to school, fishing and swimming, all with the same objective: stabilising the new family image in different contexts.

When we had done that I asked Sharon to grow up, in her mind, from that time until the present and to experience all the changes caused by the new family image (Technique 45). She took at least 10 minutes to do this.

Now it was time to try the test case, discussing her mother's birth-day with her sister. She was visibly happy about the different feel-ings and possibilities that occurred to her this time (Technique 46). Now the mark she gave the 'bad' feelings was only two.

Three months later I met Sharon again. She told me that all three of the complaints she had consulted me about had seemed to dis-appear after this therapy.

6.12 Standard order of family panorama techniques

Over the years I have done more than 200 sessions with a similar structure to Sharon's. From this a strategy has developed that I have incorporated in the following techniques. If you want to repeat this literally, you should use these techniques in the order in which they are presented.

SYNOPSIS OF THE TECHNIQUES 38–46
A therapeutic objective can be blocked by a deep-rooted social behaviour pattern. Use exploration of the childhood family panorama to find out which personifications are missing abilities.

These abilities should then be transferred to the personifications as children and the client should then visualise the alternative course of history until his own conception. After that he should experience his further development, complete with all the feelings involved. This will mean that a new life history comes into being. The childhood family panorama can then be explored for changes that have been made as a result of the transferred abilities. These will usually have brought the family image nearer to the ideal. All personifications should then be checked for agreement with the new situation and adjustments made wherever necessary. Once everything seems to be right the whole should be assimilated in different contexts and then the client should grow up, in their imagination, until the present day. That is the moment at which the results should be checked.

Technique 38: Determining indications – a flexible occupation

Doctors learn to think in terms of 'indication', which is the connection between diagnosis and therapy (Derks and Hollander, 1996a). The question here is, therefore, is there such a connection when working with the family panorama?

Diagnosis: Limiting social beliefs

One way to look at it is to see the family panorama as the 'non-verbal' part of someone's social beliefs. If a person believes, 'I am worth less than other people', they can say this sentence to themself or to others and they can also write it down. When they do that they are expressing the verbal part of a limiting social belief.

But a belief is much more than just a piece of language. Contrary to what many therapists believe, words are more a result of images, feelings, sounds, smells and tastes. Beliefs do not form a separate (meta-) category of thought; all thoughts have their own degree of generalisation and certainty. What we call beliefs are usually generalised and very certain thoughts, but they don't need to be captured in words. Beliefs can also exist outside language. Beliefs can even function very well when they have no linguistic component at all (Mervis, 1984).

In the example of someone who says 'I am worth less than other people' to his therapist, we can be sure that this person has, at the very least, an image and a feeling about this as well. Probably an image of all the people in the world being higher than them, together with the feelings and voices that go with that.

We can ascribe a 'linguistic' and a 'non-linguistic' element to all a client's expressed beliefs about social behaviour. The non-linguistic component is, by definition, a social panorama construction. The connection between the linguistic and the non-linguistic elements is so strong that when the linguistic component changes, the non-linguistic also has to change, and vice-versa (Toivonen and Kauppi, 1993)

Therapy method: Family panorama techniques

Summing up the above, I can say that when a therapist, by whatever means – Ellis' rational emotive therapy (1973) is an example – helps to change a social belief so that the client expresses it differently, 'I am as good as the next person', then there will automatically be a change in the social panorama. It would therefore be an exaggeration to say that the techniques I present here are the only way to treat the family panorama; they are a useful addition to the many different forms that already exist.

Psycho-diagnostics under fire

In spite of the fact that psycho-diagnostics have taken off in the last decades, Hubble, Duncan and Miller (1999) can find no evidence that this has contributed to therapeutic success. In practice they see no connection between DSM[63] diagnoses and the different therapy methods used. Cladder (2000) is of the opinion that psycho-diagnostics can be left out of therapy training. The tendency to use 'evidence based therapy' (keeping notes on the computer) and standardised protocols comes more from care authorities and their ilk who are looking for certainties than from people who are expert in the field of psychotherapy. The latter know that flexibility and creativity are the most valuable attributes (Erickson, Rossi and Rossi, 1976). If the therapist is creative and flexible then it rubs off on their clients, and that is a very good start (Derks and Hollander, 1996a).

---

[63] Diagnostic and Statistical Manual.

Day to day practice

I would recommend we exercise restraint in the use of the family panorama when diagnosing. For day-to-day use it will be enough to make the distinction I have already mentioned between:

1. Current problems with relationships within the family, and
2. Deep-rooted limiting social behaviour patterns that appear to stem from the early family situation.

This distinction is neither exhaustive nor exclusive. After all, many current problems can be connected with deep-rooted social patterns of thought. As well as this, current problems can cause patterns of behaviour, which have hitherto functioned very well, suddenly to become limiting. In practice, all participants in my trainings seem to be able to find a limiting social behaviour pattern. This is also true of my clients; if I look for such patterns, I find them. And the therapy that follows from that is always useful.

If someone complains about current relationships then it is preferable to have a look at the current family, usually we will then automatically find out if we need to deal with someone's past.

Technique 39: Therapeutic objectives

In order to avoid therapy being an endless and frustrating affair, Bandler and Grinder (1979) emphasise the usefulness of formulating therapy objectives in advance. This is a habit that comes from behavioural therapy.

Solution-focused therapists ask the so-called 'miracle question' to get to a therapeutic objective. 'Imagine that you wake up tomorrow and your problem is already solved. What difference would you notice?' or, 'Imagine that you meet a magician who can conjure up the solution. What would you ask him for?' In short, 'How do you want it to be?'

Any attention paid to the desired outcome can lead (family panorama) therapy in the right direction. Referring back to the objectives makes it much easier to discover which configuration of personifications is blocking the client.

Bandler and Grinder (1979) give a number of conditions to which, in their opinion, objectives must conform if they are to be workable (Derks and Hollander, 1996a):

1. The objective must be formulated in positive terms (without negatives in the expression).
2. It must be within the personal control of the client.
3. There must be clear, sensory proof to the client when they have succeeded.
4. The context within which the objective should be achieved must be clearly described.
5. There must be no objections to be found against reaching the objective.

Technique 40: Deciding on a test case in advance

Indication: To create a check for the effectiveness of the change

It can be difficult to decide afterwards whether a therapy has been successful, particularly when working with deep-rooted social behaviour patterns. Sometimes the therapist can play a provocative part in order to check the effect, but that is not always possible. Cladder (2001) advises using special questionnaires or the giving of marks to the intensity of the complaints.

In my experience it is often enough to ask the client initially to think of a convincing test case which can be used to check the measure of success at the end. Awarding marks makes it stronger.

The reliability of such a test is, however, completely dependent on the degree to which the therapist is open, verbally and non-verbally, to failure. After all, the client understands that the therapist, after several hours of work, would like to hear that the problem has gone. To avoid the client's response being affected by social desirability, the therapist must, from the start, invite negative feedback. 'If something doesn't feel right please tell me. I depend on what you feel and say.'

The downside of this is that some clients can feel rewarded for discovering obstacles and will be more resistant than necessary and this will undermine the therapy. The great art here lies in finding the right balance between being open for negative feedback and rewarding success.

Technique 41: Finding deviations from the ideal image by use of universal, collective and individual family panorama patterns

(see also section 6.7)

When the therapist has made a sketch of the client's family panorama they can find out, together with the client and using the information from section 6.7, if there are any deviations from the so-called ideal image. That will give them a direction for possible changes.

In my own work I use the patterns from section 6.7 only as an orientation. I rarely tell the client that a pattern is a deviation or give an interpretation for the simple reason that such an 'oracle' activity will make the client dependent on my expertise. I would never say something like, 'Hey, you have a family member inside your own body. Oh dear, that's all wrong!'

Being an oracle can create a placebo effect of a therapy by making the healer seem more authoritative and plausible (Derks and Hollander, 1996a; Hollander, 1997). An oracle may stimulate the client, but it can also paralyse them by making them dependent and powerless. A great dependence on the therapist will decrease the ability of clients to solve problems themselves. A client, when with the therapist, should feel competent enough to take part in finding solutions. The client's contribution is absolutely vital for changing a family panorama because of the existence of individual family panoramas, which make it impossible for another person to know what a particular configuration of personifications means for any given client. In the interpretation of the social panorama, the more the therapist leads, the more dependent and passive the client will become.

It is better to show the sketch to the client and to ask, 'What do you think that it means that your father is in two places? And why is your mother so far away with her back to everyone?'

The explanation clients give of their family panoramas when they use such sketches or arrangements to look at them objectively can often be extremely informative. From this the therapist, aware of the patterns, usually has enough to work on.

Technique 42: Transference of abilities to the distant family past

This technique is one of the most effective in this book. It was developed on the basis of Janet's 'Substitution' technique (1889), Erickson's 'September-man' approach (1967), James and Woodsmall's 'Time-line Therapy' (1988), Andreas and Andreas' 'Core transformation' (1994) and Dilts and McDonalds' 'Reparenting' (1996).

I start here at the point where an objective that involves a deep-rooted social behaviour pattern has been formulated and an early childhood family panorama has been mapped.

1. In your family, whose lack of abilities stimulated the development of the limiting social behaviour?

2. Once that family member has been found, the missing abilities are given names (X, Y, Z …).

3. Call up these abilities one at a time. Choose a specific moment when you had the ability very strongly. Get right into the situation. Associate each ability with its own colour and prepare it for a metaphorical transfer with a time machine.

4. Go back (with the time machine) into the past, taking the abilities with you (X, Y, Z …). Find the family member who needs them when he or she was a young child (e.g. Go back to the time when your father was six years old, taking with you the abilities he lacked).

5. Make good contact with the young family member and transfer the abilities to him or her, one at a time, by using their colour.

6. Visualise how the family member grows up enriched by the abilities (X, Y, Z …). Take your time, follow that line to just before the moment that your parents first met.

7. Visualise the contact between your parents with the abilities present. Continue until your conception.

8. Experience how the abilities (X, Y, Z …) affect your older siblings. Take your time to feel the abilities (X, Y, Z …) being present all

around you when you are in the womb, and then experience an easy birth.

9. Experience how you are received and grow up in a family in which the abilities (X, Y, Z ...) affect everyone. Grow up until you reach the age at which you have explored the family panorama (e.g. five years old).

10. Check how the abilities (X, Y, Z ...) have helped to change the family panorama.

N.B. It is better to do the next two techniques (Techniques 43 and 44) before you get the client to grow up to the present day (Technique 45).

Possible problems (P) and solutions (S) for Technique 42

P: It is difficult to choose a family member who was lacking abilities.
S: Choose the parent with the least influence.

P: A parent's faults are blamed on grandparents.
S: Give the abilities to the grandparents.

P: There is more than one family member with missing abilities.
S: Give both parents or both grandparents as young children the missing abilities. Let them both grow up until just before their first meeting. Then let the client look at the family history up until the time of his conception.

P: The abilities don't reach their target, are refused or the client begrudges them to the person involved.
S: Have the client send the abilities directly, in the best possible way they think would work, from the here and now into the far and distant past, where the parents or grandparents will receive them in their cradle.

P: The family panorama only partially changes, some children stay in their old positions.
S: These children have to be told separately that their parents have better abilities.

Technique 43: Testing locations in the second perceptual position

Indication: To prevent inconsistencies in the family panorama

As a result of Technique 43 or another technique one or more family personifications have been moved. In order to make sure that these changes are in harmony with the client as a whole, and that no personifications protest, you can do the following steps:

1. Move, in your mind, to the location of a random family member (second perceptual position). How does that family member like the new situation? What does it feel like to be there? How do the others appear from that spot?

2. Notice any objections that arise.

3. Make small adjustments until you know exactly where the objections are.

4. Move on to the next personification and do the same thing. Experiment with small changes in location and direction of gaze until this one, too, is satisfied.

5. Go on until all personifications, including yourself, are satisfied.

Possible problems (P) and solutions (S)

P: Putting yourself in the place of the personifications is confusing.
S: Put papers on the floor in the exact locations of the personifications. Put their names on them. Now the client will be able to step from paper to paper. Have the client move the papers around each time a change is made until he is satisfied.

P: Adjustment does not produce a solution.
S: Transfer abilities from the self-personification to the personification that is dissatisfied. Question: 'what does this person need to be able to do in order to stay in this position?' Abilities can also be transferred to personifications in their youth, or transferred from family member to family member.

Technique 44: Stabilising the family panorama

Indication: To promote the transfer from the therapeutic context into real life

Once the new family panorama has been approved by all the family personifications:

1. Let the client assimilate the new image.
2. Move around in and possibly outside the space in which you have been working. While you move, have the client imagine different contexts: holiday, work, shopping, visiting, alone in the woods. Let the client imagine the new image in those contexts.
3. Repeat this for as long as necessary to be sure that the client will remember it always and everywhere.

Technique 45: Growing up into the present

Indication: To integrate the new image in life history

Now ask the client to grow up from their new (five years of age) family panorama into the present. Give the client as much time as they need, and encourage them to imagine all the changes which might have happened as realistically as possible, complete with feelings. This reliving has a particularly stabilising influence (Isert and Rentel, 2000). If necessary, if the client's attention has been taken by regret about missed chances, help them to get back a future-oriented attitude.

Technique 46: Application to the test case

As soon as the client has arrived back in the present you can test the effect by using the test situation you chose in Technique 40. How has it changed? Can the client give it a new mark? Sometimes it takes days or weeks of patience before you can judge the results. The simplest test is to check the social panorama at the next meeting. Are the changes still there? Does the client remember them? Can they still call them up and feel them?

In one case, the personifications of the parents, who had been moved behind the client, had spontaneously moved back to their old places within a week. Asking the positive intention behind the return elicited the reason for it, 'My mother has had a stroke. I have to keep watch on her to see it doesn't happen again.' With this insight the client could solve the problem. She moved her mother behind her again but kept an eye on her condition by means of an imaginary rear-view mirror.

A behavioural test in reality is even better, as when the client reports that there is improvement in the social behaviour in a context where there used to be problems.

6.12.1 Final word about family panorama techniques

Deep-rooted social behaviour patterns come into being after long continued unconscious exposure to a family situation. The child sees the way the family functions as 'obvious'. The social-cognitive patterns that spring from this are in some cases never discussed. If the client does not have the words to describe it, a sketch of the family panorama will make it very clear. When a therapist works with a group, a family constellation can be made for the same purpose and the rest of this chapter is about the pros and cons of this method. Readers who have no affinity with it can skip to Chapter 7.

6.13 Use of the constellation method

As I already mentioned in Chapter 1, it is impossible to follow your unconscious thought processes by conscious introspection. Consciousness is too slow and not sensitive enough. We all miss an unbelievable amount when we talk to one another. When we have a conversation we are only conscious of tiny fragments of what is happening within ourselves and the other person. Looked at like that, communication between people is very limited indeed. The therapist should not try to talk to a whole family and follow their thoughts as well, as this is a completely impossible task. In light of this we might ask ourselves what theoretical framework would fit a quarrelling, squabbling and impatient family? System theory or chaos theory? Family therapists have been stumbling over the limits of system theory for some decades so it is logical that they should now be searching for alternatives.

THAWING A FROZEN FAMILY PANORAMA

What happens when we ask a client to use a random group of people to help make a representation of his family panorama: 'You take the place of my mother, you are my father, you play my sister, you stand in for my little brother and you are my substitute grandmother – stand there and say nothing.' Is such a 'still life' of family relationships manageable for a therapist? Is this a useful tool to bring clarity into the relationships?

To a certain extent it is. Particularly at the start, when people are taking their places. But it has appeared from Bert Hellinger's Family Constellation Method that usually, within a few moments, all sorts of completely incomprehensible things start happening. The apparently frozen substitutes thaw as soon as they are arranged and mysterious interactions that perplex most people start happening. 'Oh, my! Gee! My Goodness! What is going on here?'

As a scientist I had a confusing time witnessing this. Things got even worse when people asked me for an explanation. How do you explain the fact that substitutes who do not know the client, his family or one another, together give the impression that they know exactly what is happening emotionally in the real family, and even what happened in it a hundred years ago? And how is it possible that the substitutes uncover facts that even the client did not know? Facts that turn out to be true when, later, grandmother is asked about them! No social cognition theory can say anything of value about that! And how can you explain psychologically that when the substitutes in such an arrangement have made peace with one another clients can suddenly, after years of bitterness, find themselves in a sea of peace? Lucas, you say that it is unconscious communication? But please tell me how; the client has not spoken to or seen any of their relatives! Sometimes substitutes even feel pain in the place where the previous week the family member whose part they are playing was diagnosed to have cancer! Or they automatically grab their throats when they play an uncle who hanged himself. Or someone suddenly starts to tremble when he is near another who is playing the part of a person who turns out to be his murderer. Lucas, can you, as a social scientist, explain that? That someone avoids all eye contact with the substitute who is playing the father who turns out not to be the biological father? And how can substitutes, who start by just standing passively in the place they have been given, suddenly get very emotional and become besotted, angry or grief-stricken and burst into uncontrollable tears?'[64]

For anyone who is aware of the complexity of unconscious social cognition, none of this will come as a surprise. As I have already said, nobody can completely comprehend this complexity intellectually, so it makes sense that we should be baffled by what might happen with the constellation method. The wonder that people experience can be compared to the reaction of Westerners when they are confronted with 'psychic surgery' or a 'possession ritual' in a voodoo séance (Derks and Hollander, 1998).

However compelling paranormal explanations may be, in this book I will maintain a view that fits within the framework of social cognition theory.

HELLINGER'S SYSTEMIC PSYCHOTHERAPY
Hellinger's star is rapidly rising over the European therapeutic world. No wonder, because his constellation method has wonderful magico-religious aspects and it puts established psychotherapy out of the picture. A systemic psychotherapy workshop in which the constellation method is central is usually a very moving event. Most people who have been emotionally affected by it reject rational explanations that threaten to take the miracle out of it; they tend to defend their experience against intellectual disqualification.

I am aware that I cannot do justice to Hellinger's systemic psychotherapy in this chapter because I intend to limit myself to themes that have to do with unconscious social cognition. I would advise you, therefore, to study the work of Hellinger, Weber and Varga von Kibel and their colleagues if you want to explore the world of thought behind it. For me, as a researcher, the constellation method is a great social, psychological and anthropological

---

[64] People who are very enthusiastic about the constellation method always use these arguments. This illustrates that wherever magical explanation surface, one has to do with the underestimation of the human unconscious capabilities. See Derks (1992).

experiment that has provided a number of very surprising insights. I will present a few of them in the rest of this chapter.

ANCESTOR MAGIC

From an anthropological perspective it is noticeable that Hellinger practises a form of 'ancestor magic' that is adapted to western culture. He re-introduces a number of age-old healing principles that were probably lost to us at the end of the Neolithic period, but which are still very much alive in many other cultures (Lewis, 1971).

Hellinger confronts us with the fact that the fates of our ancestors can seep through into our own lives with sometimes disastrous consequences. Hellinger's message comes as a bolt from the blue in our culture, where we pretend that our family history is of only anecdotal interest. Seen from the usual western point of view of individualism, the idea that your ancestors can upset your life is an anomaly (Pouwel, 1992).

A family constellation is often a ritual to make peace with ancestors.[65] Such ancestor-placating rituals – sacrifices, prayers, dance and fancy dress – are, in many cultures, important for healing and maintaining psycho-social balance (Bourguignon, 1968; Lewis, 1971; Derks and Hollander, 1996a, 1998).

In our culture we lack this possibility,[66] which means that we are often stuck with any problems that originate with our ancestors. Within the theory set out in this book it is reasonable to assume that personifications from the distant past can reach us through our parents and, almost unnoticed, can occupy central positions in our social panorama. Think of great-grandparents who were poor, family members who were killed in a concentration camp or fighters for a socialist ideal. If you break your family taboos – waste money, go on holiday to Germany or Japan or fire your workers – you come into conflict with the personifications within you who

---

[65] Especially when the dead play a major part in a constellation. In Hellinger's work this is very often the case.

[66] Apart from the Catholic 'All Souls', the memorial services for victims of war or the burning of candles on graves such as in Austria (permanent) or Finland (with Christmas).

normally make sure that you follow the rules. But how can you solve such a situation? In many cultures this is done with a festive ceremony.

In Africa and South America they hold ancestor rituals in which living people dressed up as ancestral spirits dance through the village. Members of the community have absolutely no difficulty in believing in the reality of this. The substitute ancestors are hugged, receive presents and call up sometimes intense emotions. In short, what ancestor magic does in the far corners of the earth, systemic psychotherapy does for us.

AN INTENSE SOCIAL EXPERIENCE

The constellation method, however, is not only used for relationships with ancestors, but is effective for almost any type of problem. One of the things I, as a social psychologist, find remarkable is the size of the groups of participants, as this method is sometimes used with groups of hundreds of participants. The intensity with which this is done quickly fosters a strong connection, but it goes a lot further than anything a sensitivity training can unloose. Groups in the constellation therapy often undergo collective spiritual experiences on the lines of, 'universal human connection' and 'a link in the chain of the generations'. Hellinger, an ex-priest, who was born in 1925, leads such groups in a very infectious manner. By using archaic language and virtuoso techniques to overcome resistance he convinces almost everyone that his method is far superior to all other, 'ordinary' therapies.

Hellinger's experience in the fields of group dynamics, primal therapy, psychoanalysis, transactional analysis and hypnotherapy makes him particularly good at finding very simple connections. However, anyone who tries to discuss with him the therapeutic effect of his work gets nowhere, 'It's not about the effect. It doesn't matter whether or not the client feels better afterwards. It's about letting love do its work.' Anyone who confronts Hellinger with the often mentioned risks of his methods will be told, 'Yes, of course, it is a dangerous therapy!' And, as Hollander (1997) says, people logically see a dangerous therapy as a powerful one. It attracts most people, they want to find out if they are up to it. The danger works more as a challenge than a deterrent.

ADMIRATION AND CRITICISM

Hellinger, who was inspired in 1981 by the work of Ivan Boszormenyi-Nagy to become a family therapist, has both followers and critics. The latter often call him an arrogant guru who forces his views on people – 'I unearth the reality.' Others criticise the lack of follow-up and the passive role he gives his clients. Some doubt the effect of his therapy and others call it counter-productive, but I have never yet heard a critic accuse him of plagiarism. For me his originality alone would be reason enough to admire him. He is an autonomous thinker who does not step aside for anyone or anything, a non-conformist who is contributing a great deal to the development of psychotherapy.

6.13.1 Constellation: The ritual is put central

Hellinger and his colleagues often speak of 'systemic family therapy' but the German word that dominates this field is 'Aufstellung', which literally means 'to put in position'. In English this was translated into 'Constellation', a word that fails to convey the activity of getting people to stand in particular places in space. In titles of workshops the word 'Aufstellung' is nearly always present, as in 'Systemic constellations (Aufstellungen) according to Bert Hellinger', 'Healing with family constellations (Aufstellungen)' and 'Constellation (Aufstellungs) work with companies'. Weber, Gross and Essen developed 'Organisational constellations (Aufstellungen)' (Isert and Rentel, 2000), and the terms 'Structural constellations', 'Problem constellations' and 'Tetralemma constellations' come from Sparrer and Varga von Kibet (1998).

This illustrates the central place that the ritual of putting substitutes in standing positions on the floor takes for these therapists. The therapeutic effect of it, however, is seldom spoken of or tested (Weber, 1998). What makes the 'Aufstellung' so important? Hellinger himself emphasises that the arrangement ritual 'makes reality visible' and that, through it, psychological problems can sometimes be solved. 'Such a constellation helps people to get into harmony with their fate.' He does not define this method as a 'therapy' in the traditional meaning of the word. Therapeutic change of cognitive social constructions, which for me is the main objective, takes second place in constellation work.

As we have already seen, constellations can be used for other things than making family panoramas visible. Varga von Kibet (1995; 2001; Varga von Kibet and Sparrer, 1998) uses them for treating any type of problem, both social and non-social. Remarkable in his work are the metaphorical personifications that are played by substitutes. Hellinger uses them, too, when he has substitutes playing 'death', 'illness' or 'my country'. The therapeutic power of the use of metaphorical personifications comes from involving the social operating system in the solving of problems that would otherwise have to do without its enormous capacity. In the work of Weber (1998, 2001) we see the use of group-personifications – he will, for example, depict a department or an organisation with only one substitute.

BEFORE THE ARRANGEMENT

Before he starts making a family constellation, Hellinger asks his client about genealogical facts and important events in family history. 'Did anyone die young?' 'Has either of your parents been married before?' 'Has your mother ever lost a child?' He seems to concentrate on events such as early death, conflicts, illness, crime, loss, war, marriage and divorce. He does not ask what these things mean to the client.

'If a significant person is mentioned I go straight to work. I will get the rest of my information from the constellation,' says Hellinger (1995).

Whenever Hellinger sees a reason for a constellation, which is nearly always the case, he asks the client to choose people as substitutes for his family members. The client will then usually ask other workshop participants, 'Will you be my uncle?' 'Will you be my dead sister?'

To find the right places for the substitutes the client will be asked for good, introspective concentration. If the client has difficulty concentrating, most constellation therapists tend to break off the session; they do not make any trance-inducing suggestions to make it easy for the client. The instructions Hellinger gives his clients can go as follows:

'Take the people you have chosen, one at a time, by the shoulders with both hands and put them in the place that you feel that they should be in relation to one another. Once it feels right, stop. Follow your feelings, do it in the way that you experience it right now. Check if it feels right and then sit down' (Hellinger, 1995).

The client will usually choose a substitute for himself so he can sit and observe the arrangement from a distance. He will then watch the actions of the therapist and the substitutes.

TWO DIFFERENT CONSTELLATION ACTIVITIES
When studying the constellation method it becomes clear that the activities can be divided into two parts:

1. *Making inner experience concrete.*
A family panorama or other internal image can be made visible and tangible. In this way it becomes available to the client, the therapist and also to the audience, which is always present in this work. The fact that everyone can see what is happening gives this form of therapy something of the character of theatre, so a comparison with psychodrama fits very well. That everyone can follow the process as a live play is a very attractive aspect of constellation work; it makes all other therapy demonstrations look very dull in comparison. It is also pleasant to have so many participants actively involved in a workshop.

As well making someone's inner social experience tangible, there is also a second category of activities.

2. *Use of the substitutes' impulses.*
Once the substitutes are in place it is easy to bring them to express their thoughts, motives and feelings. This ease comes from the fact that substitutes in a constellation find it very difficult to act as lifeless dummies. As I already mentioned, the constellation itself and the stories they hear automatically bring something to life within them. Their own social operating system starts automatically giving social-emotional meaning to the information, in particular the position they find themselves in. It does not take much expertise on the part of the therapist to activate the substitutes to express

their perceptions. A question like, 'How does the father feel?' is often enough.

If a constellation is not strongly directed, the substitutes will quickly start to follow all their impulses. They will move around in the space and start all sorts of interactions. In order to prevent them interfering with the constellation, most therapists use a fairly authoritative leadership style. Hellinger uses a single microphone that he keeps to himself. The substitutes may only speak or move if the therapist has given them permission or instructions to do so.

LOCATION IS THE INCARNATION OF RELATIONSHIPS

A number of the things that happen during constellations would not be very surprising to anyone who has read this book from the beginning. We already know that the unconscious social cognitive abilities react strongly to the factor 'location.' People will automatically give a relational meaning to the space between them. If someone in a constellation is given the instruction to 'feel what you feel', an easily acquired light trance will facilitate the experiencing of social feelings. My view is that every person who has a social panorama in his head is sensitive to the spatial positions of (standing) people. In a constellation this sensitivity is optimised so that people can experience intense social emotions.

ROLE IDENTIFICATION

As well as this, it has been my experience that minimal information about someone's background, for instance, 'My father was a carpenter,' gives enough for anyone to build a sufficiently formed personification. As soon as the personification is formed, the substitute will be able to take the second perceptual position with it. Once there, they can construct a second position self-image in a flash. Then they are ready as an active substitute.

Children identify completely when they 'pretend'; the instruction 'you are the police' will enable a child immediately to 'be' a police officer. Within a workshop, asking a client, 'Will you be my sister?' works in an identical fashion. Apparently adults never lose their childish ability to identify with a role – they spend all day playing games like 'father and mother' or 'salesman and customer'

(Johnstone, 1979). As they get older this capability may even get stronger.

In the cinema a one-second shot of a still, expressionless and passive actor will easily be interpreted as an alien in human form. The same speed of understanding happens in a constellation. Our unconscious mind can apparently generate a lot of information on a minimum of instruction; for example, 'you are my grandfather' – we don't even need consciously to decide to take the part to 'become' that grandfather.

For instance, once, when I was a substitute, all the information I had was that I was the oldest son of a family of nine, that my mother had married beneath her and that there were no wedding photographs. My unconscious immediately went to work on this information without my being aware of doing very much thinking at all. When my substitute mother said to my substitute father, 'Look, these are your children', my substitute father automatically shook his head several times. When he came closer to me I felt a sensation of intense cold. Only then did it occur to my conscious mind that I was not his biological son.

6.13.2 Not social cognition, but 'the system'

Making a family panorama visible by means of a constellation is only the beginning, the next phase is to change it. One of the most practical aspects of the use of a constellation is that it is easy to move the substitutes around. By turning and relocating them, a constellation can quickly be changed.

Logically speaking, the client should be encouraged to make the same changes in his social panorama, but most of the constellation therapists I have observed spend little or no time or attention on imprinting the client with the new image. This can indicate two things:

1. The therapist knows that the unconscious mind will record the new configuration fast and reliably enough automatically.
2. The therapist does not have changing the client's social constructions as a primary objective.

That many therapists do not view the changing of social cognitive structures as being important becomes evident, in the first place, from their meagre use of expressions – such as 'inner image' or 'social representation' – that deal with social construction. They speak more often about something else that is changed by the constellation, namely 'the system'. Apparently, what they mean by this is something different from what the Palo Alto tradition speaks of. Constellation therapists seem to have the view that 'the system' is something autonomous and separate from the client and that it will automatically absorb any changes that have been made.

Let us try to reason from this vision of 'the system'. The first leap we need to make is that constellation work does not necessarily change anything in the psyche of the client; what changes is the system within which the client operates. The question that arises from that is, "What does 'the system' consist of?" Therapists often see it as a field of energy that is not bound by time or place. That means that the system falls outside the boundaries of 'normal' psychology and enters the world of the paranormal.

The fact that the system is very sensitive to spatial position does not generally seem to have attracted any particular attention from constellation therapists. They speak very little of this remarkable phenomenon. Some of them think that the locations are nodes in the systemic energy, but the locations are certainly not the same as the system. Quite possibly, in their view, the system can exist totally without the locations. Many say that they believe a change of location directly influences someone's place in the system. It seems that they see the system glimmering somewhere behind the locations, which for them are only a metaphorical or material expression of the system.

'SYSTEMAGICAL' CHANGES

The next question that arises when we try to follow this view is, 'what does the constellation do to the system?' In this view it is the constellation ritual itself that awakens the system – or, rather, invokes it. For someone is sitting quietly and watching, their system will not be very active, but as soon as the client on the podium starts to talk about his family, and certainly as soon as he starts to choose substitutes, the forces of the system will spring into action. The substitutes soon begin to work as emotional antennae for its signals. It is not clear to me from the explanations of constellation therapists whether they ascribe a special relay function to the client as a switching station in the transference of information from the system to the substitutes. Some even seem to suggest that a client's system can be called up without the client actually being present.

If we follow the vision of the system, as some constellation therapists understand it, the consequences are preposterous. It would mean that every single relative of the client would have a place somewhere in the system – including the unknown ones. In order to communicate adequately with the substitutes the system would have to know the family history for at least four generations back, including all family secrets and taboos.

It would also be true that the substitutes, who first did not belong to the system when they were sitting in the room, become part of it as soon as they are arranged in a constellation. The node of systemic energy from the location in the constellation would open a direct channel between the substitute and the person they are representing.

This view has the consequence that therapists who work with constellations often completely ignore the fact that the substitutes are not the 'real' people. They confuse (on purpose?) symbol with reality – in anthropology that is called 'representation magic'. The substitutes, too, to judge by the intensity of their emotions, seem often to forget that they are only playing a part. The term that most aptly describes this is 'possession' (Bourguignon, 1968; Johnstone, 1979:156–164). We also see this complete absorption in the role in actors, mediums, politicians, hypnotic subjects and children at play; it occurs everywhere as a normal human social skill.

Many constellation therapists seem to believe that the substitutes are accurately informed by the system about the social emotional status of the 'real' family member that they are representing (Varga von Kibet and Sparrer, 1998), but if this subject is mentioned during a session, they will dismiss it as irrelevant theorising. Within such a discussion lurks the danger that, if the substitutes are not proven to be a reliable source of information, much of constellation work loses its credibility.

It may be an irrelevant point in practice, but for theoreticians like me a concept like 'the system' is a dead end that has no connection with any other psychological concepts.

From experience I know that many constellation therapists find the vision of the system as an entity outside the client more attractive than the one I propound in this book. Clearly, belief in the system gives these therapists a great deal of freedom, particularly when the therapy is not called therapy and the results may not be compared to those of other therapies.

By suggesting that they have more access to knowledge of the system than anyone else present, the therapist reserves the exclusive right to interpret and make prophetic announcements. Followers of 'the system' would find the social panorama lacking in many of these attractive aspects (Derks and Hollander, 1996a, 1998; Hollander, 1997).

Where many constellation therapists talk of the system, Hellinger himself speaks of the 'system soul'. This is a life philosophy in which an 'external locus of control' predominates.[67] The individual is subordinate to 'higher powers'. Hellinger calls one of those higher powers, 'fate' (das Schicksal) and the other is 'love'. Fate and love decide what happens to us. Fate and Love rule a host of system souls in Hellinger's pantheon, which in their turn are more powerful than individual souls. The system soul is also a manifestation of a higher cosmic order that cannot be bargained with. The therapist's role is not to flout the law of Fate and Love and it would be very presumptuous even to try.[68]

Postulation of the system soul gives Hellinger's work a religious character. People come together in his workshops to communicate, under inspirational guidance, with something that is greater and stronger than themselves.

---

[67] See D. van Kampenhout (2001), 'Healing comes from out there; Shamanism and Family Constellations' (Die Heilung kommt von Ausserhalb; Schamanismus und Familien-stellen) Carl Aur-Systeme Verlag, Heidelberg.
[68] To transfer resources from children towards their parents is considered a kind of blasphemy by Hellinger: Grandiosity.

In our article, 'Systemic Voodoo' (Derks and Hollander, 1998), we give a summary of the magic-religious characteristics of constellation work. The fact that Hellinger was brought up with religion and magic in South Africa has certainly contributed to this. He observed the Zulus performing constellation-like rituals with ancestors. Many such magic-religious patterns also occur in Afro-American religions, of which the 'Winti' from Surinam is the best known in Holland (Stephen, 1995). I will list a number of points of similarity:

1. The constellation is a pattern oracle that is interpreted by the therapist. (In Winti the 'Lukuman' does this with a pattern of coins, stones, shells or bones.)

2. The system soul is the great family spirit that is called up by the ritual. (In Winti, they speak of 'the Bere', which means 'stomach' but also 'family spirit'.)

3. The substitutes are possessed by family spirits, particularly ancestor spirits. (In Winti, people can go into a trance because they are possessed by 'Yorkas' in a 'Banya'.)

4. Representational magic is practised by treating the symbolic representation by the substitutes as the real family. (In Winti, the black magic 'wisi' practice of ' poppie prikken'; a doll is hurt in order to hurt the person it represents.)

5. The community of substitutes works on the healing of the individual. (In Winti, a 'Winti-Prey' and a 'Yorka-Prey': parties with music, food and dances).

6. The therapist contacts family ghosts in the form of the system soul. The therapist's relationship with his or her own soul must be good, just as is true for a shaman who heals others through contact with his guiding spirit. (In Winti, the 'Bonuman' (shaman) and his 'Kra' (guiding spirit) must work well together in order to heal people)

7. Problems are ascribed to systemic entanglements, usually identifications with ancestors. These have the same structure as the forms of possession by tortured ancestor ghosts, misuse of power, conflicts, rape victims and family curses in Winti.

(In Winti, they are called 'Fyo-fyo', 'Kroy', and 'Kunu'.) In Afro-American religions the spirit world is viewed as a field of real entities outside the person, just as the system is seen by its advocates. The ghosts are an objective fact; they are 'real' and are not experienced as cognitive constructions. The priest uses his rituals to reveal the reality of the spirit world.

6.13.3 Why do you want to know?

Because it is impossible rationally to understand the phenomena that occur in constellations, we could view the system ideology adhered to by constellation therapists as a logical choice for filling a conceptual gap. The theory in this book is an attempt to fill the same gap in a different way.

Some constellation therapists (Weber, 1998; Isert and Rentel, 2000; Hellinger and Beaumont, 1998) seem to choose to say as little as possible about the character of the phenomena. They do not postulate a system or a system soul but nor do they speak of unconscious social cognition. Seen pragmatically, these two views appear comparable and as far as the practical application goes they seem, at first glance, to have similar consequences. But that can also be said of Winti.

In my opinion, however, this comparison fails when we look at integration with science and the connection with other forms of psychotherapy. The social panorama model offers better possibilities than either of these other visions.

The representational magical assumption that the feelings of a substitute really are the feelings of the family member he represents contradicts the assumptions of 'normal' science. It also immediately occasions questions like, 'Is it done by telepathy?' 'Is this a manifestation of Jung's Collective Unconscious?' or 'Does this prove Rupert Sheldrake's Morpho-Genetic Field theory?'

Constellation therapists see the contrary assumption – that the feelings of the substitutes are *not* the same as those of the people they are representing – as a challenge to the legitimacy of interventions carried out on the basis of substitutes.

Varga von Kibet (Varga von Kibet and Sparrer, 1998) says explicitly that the feelings of substitutes are the same as those of the people they are representing. Beaumont (Hellinger and Beaumont, 1998) says that he is not so sure about that, but that it is useful to use the feelings of substitutes as pointers in the therapy. He sees these feelings more as a source of synergy. The alternative family panorama that is created within a constellation helps the client broaden his vision. Hellinger's opinion seems to vary. In 1995 he said:

> I don't explain anything. I just watch what happens and see that it works and that you can check whether the people who are being substitutes in a family constellation can really feel what is happening in that family. For my work that is enough.

CONSTELLATIONS WITHOUT SUBSTITUTES

When someone participates in a constellation as 'him-' or 'herself' and not as a substitute, then there is no doubt about whether the feelings are 'real' or not. In that case everyone believes that their position in the constellation calls up accurate feelings.

When, as an exception to my normal practice, I make a constellation with a couple or with a team in which the participants play themselves, the feelings seem to be as strong and clear as those in a constellation with substitutes – the only thing that is missing is the amazement.

The fact that the same sorts of emotions occur in constellations with or without substitutes shows that there is very little difference as far as the unconscious social cognition is concerned. In both cases the result is a 'real', intense social experience.

6.13.4 Experimenting with family constellations

We are still left with the question, 'Does a substitute feel the same as the person they are representing?' If that is so, then different people representing the same person must experience identical emotions.

To obtain more insight into the reliability of the emotions experienced by substitutes I did the following experiment.

On the 21st March, 1997, I gathered a group of 13 students together, of whom, to my knowledge, none was familiar with either family constellations or the social panorama.

I explained that this experiment was very important to me, and that it would require great concentration and discipline on their part.

I asked if there was anyone who came from an uncomplicated family. A man of 50 said that he only had one brother. I helped him (= client) to arrange his family as he had experienced it when he was seven years old. I worked in exactly the same way as I had seen Hellinger do. As soon as the client was satisfied with the constellation we had made, I asked the other participants to concentrate on their feelings. The family constellation consisted of only four members, the client, his mother, father and brother. They were arranged as follows:

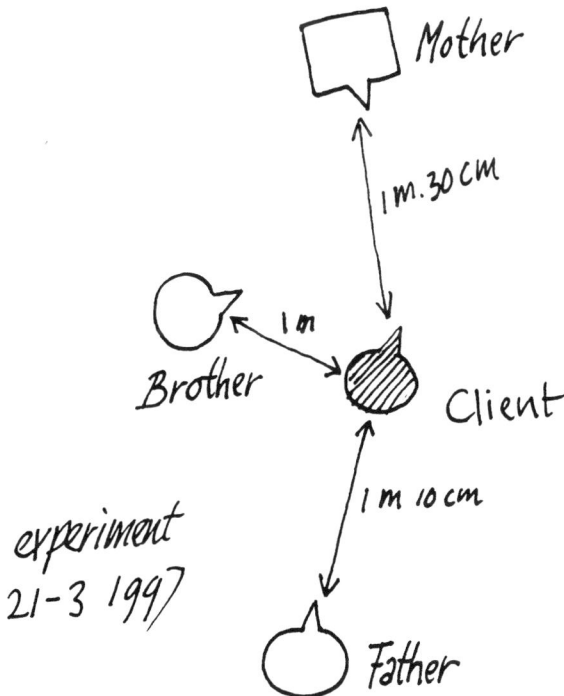

267

I drew with chalk an outline round the shoes of the people in the constellation to make it easy for them to stay in the same place for some time.

As he stood there, the client was asked to fill in a list of questions – questions that all the test subjects had just answered about the emotion 'love'. I used this questionnaire to determine the structure of emotions; it was based on the dimensions of emotions as developed by Cameron-Bandler and Lebeau (1986).

I then asked the client to choose someone as a substitute for himself. First I allowed the substitute to get used to his place and then he filled in the same questionnaire as the client. Once he had done that he was set apart and replaced with a new substitute who was put on exactly the same spot. The new substitute received exactly the same instructions, he was asked to concentrate on his feelings and then fill in the list of questions without leaving his place. This was repeated eight times.

The first two questions gave a clear picture of the social emotions of the substitutes:

Q.1: How would you describe this emotion?
Q.2: What is the most important thing that you want or want to avoid when you are experiencing this emotion?

The client called his emotion 'loneliness' and said that what he wanted was 'love'. Here are the answers of the eight substitutes:

Question 1: What emotion?	*Question 2: What do I want?*
Substitute 1: Longing	Mother love
Substitute 2: Fear	Harmony
Substitute 3: Pressure	Not to be between parents who do not communicate
Substitute 4: Limitation, anger	More freedom, that they stop watching me
Substitute 5: Rage	Closeness
Substitute 6: Threat	To see my father
Substitute 7: Being tied down	Freedom
Substitute 8: Restlessness, unease	To look back

All these emotions are characterised by negativity, but within that they show a remarkable diversity. At question 8 (see later) they were asked to give a mark between one and seven to 'intensity' of the feeling. The average was 6.11, which was 0.1 higher than the intensity given by the client.

Here are the other answers. They speak, for the most part, for themselves. The number of responses per alternative is given after the answer. Some respondents gave more than one answer. The **C** is the client's answer.

Question 3: Where is your attention when experiencing this emotion?
Answers: Past (2)   Present – **C** (6)   Future (4)

Question 4: Which verb fits this emotion?
Answers: need – **C** (1), must (1), must not (1), want (3), not want (1), shall (1), might (0), might not (0), can (0), cannot (3), may (0), long for (1), hate (0), fear (1), love (0)

Question 5: When you are feeling this emotion do you feel active or passive?
Answers: Active (4), Passive – **C** (5)

Question 6: When you are feeling this emotion, which do you notice, similarities or differences?
Answers: Similarities – **C** (2), Differences (5)

Question 7: What is the musical tempo of the mood associated with this emotion? (From 1, slow to 7, fast.)
Answers: slow – 1 (1), 2 (1), 3 (2), 4 (0), 5 (0), 6 – **C** (3), 7 (2) – fast

Question 8: What is the intensity of this emotion? (From 1, low to 7, high.)
Answers: low – 1 (0), 2 (0), 3 (0), 4 (1), 5 (0), 6 (5), 7 – **C** (2) – high

Question 9: When you are feeling this emotion, do you generalise or pay attention to detail? (From 1, detail to 7, generalise.)
Answers: detail – 1 (0), 2 (0), 3 (3), 4 (0), 5 (2), 6 (3), 7 – **C** (2) – generalise

One thing that this test, with only eight test substitutes, proves is that they don't in any case feel exactly the same thing in the same location in the constellation. Remarkable is that the emotions were all negative and all very intense. The behavioural tendencies (Frijda, 1986) and motivations associated with the emotions were very different. This experiment suggests strongly that the direction that different substitutes give to a constellation will not always be identical.

6.13.5 *Epilogue*

Anyone who has seen a therapist working with constellations and who can manage to get a group of about 10 people together will be able to give a family constellation workshop. I am not speaking about quality or effectiveness but about the calling up of impressive phenomena by use of the constellation method as described in the last part of this chapter. The fast increase in popularity of the constellation method in the last decade shows that there is a huge market for the deep, dramatic, magical and emotional.

In 1995, Hellinger defined therapeutic success as the improvement of the client's social representation. He says the following about Bruno, a client of his:

> He had an inner picture of the relationships within his family. The fruitless efforts of the family to solve their problems led eventually to the death of his sister and his mother. Bruno had brought his inner image out into the open (in the constellation) so it was visible to us. Now that he had it there in front of him, he could find a better solution by making changes to it. We didn't need to change anything in Bruno's real family to be sure that this solution would work for him. His father does not need to change; he doesn't even have to know anything about what happened here. And the dead will stay dead. Bruno, on the other hand, can lovingly absorb this new, improved image into his soul and it will be effective.

In the end, the most important thing is that everyone is in the right place.

Chapter 7
The spiritual panorama

7.1   *Psychology and religion*

In 1902 William James published a series of readings under the title, *The Varieties of Religious Experience*. Together these formed a psychological study in which James concludes that religious experiences – such as visions of the Virgin Mary, possession, religious ecstasy, mystical experiences, 'seeing the light' and suchlike – have a lot in common with their everyday equivalents. In James' opinion these phenomena get their supernatural qualities only from the context in which people put them and the conclusions they draw from them.

James compared each supernatural experience to a natural one in which the same phenomena occur. One example is a man who is reading and knows for certain that his wife is in the room with him and talks to her for a long time – only then to discover that she has gone shopping, compared to someone experiencing the presence of the holy virgin.

James studied the structure of the subjective experience in a similar manner to the one I use here. As well as being a founder of American psychology, James was also the most well known spokesman of the philosophical stream that is known as 'pragmatism' (James, 1907). Pragmatists look at the consequences of religious beliefs; they are interested in the practical pros and cons of beliefs, and not the 'truth', 'reality' or 'exactitude' (Peirce, 1876).

CRITICISM
Not everyone was pleased when James turned religious experience into a normal psychological study object. Even though he virtuously summed up all the advantages of religion, he was not thanked for it. Religious leaders called it blasphemy and even the Pope condemned him for it. Although James was himself the son of a reverend, he took very little notice (Cotkin, 1990).

The problem that James encountered was typical for the subject. Religion and spirituality seem to be territories that are fanatically defended by church authorities and other people who seem to think that they have exclusive rights to them. I assume that this chapter, too, will upset people because it will automatically sow doubt in affairs that they consider to be holy truths. Psychotherapeutic interference in religion also means an advance of social sciences into the terrain of soul care, in which priests previously had the monopoly. Thanks to psychologists like James, soul shepherds can only look on while religion is secularised and the spiritual world that they used to rule is gradually broken apart.

APPLICATIONS
In this chapter we study the patterns of unconscious social cognition with regard to religion and spirituality. The direct application of this can be found in therapy with clients who have problems with religious questions and grief, and in working with clients whose religious beliefs are very different from those of the therapist. Another particularly useful area of application is helping clients from other cultures, so this research can make a contribution to transcultural psychotherapy (GGZ Nederland, 2001).[69]

7.2 *The power of spirituality and religion*

Geological research shows how humanity has repeatedly been plagued by nature's violence. Climatic changes, meteors, earthquakes, major volcanic eruptions, floods and ice ages regularly threaten our kind with extinction. The cosmos sometimes shows itself to be merciless and even the earth can try to shake us off, wash us away or burn us.

The frequency with which disasters overtake us, however, is so low that we seem, time and again, to forget our collective desperation. According to some people (Hancock, 1995), the early Neolithic monuments (like the ones that were built at the end of the ice age) were meant by their builders to remind us of these disasters, but even so, we have all forgotten them. All we remember are the myths, which we rather prefer to see as parables than as history. And still further Armageddon movies haunt our nightmares and make box office hits.

---

[69] The spiritual panorama was the main subject in a transcultural therapy workshop held in Paramaribo, Suriname in 2004.

We modern primates have developed brains with which it is possible to philosophise about the distant future. The greater the ability to look into the future, the greater the need to answer the question of how we can still have a quiet, pleasant and enjoyable life in spite of the fact that we know for certain that there will be a next cataclysm.

RELIGION IS THE ANSWER

First of all, religion can help a person to believe that they and their community will be the ones to be spared when the next disaster comes and if things go wrong anyway, then they can still be absolutely certain that the cataclysm will be followed by a perfect world.

Secondly, religious frameworks can give form and content to spiritual experiences. These experiences teach one to see beyond the limits of one's own individuality and mortality. A glimpse into eternity makes it possible to put the immediate fear of one's own death into perspective.

Thirdly, thanks to the comfortable certainty that religion gives, it allows for the required peace and scope in the community in order to build a higher level of civilisation. Saving one's own skin and one's children are no longer the only important things, so communication, creativity and community spirit can be given a place within a society. In world history, important cultural developments always seem to be accompanied by important religious developments. The existence of greater social bonds seems to be very dependent on collectively held ideologies.

RELIGION AS AN ORGANISING PRINCIPLE IN SOCIETY

Political and religious leadership went hand in hand for our ancestors. Emperors, popes, caliphs, Maya kings, imams, hermits, dukes, lamas, bishops, priests, knights, tribal leaders, cardinals and presidents have together created our modern world. But it has not been easy. Often the secular and the sacred were at each other's throats. Sometimes religion won, and sometimes politics. But now the religious and the political leaders of the Western world have finally come to an agreement: the secular powers get everything except the most important area, which is kept by the church.

But the division of church and state is not automatic, and the friction which we sometimes see arising can also be seen between leaders and shamans in all four corners of the earth.

As a social psychologist I cannot speak of spirituality without thinking of power. The main question is, who is the boss of the most important things in life?

7.2.1 Unreliable sources of information

If we want to discover the patterns in spiritual life we can write off most spiritual leaders as trustworthy sources. Even if they did know the patterns, they would probably tell us nothing about them. They would be more likely to confuse us laymen with metaphors, theological riddles and paradoxes (Alstad and Kramer, 1993). Or they would want to excommunicate us as heretics so we can thank God that secular power is no longer in cahoots with the cloth, as it was during the Inquisition, and that conflicts on a spiritual level are no longer settled here on earth.[70]

When we are doing psychological research into religion, we have to be aware that the authority of religion will be undermined as soon as we subject the source of its power – a special bond with a higher authority – to critical questions. Religious authorities are in danger of losing their position if we laymen understand more about spiritual life than they do, particularly if we sow doubt among their followers with our knowledge. Religious leaders are not worth much without followers and when those followers have doubts, their belief is no longer of any value.

An interesting present-day Dutch example of the establishment's reaction is the theologist Matzken (1995; 1996) who, in his publications, represents 'pragmagic' – the psychological analysis of the subjective experience of exotic religious practices (Derks and

---

[70] In 2001 we saw the truth of this in Afghanistan.

Hollander, 1996a; Hollander, Derks and Tanebaum, 1996) – as a devilish and occult doctrine.[71]

It is logical that a radical humanistic psychology (Rychlak, 1988) such as the one in this book will conflict with any ideology that seeks salvation outside humanity – with god. A psychology that denies an external power brings people closer to their own power and vulnerability and to their fear of death (Mandell, 1980). Such a psychology opens people's eyes to the threat of social, ecological and cosmic disasters. That fear is, in many religions, the equivalent of evil because it de-stabilises social relationships. Just as the warnings of Greenpeace are impossible to combine with the belief that god will automatically take care of everything for us.

7.2.2 *Spirituality in clinical psychology*

Many clinical psychologists are convinced that spirituality is of vital importance to personal development (Sperry, 2001). Concrete therapeutic interventions on the 'spiritual level' have been developed by Dilts (1990), Andreas and Andreas (1994), Wrycza (1996), Bolstad and Hamblett (1999) and many others. As well as these there are many streams that have their roots in yoga and Zen Buddhism, such as avatar (Palmer, 1994), which have produced directly useful methods for therapists.

---

[71] Matzken (1996) is a theologian who wrote against NLP and in particular against 'pragmagics', a transcultural development in NLP.

The above-mentioned techniques have helped to make the fear-reducing, healing, integrating, problem-solving and conflict-reducing effects of spiritual experiences applicable for use in non-religious counselling practice. Spiritual experiences, which used to be evoked only by initiated priests, are nowadays called up by psychotherapists with their 'step plans'.

Experience has taught that such experiences are much more accessible than most people think. With the right steps in the right order the client can be in the middle of a spiritual experience within half an hour.[72]

As soon as an experience with spiritual characteristics has been initiated, it can be 'let loose' on someone's problematical thoughts. When that happens, the client usually immediately experiences how problems lose their emotional weight, and how it is possible to reflect from a cosmic point of view and put things into perspective. What at first seemed to be a problem turns out to be an essential element of existence and the person in therapy learns to see it as an inner enrichment.

7.3 *Patterns in unconscious religious social cognition*

As I emphasised in the last part of Chapter 6, the supernatural is seen as so pervasive that people underestimate their unconscious abilities. In that chapter I spoke of seeing the phenomena called up by the constellation method as being supernatural and explained them away as the 'system,' the 'collective unconscious' or the 'system soul'. The unconscious dynamics of personifications as I describe them in this book are a rich source of the sort of phenomena that are usually labelled 'supernatural'.

This basic pattern is characteristic and marks, at the same time, the border between psychology and religion. If a person claims that human beings have almost unlimited unconscious powers, then the supernatural and religious sides of his image of the world

---

[72] The so-called 'Core Transformation' technique by Connirae Andereas and Tamara Andreas has an especially solid reputation in this area.

disappear and only psychology is left. Reversing the reasoning, we can say that the fewer unconscious capacities a person ascribes to human beings, the more supernatural explanations will be needed to explain the social and spiritual world.

THREE QUESTIONS ABOUT SPIRITUAL PERSONIFICATIONS

In this chapter I take a look at religion and spirituality from the point of view of the social panorama model, in particular the spatial arrangement of personifications. The first question that this raises is, what is the role of location in differentiating between personifications of the living and those of the dead – spirits and gods?

The second question is: 'Where do people localise the healing powers that come from spiritual experiences?' In their self-personification or in (godlike) personifications that are located outside of themselves? In short, is the power something that is inside you, or does it come from outside?

The third question is, what configurations of personifications occur in spiritual and religious experiences?

SOCIAL PANORAMA AND SPIRITUAL PANORAMA

The foregoing questions arose when I was working with clients who spontaneously told me about spiritual personifications. When I started to formulate the social panorama model it turned out that the locations of dead people, ghosts and gods, were just as easy to find as personifications of living people. In this way it quickly became clear that many Westerners have made themselves a spiritual panorama – heaven – above their social panorama.

The social and the spiritual panorama are, however, for most people not two separate worlds but are interwoven in a complex way. People who die move from the social to the spiritual domain, and sometimes living people get information from 'the other side' (Derks and Hollander, 1996b).

RELIGIOUS RULES

Every religion dictates how the social/spiritual complex should be constructed. Religious cosmology tells where the dead should go, where the gods and the spirits live and how their connections with the living are supposed to function (Cipoletti, 1989).

The Celts in their cosmology, saw the spiritual world under the surface of the earth as an upside-down world. Caves were for them the holy gates of the underworld where they went in their dreams (Campbell, 1964). An interesting question is: 'In the last 20 thousand years has humanity evolved from cosmological rules in which the earth is central towards a more celestial orientation?'[73]

'Heaven' is a conceptual metaphor that is founded in the common basic experience of seeing clouds, stars, planets, sun and moon. Until a few centuries ago observing the night sky was an alternative which people could enjoy before going to sleep. The personification of heavenly bodies is natural, and a heaven peopled with spiritual beings seems to be the next logical step.

But the astronomical knowledge of the old Egyptians, Babylonians, Chinese, Mayas and Incas makes it unlikely that all astronomers in ancient times believed that the planets were conscious entities. In those cultures, too, there may have been advocates of a de-personified cosmology who were like the present-day advocates of the 'scientific cosmology'.

7.3.1 Patterns in the difference between life and death

In earlier chapters I spoke of 'person permanence' (paragraphs 4.5.1 and 6.7.1) meaning the cognitive awareness that people continue to exist whether or not we actually see them. Because of that

---

[73] The Australian Aboriginal culture is probably the oldest on earth (between 30,000 and 60,000 years). The earth is central in this culture. After the ice age (about 12,500 years ago) it seems that cultures with a more heavenly orientation came into existence. Did the earth lose its reputation as solid ground after the ice age? Speculations about how the ice age came to an end, and the natural disasters that went along with that, may provide an explanation (Hancock, 1995).

awareness, human social cognition can function independently of social observation. We can think about people when they are not there. That can go so far that people can focus on their inner social constructions to such an extent that they ignore observed facts: as in the case of positive or negative hallucinated personifications; seeing someone who is not there or failing to see someone who is present.

The ability to create personifications makes it possible for a small child to give his grandmother her own place in his social panorama even though she lives on the other side of the world and he may never have seen her. He can personify 'grandmother' purely on the basis of a few stories combined with the products of childish imagination. The same goes for a father who leaves his family after a divorce. He still has a place in the family's social panorama in spite of the fact that he is not there.

But what happens to those personifications when grandmother or father dies? Does person permanence allow those constructions to survive?

Most religions dictate what should happen to the body when someone dies – give it to the vultures, bury it, mummify it … If people identify the body with the personification a burial or a cremation will give guidance for the relocation of the personification (Cipoletti, 1989). They can then be put in a certain place in the earth or as a cloud of dust in water or air.

But if religions preach the separateness of body and soul, then a funeral will still leave the soul to be dealt with, and people will keep meeting the continuing presence of the personification in their thoughts.

That is why religions give directions for what to do with the personification, as well as the body – each uses a radically different form of person permanence. Grandmother must move from being close by and on the ground to floating far off in heaven. Daddy must be moved to a great distance away in the eternal hunting ground. Auntie may go down, deep into the underworld. And if you are used to visualising the personifications of your living tribe close round you, then you must move them, in your mind, to the ancestor tree outside the village.[74] You could also reincarnate them among the living, or give them 'spirit permanence' in the mountains or among the stars (Abrams, 1999).

But why don't we just leave the personifications of dead people in the locations they had before they died?

You don't need to be very observant to see that being able to differentiate between the living and the dead is a universal human need. And the source of that need is simple – if there is no difference, you will constantly be expecting the dead to reappear. You will think that they do things and have opinions; you will rely on their abilities, motivation and contributions. You will confuse them, daily, with the living and you will continue to be dependent on them.

As long as your dead partner is still next to you in your social panorama you will be unable to marry again. It will also be difficult to deal with the estate of someone who still belongs within your intimate circle.

In order to get over your loss you eventually have to be able to let go of the dead (Klass, 1999) and this requires you to localise them a long way away in a peaceful place. It could be with gods and other spirits of the dead, or it could be waiting for a heavenly reunion (Rosenblatt, 2000).

Some cultures, Christianity for example, teach people to make a very strong spatial separation between the living and the dead. In other religions this distance is less great. In some cases people believe that the dead are close to or within the living as in Afro-American cultures. In such cultures the dead, in the form of ancestral spirits, continue to play an important part in daily life.[75]

Even more interesting is the question of why this pattern is universal. Why must all people in all cultures at all times move their personifications of dead people to other locations in order to

---

[74] Cipoletti (1989) describes how complex this is within cultures like the Dajaks on Borneo, the Sadan Toradja on Sulawesi and some Pacific, African and South American tribes.

[75] We see people very occupied with offerings and rituals to appease the spirits.

complete the grieving process? Why cannot people just delete people from their social panorama? Why are they not just wiped out of the mind – dead is dead and gone is gone? Why don't we press the Delete button?

We advocate the hypothesis that this comes from a psycho-physiological law (Sinclair, 1982; Derks and Sinclair, 2000). Because it is not practically possible to continue to treat the dead as if they were alive we continue to find ourselves missing them. Our mind seizes up and we automatically start to turn off the 'unnecessary' personifications. 'Extinguishing' is the limited form of 'deleting' that our brains possess and it is accompanied by intense emotion. If the personification were never to be activated again, then having one good cry would theoretically be enough to make the extinction permanent, but that seldom happens. Usually the missing person will be brought to mind again, which will reactivate the 'unnecessary' personification. During the interval between the extinction and the next activation the brain has been using its 'automatic restore' function on the extinguished personification, so that it is complete again (Sinclair, 1982).[76] We can cry again until it is extinguished, but time and again the personification will be restored. In short, extinction is seldom permanent (Derks, 1988; Hollander, Derks and Meijer, 1990). This same mechanism is what limits the efficacy of emotional venting therapies (flooding, implosive desensitisation, exposure, etc.). With these, too, emotional extinction is no guarantee of permanent therapeutic results – changes on a cognitive level need to be made as well (Folette, Ruzek and Abeug, 1999).

In other words, a change in location is necessary because of the inability of our brain to delete 'files'. We are stuck for all time with the personifications of dead people on our mental hard disc (Derks, 1989). Deleting does not work, but we can move them to the far corners of our social panorama.

We do not necessarily need to put our dead with the gods, of course; we can localise the dead below and the gods above, or the

---

[76] Inhibitory inter-neurons switch on automatically to provide rest to tired neural connections, giving the latter an opportunity to strengthen themselves (Sinclair, 1982).

other way round. But the followers of most of the major religions have learnt to put both types of personification in the same place, which makes death a divine destination.

William James (1902) also studied the various forms of heaven. But when he tried to make a realistic image of it he ended up with a less attractive picture: it was far too crowded, with all those souls pushing round god's throne. And he wondered where in evolution the 'going to heaven' of dead souls began. Was that at Easter in the year 38? After the last ice age in 10,534 BC? Or as early as the Pleistocene? Must we share heaven with the Neanderthals and Homo Erectus? He preferred, as a pragmatist, the idea of reincarnation because that would solve the unpleasant finiteness of life, the overpopulation of heaven and the evolution of the soul all in one go. Yes, James had a lot of insight into the use of an afterlife. Belief in it solves a lot of insoluble problems around life, suffering and death. But James also demonstrated that you should not be too critical about this idea of an afterlife because it can cause more problems than it solves.

7.4   *Patterns in spiritual experiences*

If we want to understand the patterns in spirituality by using the spiritual panorama, we must first make a distinction between 'spiritual experiences' and 'experiencing spirits' (Derks, 2000c) because confusion of these categories results in messy theorising. This distinction defines the difference between social and non-social spirituality.

NON-PERSONIFIED SPIRITUAL EXPERIENCES
Spiritual experiences are subjective events of an extraordinary quality and intensity that are known for their healing power and their ability to forge a person's psyche into a whole. The intensity of 'sudden' spiritual experiences often exceeds anything a person has ever known, and is impossible to compare with anything else. Spiritual experiences are unique and indescribable.

Personifications need play no part in spiritual experiences. People can have 'non-personified spiritual experiences' in which they experience, for instance, 'unification with nature'. If their self-personification is not activated at the same time, there will be no self-awareness. In that case they may speak of being 'totally absorbed' or at 'complete oneness with nature'.

Further on in this chapter we will deal with spiritual experiences in which personifications do play a part. That is a social experience combined with a spiritual experience.

INDIVIDUAL OR COLLECTIVE?
It is useful to make two further divisions within the category of spiritual experiences:

1.   Individual spiritual experiences.
2.   Collective spiritual experiences.

The first can be characterised as an intensive cosmic experience that someone experiences on his own. The second is such an experience within a group.

SELF-AWARENESS AND THE US-FEELING IN THE IMPERSONAL COSMOS
Although the awareness of personifications does not need to play a role in spiritual experiences, it often does.

In individual spiritual experiences the self-personification can play a part, and people perceive themselves in relation to the universe. This personification can also have a collective character and a group will similarly experience itself as 'us' in relation to the universe. We also see the form in which the self-awareness and the group awareness are aligned together in relation to something higher. In that case the kinaesthetic self is the centre of the social panorama with the group feeling encircling it like the rings of Saturn.

In the aforementioned individual version, people feel themselves and see their self-images in combination with an awareness of an impersonal universe or impersonal Nature, and there will be no further activity of the social panorama. This sort of experience is accompanied by feelings that vary from 'complete self-consummation' to 'deep existential aloneness' (Derks, 1999b).

Religious hermits are searching for the positive version of it, just as solitary nature lovers claim to be. It can come as a shock when a person is suddenly assailed by such an experience. People sometimes describe how a 'social curtain' is suddenly pulled aside for a moment, all internal imaginary interactions cease and the person comes into direct contact with the universe. This can happen when someone sails for weeks alone on the ocean or stands alone on top of a mountain – 'just me and the cosmos'. When this happens people may feel themselves to be the only 'conscious creature' in the universe.

PERSONIFIED SPIRITUAL EXPERIENCES

As well as the self-personification or the group-personification, other personifications can also play a part in a spiritual experience. That happens when, for instance, the universe, nature or parts of nature are endowed with personification factors. The social panorama model reverses the Genesis text: 'Man created God in his likeness'.[77] The spiritual panorama is a pantheon that comes into being when the universe, nature or natural forces are personified.

People can have a personified spiritual experience both in groups and as an individual. Moses is a classic example of an individualised personified spiritual experience; he met God while he was alone at the top of the mountain, after which he went down again to the social domain of his people, bearing the Ten Commandments.

In Ecuador I was told about a recent collective personified spiritual experience: three children saw the Holy Virgin high in the Andes.

INTENTIONAL AND UNINTENTIONAL SPIRITUAL MEETINGS

Searching for an individual spiritual experience, personified or not, takes a lot of courage because such an experience will involve the insignificant individual being brought close to something

---

[77] In Julian Jaynes 1976 book, *The Origin of Consciousness in the Breakdown of the Bicameral Mind*, many issues considering consciousness and unconsciousness are used to explain how people come to create gods and rituals.

immense. Meeting God or the Universe in its totality can be frightening when you are all on your own. It is not something you begin without thorough preparation. Moses, as a king, probably had an enormous awareness of self, which allowed him to feel less insignificant when meeting God than a lesser man would have done. People who see death as the moment that you meet your (judgmental) maker can come to see death as either more frightening if they are sinners or more peaceful if they are not.

Religious traditions can teach people to call up spiritual experiences through meditation. In general this is known to be a difficult way, a long narrow path that leads endlessly upward.

Building up a strong, positive self-image should theoretically be part of the preparation for a personified spiritual experience, but many religious traditions prescribe humility instead. Making the self-image very small is what gives access to the spirits; making yourself small allows the gods to dominate you at will. That is the way it usually seems to happen. In fact, people don't usually prepare themselves for spiritual meetings, they are totally surprised by them. They don't choose 'it', 'it' chooses them, which is why they feel like a chosen one after such a rendezvous. A sudden individual spiritual experience is the sort of experience that has the greatest impact on people. You could say that it is the opposite of a trauma. Most religious leaders become what they are because of such an experience. It inspires them to share what they have learnt from it with others. Even many active nature conservationists only became such after they had had a spiritual experience with nature (Derks, 1998c, 2000c).

THE GENERAL DISTRIBUTION OF SPIRITUAL EXPERIENCES

Whenever my colleagues and I ask our clients and workshop participants about their spiritual experiences they can usually name several examples. From this we conclude (Derks and Hollander, 1996b) that most people have known an experience that fits within the framework we could call 'spiritual'. The place in their lives they give to this experience can vary a lot. Because it is difficult to talk about, the experience can just as well become an isolated island in their existence as the basis for all they think and do.

However common spiritual experiences are, actively searching for a spiritual experience is beyond most people. If they want a spiritual experience they will usually prefer to search for it together with others. In most cultures searchers for solitary spiritual connection are a religious elite. The common man approaches God as a group, led by an expert and most spiritual authorities prefer that. People who search for their own way to the gods threaten the status of the religious establishment. This, of course, is not true of religions in which the striving for individual enlightenment is central. In those, the individual who searches for spiritual experiences is automatically an authority himself, as in the Hindu sadhus.

Collective spiritual experiences are often undergone in group rituals that are specially organised for the purpose. If such an experience is evoked, a group member will feel a great degree of team spirit together with a connection with nature, god or the universe. This is the experience on which society is built, and how cultures develop. It is the type of experience that most religions are trying to attain in their group rites. Priests guide the congregation to a collective spiritual climax and then bring them safely back down again.

7.5   *The spiritual top level*

There has been some criticism in the last few years on the way in which Dilts (1990) has translated the notion of 'neuro-logical levels' from Bateson's 'logical types'.[78] The critics particularly object to the fact that this has resulted in six discrete categories – environment, behaviour, ability, belief, identity and spirituality (Grinder, 1998; Woodsmall, 1999; Flanagan, 1999). Grinder says that Dilts' list is a 'content model' and not a 'process model'. It does, after all, prescribe what a person 'should' be thinking.

This criticism, however, does not apply to the hierarchic structure of thought and we can probably solve all theoretical differences by saying that human thinking has a tendency to organise itself hierarchically. One thought can dominate another, but which thought is placed above which is the business of the individual and their

---

[78] See also section 3.7 on page 107 for an introduction of Dilts' idea.

culture. An essential question for cognitive linguistics is, 'How does an individual make one thought more important than another?'

Working therapeutically, we find a satisfactory answer in the hierarchy of values (Bandler, 1985; Andreas and Andreas, 1989). This shows that a certain value can be made more important by giving it stronger sensory qualities. The person must make the cognitive schemes that represent his value bigger, closer, lighter, shinier, higher or more central. This surely applies not only to values, but also to all other categories of thought. I, for one, assume that people arrange all sorts of thoughts in the same way as their values. So if their relationship with the universe (spirituality) is more important than who they are (identity), a person will give form to that by a difference in the strength of the sensory qualities of these domains of thought. If that is so, then we can assume that most people give spirituality the strongest sensory characteristics.

The question here is, what is it that is represented with these strong sensory qualities? It is certainly neither the nature of the universe, nor all-encompassing love. Sometimes it is humanity as a whole or a superior being. But it can also be things like 'freedom', 'science' or 'my country' that have the highest value in the world.

The strength of the sensory qualities seems, however, to have neurological limits. The brain has, for instance, only one location above it, and, although you can think higher and higher, it stops at 'highest'. Similarly, the brain can imagine nothing lighter than 'the brightest imaginable light in the universe'. 'All-encompassing' and 'all-penetrating', too, seem to have upper limits.

Therefore we can say that matters which are experienced in the strongest sensory qualities automatically dominate thought. Spirituality, therefore, usually means that the brain is going 'flat out'.

INTENSITY AND QUALITY OF SPIRITUAL EXPERIENCES
It is important for a therapist to look at the intensity and quality of spiritual experiences. Intensity will reduce with usage. Every time

a person thinks about a particular spiritual experience the intensity of the memory will decrease. Quality, however, is retained over time, and it is, in the end, the quality that determines what a person can do with that experience in their life. The healing power is in the quality; motivation comes from the intensity.

A good example of a spiritual experience is a positive near-death experience. People often report a glimpse of heaven or contact with the all-highest or one of his representatives. The intensity of such experiences is very motivating; their healing work has been demonstrated (as a resource) in many therapy sessions. Often, the birth of children is described as a spiritual experience.

As well as this type of very intense spiritual experience there are the everyday connections with nature, the universe, the dead, gods and spirits. These experiences, with their 'normal' intensity make up the greatest part of religious life. People talk to nature (beastly rain…), to spirits (Holy Mary, Mother of God…) and gods (Good Lord, what is this…) and as they pray they orient themselves towards the locations in the social panorama where they have put their personifications (Our father, which art in heaven…).

7.6   *Experiences attributed to spirits*

The most significant social phenomena that exist are associated with meetings with spiritual entities. William James (1890, 1902), with a completely open mind, performed psychological research on them. He was not so much interested in whether ghosts exist, but rather *how* they exist, and what their effect on society is.

The importance of ghosts and meetings with ghosts has been collectively trivialised by modern psychologists. It is only studied by some para-psychologists and religious psychologists, but they seldom receive any serious interest from colleagues (Derks, 1992). Successful scientists who study 'the other side' seem only to exist in Hollywood films. Films like *Poltergeist*, *The Exorcist*, and *Ghostbusters* illustrate the enormous public interest in the subject. It is ideal for the provoking of goose bumps.

SPIRITS ARE EVERYWHERE

This subject becomes much less obscure when you realise that the Bible, and almost all other religious books, report meetings with spiritual personifications. Anyone who swears an oath implicitly declares that they believe in spiritual entities. The influence of the dead upon the living was discussed in the previous chapter; people very often declare that they are in contact with dead relatives. And we haven't even mentioned all the spirits with which we live in multicultural Netherlands.

... AND SPIRITS DICTATE THE TRUTH

Almost all world religions are based on holy texts that have been dictated to the living by the voices of spirits. In short, a significant part of the world population is steered by the poetry of spirits. Holy books are usually themselves personified, 'the Bible can...', the Bible will...', 'the Koran says...' 'the Torah says...'

Modern spirit products are the Seth books (dictated by guiding spirit Seth to the medium, Jane Roberts), *A Course in Miracles* (dictated by Jesus of Nazareth), and *Conversations with God* (dictated by God). Oddly enough, Jane Roberts of the Seth books has also written a book in which she reports her contact with the spirit of William James (Roberts, 1978).

When I tuned in to the spirit of William James he told me loud and clear that the experience of 'dictation' happens to every writer. Also he mentioned the example of 'automatic writing' from hypnosis, where an unconscious part of the person takes over the writing – sometimes even with a person's 'wrong' hand (Hilgard, 1977). James himself constantly experienced an inner voice telling him the sentences but he regarded that as coming from his own unconscious thinking and not as a voice from the future belonging to someone like Lucas Derks or Jane Roberts.

Alstad and Kramer (1993) point out how 'channelled' texts automatically have unquestioned authority. If you indeed believe that *A Course of Miracles* comes from the spirit of Jesus, then that will preclude all critical questions: all you can do is to try and understand the text.

THERE'S SAFETY IN NUMBERS

Just as is true for spiritual experiences, it is useful to distinguish between collective and individual meetings with spirits, gods, ghosts and angels. Firstly, because the report of a collective experience with a spirit has much more social impact than a story about an individual meeting. After all, an individual can be deluded,[79] but when a hundred people see a ghost together it is statistically unlikely to be a coincidence. Also it will lend social confirmation when thousands go to listen to someone who tells them about meetings with angels.

IT MUST HAVE BEEN A SPIRIT

The experience of a spirit or other supernatural entity is not necessarily accompanied by seeing, hearing or feeling it. Often the experience of a spirit is only a matter of attribution. A person will attribute a certain (extraordinary) experience to the influence of a spirit without that spirit actually being 'in the picture'.

The reasoning behind this is often simple; someone has an incomparably intense and rich spiritual experience that is so overwhelming that he cannot put it into words and finds it impossible to believe that it is only the product of his own neurology. That means that he is forced to ascribe this experience to something outside himself.[80] What options does this person have? Who can have caused this incredible experience? Quetzalcoatl? Hanuman? Baal?

---

[79] I (Lucas Derks) have had encounters with spirits twice in my life. Both times the experience was auditory: the spirits talked with very clear voices to me. One time I chased the spirit away by means of talking back. Recently I talked to a colleague who had seen the spirit of a dead person. The spirit lived in the guest room where he was sleeping. Probably such experiences are very widespread; but people tend to keep them to themselves fearing to be taken for mental cases.
[80] Lewis suggests that people with a small ego tend to look for explanations outside themselves when they have a spiritual experience. The same holds for extraordinary accurate intuitions. In case you have little schooling and social status, it is hard to believe in your own abilities. A guardian angel, a god or helper spirit is easily constructed as an external cause. In some shamanistic traditions it is the dominant view on how one can get from lower class into some sort of priesthood.

For these reasons it is very usual to ascribe such intense spiritual experiences to the personification of a supernatural power, and that is why they are called *spiritual* experiences.

SPIRITUAL TURNING POINTS IN LIFE

Visions of God, Christ, the Holy Virgin, Buddha or other supernatural entities can have the same sensory qualities as a spiritual experience. They are often accompanied by a central, shining, clear light, together with warm feelings of universal love and connection. This usually changes people radically: criminals and addicts can be 'reborn'. The ensuing positive feelings often give people the energy to start supporting their needy fellow beings.

MEETINGS WITH EVIL

A loving and euphoric emotional tone is the absolute opposite of the chill, sombre emptiness and horror that accompany the often traumatic experience of a meeting with a ghost, an evil spirit or the prince of darkness.

Here, too, it can be a hitherto unknown intense (in this case negative) experience that someone cannot ascribe to their own psyche. James, who suffered from depression until he was 40, spoke in such a case of the 'abyss of horror'. The devil does not need to show himself in person to get the blame for this.

The limited belief in the devil of present-day Christians is probably the reason that the number of reported sightings remains limited. This is because a personification must first figure in someone's social panorama if it is to be of influence. The Incas and the Aztecs both had European-looking gods in their pantheon, which were known to be 'good'. This is why they were so upset when the Spaniards turned out to be after their gold and their lives.

The difference between a pleasant and a frightening meeting with a spiritual personification probably has to do with the way in which the relevant personification was stored in someone's memory before the vision. If it is a personification that a person tries to keep out of their thoughts, to forget, to ban or to repress – like Beelzebub – then a meeting can only occur if the relevant inhibitory mechanisms are not working, as can happen in exhaustion, illness, drunkenness, LSD or mescaline trips, hormonal imbalance, trance and half-sleep. There the accompanying feelings are usually cold, empty and unpleasant. Seeing the spirit of a long-dead good friend, on the other hand, is usually accompanied by positive emotions.

THE GREAT IMPORTANCE OF DISTANCE

Spirits can be terrifying and upsetting, that is one of the reasons that most people usually represent their spiritual personifications far away, from about six to 100 mental meters away – much farther than they put significant living people in their social panorama. After a sudden meeting, spiritual entities are often seen at only a few metres distance. Then they are seen with almost the qualities of a living person. This is when they have the most impact.

As Mavromantis (1987) suggests, such supernatural experiences usually happen to people who are in an unusual state of consciousness. People are particularly susceptible to meetings with beings from the other side in the hypnagogic state that immediately precedes sleep. Often one of the sensory modalities is missing in such an experience – there is no image, no sound or no feeling.

NO AMNESIA FOR GHOSTS

A person will not easily forget the way a ghost felt, looked or what was said during such a meeting. The clear memory of spiritual experiences is very different from the amnesia that follows most hypnagogic (half-sleep) experiences. This is because such a meeting is immediately followed by a moment of complete wakefulness, which stops a person forgetting what has happened (Sinclair, 1982; Derks and Sinclair, 2000). The spirit wakes a person up, so the sleepy trance is immediately followed by hyper-alertness whereby everything is remembered clearly. The feelings engendered by such a meeting may therefore linger for days.

7.7 *Intimacy with spirits*

Once I asked a young Balinese man where he experienced his dead
father and he pointed to a spot one metre away and slightly to the
right. I immediately asked if that was comfortable, but he assured
me that it gave him a warm feeling of connection. Did that mean
that in Hindu culture it was typical to experience the dead close
by? Such questions should be researched by anthropologists. In
our culture, too, the departed are often seen close by. This does not
have to be a problem if someone is at peace with his dead. If, however, the person is troubled by it then it needs more attention.

As already mentioned in the previous chapter, dead family members can have an enormous influence on their surviving relatives.
In particular, suicides, innocent victims, early deaths, deserted
lovers and aborted children seem to make life difficult for their
survivors (Cipoletti, 1989). People in almost all cultures are aware
that this type of dead person has a tendency to haunt. Recently I
treated a client who had problems with a grandmother who had
committed suicide, even though she had never known her.

But even those who have gone peacefully can be experienced as
unpleasant company. In general we can say that, however sure
you are of the friendliness of a particular spiritual entity, for most
people it is an unsettling idea suddenly to have them standing
next to you. Ghosts are fundamentally 'different' from the living.
Spiritual personifications usually lack, for instance, the personification factor 'sensory perceivability'; commonly, you cannot see
them, hear them or feel them. Even if you can, there is almost
always something strange about them. Spiritual personifications
are not the equals of the living and that means that even people
who have a very good relationship with the spiritual world prefer
to keep a good mental distance between them and the spirits. But
that is certainly not true for everyone.

The presence of spiritual personifications within a person's intimate circle – at arm's length or less – will usually prevent someone
starting intimate relationships with the living. Monks, nuns,
shamans and priests can sometimes be so intimate with the world
of the gods that a celibate existence is unavoidable. The same
mechanisms that come into play between flesh and blood lovers,

where no one else is tolerated at a closer location in the social panorama, seem also to be at work in the case of disembodied loved ones.

Looking at religious art and listening to religious expressions we can conclude that the spiritual entities that lead the pantheon often appear having the sensory qualities of spiritual experiences. They are shining, large and central. Distance is, however, the deciding factor. That distance is great: usually too great to the taste of their worshippers. An angel seen at 100 metres may be 10 metres tall and as bright as the sun, but if he were experienced at five metres then the positive feelings engendered by its presence would be much stronger.

Many religious exercises are about feeling contact with the gods. In order to do that, the distance must usually be decreased. But how? As we have already mentioned, fear is the eternal enemy here. Only those who have little to fear from a god – people who are protected by their great and consistent self-awareness and those without sin – can dare to come close. That is why self-image meditation and cleansing rituals are so necessary for many shamans. The inner conflict between approach and avoidance is a problem for everyone who wishes to contact the spirit world.

7.8   Heaven on earth: Whose is the true god?

Anyone zapping across television channels in Los Angeles on a Sunday morning will be treated to many competing TV preachers who try, with the most dramatic sermons, to be the unique supplier of the personification at the top of your social panorama. A Martian, watching this competition through his super-receiver with Earth converter, would probably ask himself, 'What is all the fuss about?'

If the Martian were to do some research in the 'Earth Institute' he would soon discover that people have been aware for thousands of years that spirituality has strong healing and socially binding power. Seen from a cognitive-psychology point of view, spirituality has the highest possible level; it is naturally seen as being super-important. As we have already said, the high status of spirituality springs automatically from its totally dominant sensory qualities. Because of this, spiritual leaders who proclaim themselves to be the distributors of spirituality automatically have great social power. They will be put above most worldly leaders in the social panoramas of their followers. Add to this that the size of a person's following partly determines his income then the Martian will understand what the fuss is about. Marketing god successfully yields status, money, respect and unassailable social power.

In almost all cultures of the world power structures rise above the secular social domain. Their special connection with spiritual super-powers gives shamans and priests a 'higher' power, and their connection with the gods gives them more status than they could realise by political or economic means. Many members of a congregation must have representations of these super-powers high in their social panorama to enable this god-given source of power to function, which means that their followers must firmly believe in the world of the gods.

THE SOCIAL CREATION OF SPIRITUAL TRUTH

In this book we regard all personifications – including the spiritual – as mental constructions. Gods are personifications, and personifications are parts of the person. Therefore gods are self-created parts of an individual. This vision is, of course, diametrically opposed to what gives spiritual personifications their great prestige. A god cannot be an individual creation, it must at least be a collective one, and actually not a construction at all, but a reality. A spiritual entity must be seen as something external if it is to function properly as a being that is completely independent of the observer. According to James, the supernatural context and interpretation that give such experiences their special place can only exist if this is true. In short, a spirit must be 'real'.

A spiritual experience must be ascribed to the activities of the spirit for it to achieve the maximum psychological effect. An image of a weeping Virgin Mary or a shining angel must exist of itself and not through some technique of a priest. That is why this distinction is always so essential in testimony about miracles; it has led to the existence of recognised and unrecognised miracles in the Catholic Church. If a miracle is recognised, then it usually results in beatification or sainthood. The church is careful not to do this with living people; a living saint would be in a position to overtrump the entire episcopal hierarchy.

What do you do when you have seen a spirit? Do you shout it from the rooftops or do you keep it quiet? The uncertainty about how a report of such a vision will be received by the social environment leaves people balanced between the possibilities of psychiatric hospital admission and beatification. The social status of the person and whether or not they saw the ghost alone or in the company of others will help to decide what they do. If 10 airforce generals and 10 astronomers independently see an invasion of Martians at the same moment they will not end up taking antipsychotic drugs. But if you go out onto the street right now and shout that you have seen an archangel your circle of friends will be likely to diminish.

William James (1890) understood that the senses play a crucial role in the experience of truth. He saw that, for most people, a thing only becomes 'real' if they can touch it and get hold of it. As did James, we can view the carrying of holy statues in processions as being a way of lending tangibility to gods, just as children use objects to give reality to their imaginings. But it was only Bandler's pioneering work in the field of sensory qualities (1985) that showed us that 'certainty' and 'truth' are only a question of the right cognitive form.[81]

So it becomes understandable that spiritual leaders try to give their religious concepts certainty and truth. In their sermons they steer the sensory qualities that their congregations conceive of in order to affect, by direct suggestion, the way they represent spiritual personifications and so make concepts more certain and more true. They use powerful metaphors, strong adjectives, individual testimony and the fact that large groups of people who, by agreeing with one another, have a great power to convince.

The mental activity that believers need to strengthen their belief in the world of the gods is not very different from that used in the

---

[81] Words that point at the sensory experience are called 'predicates' in the work of Bandler and Grinder (1979). These words indicate whether a person is having visual, auditory or kinaesthetic experiences.

process of believing in bacteria, gravity or atoms (Hollander, 1997). As far as that is concerned, indoctrination with rational, empirical scientific dogma runs parallel to religious influence. (Do you believe in the social panorama?)

It can be illuminating to work directly with the sensory qualities of spiritual entities. Hollander (1997) experimented with what he called the 'operators of reality'. Which sensory qualities define the difference between real and not real? Or, more importantly, which sensory qualities does a memory need to have for us to be sure that it really happened? This question is as valid for testimony about a crime as for a vision of the holy virgin. How real was that vision?

The exact configuration of sensory qualities that are necessary to experience something as real varies from person to person. In general we can say (Derks and Hollander, 1996a) that experiences are more realistic the more colourful, solid, three-dimensional, close, in focus, opaque and comprehensible they are. These are the qualities that a priest can suggest in order to give a religious concept more 'body'.

'Seeing is believing' is therefore not true for everyone. For some people, touching, smelling, measuring and statistically testing are necessary to give something the status of a fact. Others are convinced by seeing that something has a long history; 'If the ancient Egyptians believed it, then it must be true.'

7.9   *Spiritual authorities*

In their book *The Guru Papers* (1993), Dianne Alstadt and Joel Kramer analysed the structure of spiritual power as it functions within religious sects. In such cult groups the leader is always seen as being more powerful than all worldly leaders. This is how sect leaders often gain unlimited power over their followers.

The use of this power usually becomes noticeable as soon as the practices of a cult become illegal. Bloody confrontations with the police or collective suicide as in Jerusalem, Waco, Tokyo, Jonestown and Beijing illustrate how charismatic sect leaders can use spirituality as a source of power. This makes them feared and hated by not only the religious establishment but also the secular authorities.

The religious establishment and the secular authorities often try to exorcise this sectarian evil. A traditional method for this, according to Jenner and Wiegers (1998), is to canonise the official holy writ. Sects can then be declared heretics if they do not observe the standard texts.

The combined hatred of the religious establishment and the secular authorities has often finished many charismatic sect leaders, as, for instance, in the Gospel according to St. John. In the end, cult leaders have to obey the law; all they can hope for is heavenly justice.

PLAYING INTERMEDIARY BETWEEN MAN AND GOD
Alstadt and Kramer discovered an important pattern in the connection between religious leaders and the spirit world. Spiritual leaders get their power from their ability to convince their followers that they, the leaders, have a special relationship with the spiritual domain. The leaders demonstrate such a relationship by revealing omens and wisdom given to them by the gods, or by miracles they perform 'under licence' from higher powers.

These special connections must be given form in the followers' social-spiritual panoramas. The followers visualise the leaders centrally and far above normal mortals. They see the spiritual connection between the higher power and their leader as a descending stream of light. A quick look at religious art reveals the manner in which people view such spiritual connections, usually by golden lines and shining halos.

Alstadt and Kramer (1993) observed that many spiritual leaders stay in power by suggesting to their followers that this connection with the spiritual levels is exclusive to them, the leaders, who have managed to achieve such a connection. This doctrine leads the followers to create a spiritual-social panorama in which they themselves are cut off from the gods but with whom their leaders can communicate. This structure results in a great degree of dependence. In any religious group this difference in access to the all-highest determines the amount of power the leader has.

A religious elite will also exercise power by prescribing the conditions which must be adhered to in order for a normal follower to achieve contact with the almighty, and how the soul can reach the divine terminus during or after life.

I CAN SEE WHAT YOU DON'T SEE

The followers do not need to be allowed to see what is at the top of the spiritual panorama, or where the golden light comes from. They can often even be kept in ignorance of the true nature of the almighty. It is enough for someone to have the notion that there must be something there – at the highest, all-encompassing level of their spiritual-social panorama – without any exact idea of what it is. Religious leaders can keep this information to themselves.

RADIATION OF RELIGIOUS AUTHORITY

When a priest or a shaman speaks of mystical experiences we can often observe the non-verbal expression of religious enthusiasm. Such ecstatic expressions can be ascribed to his reliving of spiritual experiences as he speaks. In general, visionary figures see what they speak of in front of them in strong, living sensory qualities. Talking about it is accompanied by visual-kinaesthetic synaesthesia with the subject matter. For instance, when a visionary speaks the words, 'The spirit is really great', he will also see a large image of the spirit and have a strong feeling of its presence. This experience will immediately show in all the speaker's non-verbal communication, which will convincingly reinforce the impression the listeners have of a 'really great' spirit. Many people will be inspired by such a visionary style; others will wish to avoid it completely.

7.10 *Beautiful words and resounding language*

Spiritual leaders often use neologisms, metaphors and broad abstractions to reinforce the spiritual/social constructions of their followers.

The spiritual/social world is often based on abstract concepts such as unconditional love, cosmic unity, the ability to surrender completely, dissociation, lack of ego, purity, unselfishness, humility, disembodiment and enlightenment. Anyone who tries to judge such concepts on their merits or criticise them can become the victim of what Alstadt and Kramer (1993) call 'guru ploys'. These are verbal tactics to disarm the critic such as, 'You can only understand enlightenment if you are enlightened yourself.' Or, if a follower were to ask, 'What is unconditional love, master?' the guru ploy answer could be, 'That I love you in spite of the fact that you have asked me such an ego-bound question.'

PRAGMAGIC WORKSHOPS

Using this view we could say that a pragmagic workshop such as those Hollander and Derks gave between 1993 and 1998 can have a liberating character. Basing our work on our research into shamans, priests and spiritualistic cults (Candomblé, Gnava and Umbanda) we taught the participants to communicate with gods and spirits without the help of an intermediary (Derks and Hollander, 1996a; Hollander, 1997).

If a person develops their own spiritual connections, then priests will lose their power over them, to the extent that that power is based on priests' exclusive access to the supernatural. Most modern religions are more and more preaching such a personal connection with the almighty.

I AM ENLIGHTENED, NOW IT'S YOUR TURN

In terms of the social panorama we can say that many spiritual leaders teach their followers to give much more importance to one particular group of human qualities. Such lessons may be, for instance, that unconditional love, total surrender to faith, altruism or enlightenment are extremely important qualities that you should possess, and that the leader already has.

The higher such qualities are valued, the better the position of the leader in the social panorama. The devaluation of antithetical qualities such as the ability to enjoy autonomy, or freedom is often done by use of verbal techniques: 'Enjoyment is nothing more than identifying with your ego.' 'Autonomy is the denial of your connection with humanity.' 'Freedom means that you can choose not only for God, but also for Satan.'

Cognitive-linguistic models in the area of reframing (Bandler and Grinder, 1982) and word magic (Hollander, Derks and Meijer, 1990) are eminently suitable for analysing guru language.[82] For

---

[82] In the verbal techniques called 'reframing' and 'sleight of mouth' the goal is the changing of limiting beliefs. Beliefs are often concluded from experiences that are taken for definite facts. The generalisation of these conclusions will lead to inner certainty that can prevent a person from achieving important goals later in life.

instance, we often hear gurus using high-sounding, suggestive adjectives in expressions such as the *highest* enlightenment, *pure* consciousness, *true pure* love, *absolute* certainty, the *higher* self, *cosmic* identity and suchlike. The use of such adjectives automatically degrades the following concept if the qualifier is *not* used. By using the concept 'true love', for instance, all other love becomes ordinary, lower or counterfeit (Grinder and Bandler, 1976). In the same way the concept *scientific* psychology degrades all other psychology to the realms of the non-scientific.

7.11 *The patterns of possession*

Until now we have spoken only about the authority of religious leaders, but gods and spirits like to have authority, too. They are often the very highest authorities. How do these work in the social panorama?

IDENTIFICATION WITH DOMINANT PERSONIFICATIONS
The 'law of the dominant personification', presented in Chapter 4, explains different forms of discontinuity in self-awareness, in particular the experience of being overwhelmed by an authority. The submissive behaviour that accompanies this is usually brought on by the 'real' flesh and blood authority coming near to a person, as when the president suddenly appears next to him.

The most remarkable effect of this in the subjective experience is the sudden move from the first to the second perceptual position: the 'me-feeling' shrinks and the person experiences a great loss of self-determination. At the same time the person will pay great attention to the needs of the authority and tend to see himself only through the eyes of that authority. Sometimes typically hypnotic symptoms appear, such as trance, suggestibility and amnesia.

In short, wherever the law of the dominant personification is at work, it will cause discontinuity in the experience of self. The brain concentrates on the most dominant personification and identifies with it. People complain that they 'lose themselves' and start playing roles that are reminiscent of the symptoms of dissociation and multiple personality (Giel, 1978; Johnstone, 1979).

DOMINANT SPIRITS

The phenomenon 'possession' is so widespread in our world that it is a miracle that we have been able to keep it almost completely out of our western psychology. Every Christian knows the concepts of 'possession by the Holy Ghost' and 'possession by the devil'. In the Pentecostal church, for instance, speaking in tongues is an accepted, highly prestigious ritual. That is a clear case of possession (Bourguignon, 1968; Hollander, 1997).

But possession seems to us to be irrational, primitive and exotic and this is probably why it is kept as much as possible out of our culture. Psychologists view it as something for anthropologists or trans-cultural psychiatrists (Giel, 1978), but using the social panorama model we can understand the mechanisms behind this phenomenon. Possession isn't as crazy as all that (Johnstone, 1979).

The spirits who take possession of people are, by definition, personifications with more authority than the people themselves. These spirits usually overshadow the sensory qualities of living people and living authorities. People tend to put the living in the 'social' sphere, at about the same height as themselves. This limitation is not true for spiritual entities. We can put a spirit straight above us or deep in the bowels of the earth. Straight up and straight down are unusual locations for living people, but they are very normal for spirits, gods and the dead. The way spirits are represented in religious art is no coincidence. The Roman Christ Pantocrator is in the middle, in front and very high and large. Or centrally above your head, as in baroque cathedral domes. Altars with colossal statues of Buddha, Shiva or Christ help believers to see their internal images in the right sensory qualities.

POSSESSION AS A PROBLEM OR AN ABILITY

Before we go any deeper into the mechanisms of possession we should first look into its effect. In most cultures where possession is common there are two types:

1. *Long-term possession:* This is unwelcome and problematical, as in possession by the devil.

2.   *Short-term possession:* This is either a pleasant surprise or it is
     called up on purpose; in both cases it is seen as a blessing and
     not a problem, as in being possessed by the Holy Ghost.

7.11.1 Long-term possession

In Western psychiatry we would call long-term possession a form
of dissociative disorder. Psychiatrists, in an attempt to give it a
medical tone, once used the term 'hysteria', but that has now been
outlawed. The Gestalt tradition (Perls, 1969) speaks of parts outside the client's control that cause all sorts of symptomatic behaviour. The fact that the client is incapable of stopping the symptoms
is the reason that these are often attributed to external causes. The
more external the 'locus of control', the more the cause of the problem will be sought in possession by a spirit.

GUILT AND INNOCENCE OF THE VICTIM
Long-term possession is a problem that has a victim, but this victim is not always innocent of blame for it. In many cultures people
are possessed by an ancestral spirit who is taking revenge for the
person having broken a taboo. The fear of possession keeps people
in such cultures on the straight and narrow. But possession can
also be blamed instead of the person, as when unfaithfulness is
ascribed to 'witchcraft', 'black magic' or 'an evil spirit', which
offers great advantages to all concerned. In a Western culture the
adulterer is always the guilty party, but put in a frame of possession he can be an innocent victim. The solution is then for the adulterer to be freed from the evil influence by a priest, after which his
wife and the whole family can celebrate his 'cure'.

PREVENTATIVE MEASURES
People can resort to all sorts of magic rituals to prevent possession.
A Malawi herb doctor with whom I once corresponded advised
the burying of certain roots under the threshold of the bedroom.
He also said that some herbal extracts were very effective. If, in
spite of all preventative measures, possession is diagnosed, then
there are roughly two remedies available: exorcism or reconciliation (Fuller Torrey, 1986).

Experienced shamans often say that reconciliation with the spirit is the only true cure for possession. And they know rituals that are aimed at such a pacification (Derks, 1992).

EXORCISM

The opposite of reconciliation is exorcism where a shaman usually behaves very disrespectfully to the possessing spirit in an attempt to force it, by the use of cursing and commands, to behave differently. The priest tries to degrade the spirit by intimidation, which, if all goes well, will cause the victim to represent the spirit less prominently. If it works, this will lead to the spirit allowing room for the self-personification of the victim. Once the experience of self gains the upper hand in the victim the total possession will be over, but the evil spirit will not be completely gone from the victim's social panorama. The devil does not allow himself to be easily driven away by a mortal with a lot of lip.

In general, reconciliation is the preferred method because cults that practise exorcism can do a lot of damage with it. The current generation of trans-cultural clinical psychologists sees exorcism as an intervention that reinforces dissociation. Not only is exorcism an aggressive, dramatic and sometimes painful ritual, but it often produces symptom substitution, in the psychoanalytical sense of the expression. The spirit often comes back in a worse form.

The problem we meet again here is that personifications are extremely difficult to erase. You can transform them, move them and improve them with abilities, but erasure seems to be out of the question.

RECONCILIATION

A shaman or therapist who immediately starts looking for the positive intention of the possessing evil spirit usually has more success. 'Six step reframing', a technique of Bandler and Grinder's (1979) is very suitable for this. What does the spirit want to achieve for the possessed with these symptoms? What is the positive intention? Should the victim, for instance, stop transgressing customs, mores, clan rules or the law and live in harmony with family tradition? Is the spirit trying to make him look after his sick brother or to stop grazing his cows on someone else's fields?

A positive effect can also be achieved by the earlier mentioned technique of enriching the evil spirits (hated personifications) with the abilities they are lacking (Techniques 6 and 7). Several years' systematic research into work with problem personifications has proved that the addition of abilities that were lacking is a widely effective formula; it is just as effective with evil spirits as it is with hated parents or dreadful colleagues (Derks, 1998c).

7.11.2 Short-term possession

Unexpected short-term possession and possession that has been called up on purpose are not viewed as a problem but as a blessing. These are things that shamans practise and that people in many cults all over the world try to achieve. They are looking for the most intimate contact with spirits – identification. They obviously do that with an object in mind, but what is that object?

FRANCHISE CONSTRUCTIONS FOR SUPERNATURAL POWERS
Sometimes the object is obvious. Many shamans can, through possession, make use of the supernatural powers of the spirits they unite with. They can work miracles and sell them under the licence of the spirit.

Although the philosophical frame of this book requires me to ascribe these powers to the one possessed, it is understandable that a shaman and his cult do not do that (Lewis, 1971). By becoming possessed, a priest is suddenly able to make infallible diagnoses from the intestines of a dead guinea pig, heal deadly diseases by singing hymns, predict someone's future by interpreting the pattern of thrown shells, magnetise, speak in tongues, exorcise evil spirits, do psychic operations or make spiritual journeys. Within the framework of possession a shaman can do a lot of useful things for his congregation.

Even if we do not believe in spirits or in the existence of such a thing as real possession, we can still understand its function.

GIVING STRONG PLACEBO SUGGESTIONS

The shaman is a member of a congregation with a special function. By his spiritual approach he can set a great placebo effect in motion (Derks and Hollander, 1996a; Hollander, 1997). His impressive performance calls forth his patients' maximum healing powers and wisdom. He can ask for favours and co-operation from powerful spirits that terrify ordinary mortals. He transforms himself into these spirits, which has a dramatic effect and makes tangible something that his patients cannot understand.

POSSESSION GIVES THE SHAMAN FREE TIME

It would make the shaman's life very difficult if he had to play the role of the spirit day-in day-out without first doing the possession ritual. Thanks to the frame of possession he is able to step out of it. He will make a bi-location for his self-personification in his social panorama, whereby one part coincides with the spirit who possesses him from time to time. He will also be given a similar bi-location in the social panoramas of his tribe.

If a shaman were to be continuously possessed, his friendships, his sex life and his family life would be seriously endangered. Certainly in a small community it would be impossible to live life in a permanent state of possession. A reincarnated person, such as the Dalai Lama, is always in role and therefore has more trouble maintaining a private life than a shaman who becomes possessed only now and then. Possession gives his role a context, and therefore as a normal person he can still have faults like bossiness or greed. It can also work the other way round, a person can be ill-mannered and foul-mouthed as the spirit and very pleasant when he is not possessed (Hollander, 1997).

POSSESSION AS A MEANS OF CLIMBING THE SOCIAL LADDER

People in many cultures view the ability to be possessed as a blessing. The blessed one usually rises several rungs on the social ladder once they have shown that they can become possessed. This elitist position is only interesting for someone with a low status. For an aristocrat or a professor, possession will not have any advantages, but for a downtrodden, poor old woman it will (Lewis, 1971).

In many cultures there is an interesting link between problematical and blessed possession. Anyone who has succumbed to evil spirits can learn from a master to control their situation by reconciliation. After that, the evil spirit can become a helping spirit that occasionally takes possession of the person, who has now become a shaman themself.

VISITING THE SPIRITS

Possession rituals are, of course, held in holy places. The spirits live there, so visiting an altar will automatically bring people closer to its inhabitants. Having spirits bound to particular places automatically makes dealings with them less dangerous – if you get scared you can just leave. Particularly in cultures such as Hinduism, where the spirits often combine a good and a bad side, it might be troublesome to have them around the whole day. If a god is omnipresent, it is better that it should have no bad intentions. If it does you will need constantly to be making sacrifices to it. The Mayan gods reflect both the creative and the destructive powers of nature, so to avoid the latter the Mayans tried to satisfy them with human and animal sacrifices. It is possible that the officiating priests went into a possession trance so they wouldn't have to be cold-blooded murderers in daily life.

The induction of short-term possession is an ability, which for a shaman can be his daily work. Usually we, as observers, can see that a combination of stimuli is necessary in order to call up this ability: incense, music, dance, stimulants… In hypnotherapy we would call these 'trance anchors' (Bandler and Grinder, 1982; Hilgard, 1977); they help a person achieve an altered consciousness. The right state of consciousness, however, does not automatically mean possession.

On Bali and Haiti whole groups of people dance, but only a few become possessed. So what is so difficult about possession?

CHOOSING THE RIGHT SPIRIT
Shamans may believe in a rich pantheon of spirits and gods, but when they want to become possessed they address themselves to just one spirit – the spirit with whom they have a special connection and who, for that reason, has a very clear image in their social panorama.

WITHOUT FEAR
Many trance mediums have learned to put their fear on one side in preparation for a confrontation with a spirit. Often they do this by purification rituals such as herbal baths, incense baths, diets, fasting and sexual abstinence. When these rituals are effective they make it possible for a shaman to expand his image of the spirit

involved. The closer it comes, the more intense will be its emotional influence.

PROXIMITY OF THE SPIRIT AND LACK OF SELF-IMAGE

Distance and ego are the issue when it comes to possession. Only the elite shamans and priests can overcome their fear of the spirit world – the normal mortal is not so keen on a real meeting with a spirit or an angel.

This fear makes it difficult to visualise gods as being close by. If you believe that a spirit is capable of making or breaking the world, then it is logical that it is terrifying to be close to it. This is also true, to a certain extent, for the spirits of ancestors. People don't want them too close because they will interfere with the whole of life.

All this means that distance is a crucial factor in religious practice, certainly by the invocation of possession. That is why we see many shamans and priests performing rituals to bring them closer to the gods. Prayers, hymns, dances and sacrifices are designed to attract the gods. The priest is active in the calling up of spirits, but the spirits stay in control. The spirit is invited with his favourite music, smell, colour and food. The believers often sing songs, just as school children in Holland do when they wait for Saint Nicholas to appear.

The first objective in possession rituals is to feel the presence of the spirits. This is achieved when the representations are visualised large and close enough. Feeling the spirits is the first step, but becoming possessed by them is a step further.

LACK OF SELF-IMAGE

Just as in contact with living authorities, the experience of self plays here a key role. The awareness of self (i.e. the self-image together with the kinaesthetic self) can get in the way. Trance states help to weaken the self, or remove it altogether, which is why we often see shamans go into a trance in order to access the spirit world. Many shamans dance in fast rhythm, others use consciousness-expanding herbal extracts. The experienced shaman knows exactly how he can achieve a trance and open himself up for the domination of a spirit.

Within this model it is logical that possession is easier for people with a weak or divided awareness of self; a strong self is a technical problem for someone trying to become possessed. Anyone who approaches the spirit world with a large self-image and a strong me-feeling has very little chance of becoming possessed. If you want to do it anyway, which of course is often the case with shamans, then you must take measures to weaken your self-awareness in order to give the spirits access.

An alternative way to make possession possible with a strong self-awareness is 'turning in on yourself'. This means that you bring your self-image so close that it turns round and merges with your body so that it is no longer somewhere in front of you, but inside you. The spirits can then be brought closer without the self-image getting in the way. This leads to a very controlled form of possession, which still makes more or less the same things possible as the uncontrolled variant with a weak self. It may, however, be that turning in on yourself will result in a possession that is less than total.

THE SUDDEN SWITCH

When spirits come closer, the same thing will happen as with living authorities: there will be a sudden shift to the second position. In the Balinese sword dance the dancers become possessed when a large, dragon-like monster appears on the scene. It may be that the close confrontation with this vast image of the spirit has the same effect as close confrontation with a real, living authority.

If the personification of the spirit engenders stronger feelings than the self-awareness, then the former will replace the latter in the central position in a person's social panorama. The self-awareness ascribed to the spirit will take the central place, which implies identification with the spirit. Up to now it has been difficult to determine whether the shaman has to move in the direction of the

spirit-personification, or whether a sufficiently dominantly conceived spirit automatically steps into the place where the shaman's
kinaesthetic used to be. It is possible that both occur at the same
instant.

COMING BACK TO ONESELF

In order to become 'dispossessed' the spirit needs to be put back
at a distance and the self-feeling returned to its central position.
Others can help in this process. They can, for instance, speak the
name of the person involved, which can work as a sort of identity
frame (Akstein, 1991). This is in contrast to speaking the name of
the spirit, which has the opposite effect. Others can also bring the
person back by touching them or putting an arm round them. In
most shamanistic cultures there is a special ritual for coming out
of a possession. Practice makes perfect; a shaman can sometimes
go from being possessed and back again very quickly.

POSSESSION TRANCE

Apart from the trance that has already been induced by the dance,
the one possessed also goes into a possession trance (Giel, 1978;
Johnstone, 1979). In trance states of this type a large portion of the
abilities are turned off and others used very intensely (Hilgard,
1977). In other words, all the mental software of everyday life is
put on standby while the 'file' containing the role of the spirit is
super-active. It is no coincidence that a possession trance is very
like the state a good actor gets into when playing a part
(Johnstone, 1979). Nor is it a coincidence that any shaman will
deny that he is playing a part when he is possessed. The belief in
external control of the possession – the spirit is doing it – is an
essential part of the system of belief in which possession is a useful way of working.

A SERIOUS, DANGEROUS, SUBVERSIVE AND SINFUL BUSINESS

Though the symptoms may be very similar, possession, unlike
role-playing, is always taken very seriously. This yields the same
atmosphere as can be found in multiple personalities (Van der
Hart, 1991; Spiegel and Spiegel, 1978). In my view it is essential for
researchers into multiple personality disorders to study the

313

similarities to possession. There, too, things such as 'out of my control' are taken very seriously. Possession and multiple personality disorder are only 'real' if the spirits or alters have control. The frame is immediately lost if the trance medium says they are playing a part. We see exactly the same thing in the constellation method, which was described in the previous chapter. As soon as the person playing the role is in control, the whole thing becomes suddenly laughable.

That is why laughter is not allowed by possession. I have heard tell that what the devil hates most is relativistic humour. Grimness and seriousness increase the total effect.

In our culture the practice of possession affects existing religious authority relationships and is usually labelled 'sinful'. Social sanctions, which in other times sometimes even bore the penalty of death, oblige people to carry on their occult practices in secret, which gives it even more of a subversive character.

Partly because of that, people are always exhorted to be very careful with it; they are warned of undefined 'dreadful' dangers. Cult leaders use the same arguments to reserve possession for the initiated. Experimenting with possession as we (Derks and Hollander, 1996a) did, is consistently frowned upon as being dangerous, unscientific and 'new age'... Incidentally, rival sects always call the possession practices of the competition, 'dangerous', 'occult' or 'black magic'.

AMNESIA AS PROOF OF AUTHENTICITY
In most cults that practice possession they believe that when someone is possessed they are outside themselves and have lost all self-control and consciousness. This last (loss of consciousness) is a misunderstanding. People confuse loss of memory with loss of consciousness. People make the same mistake about dreams (Derks and Sinclair, 2000). They think that they are not conscious when they are dreaming because they remember their dreams only partly or not at all. But the opposite is true. Dreams are intense, conscious experiences, which are immediately forgotten (Evarts, 1967). This confusion is reinforced by Freud's association of dreams with the subconscious (Derks, 1988).

Just as with any form of trance, amnesia can happen after possession (Erickson, Rossi and Rossi, 1976). Sometimes this is cultivated, but it is difficult to test whether the shaman remembers afterwards what he did during the possession. Just as in popular ideas about hypnosis, amnesia is seen as a proof of genuineness. 'I was well away, I don't remember a thing…'

This amnesia means, among other things, that a shaman cannot afterwards be held responsible for his actions. If he, for instance, made a faulty diagnosis during possession then no one can complain to him about it.

POSSESSION IS RECOGNISABLE TO OTHERS
In every cult, the members can tell, by looking at a person, whether or not they are possessed. People assume that they should treat the one possessed as a god or a spirit and will usually therefore pay the possessed person a great deal of respect during their state of possession (Hollander, 1997).

POSSESSION AS TEMPORARY OMNIPOTENCE
Possession temporarily turns people into gods. Possession takes a person from the social panorama into the spiritual panorama and at the same time lowers a god to the level of mortals. Possession only fits in cultures in which the social and the spiritual panorama communicate freely with each other, and where there is no division between church and state. Where there is such a division, spiritual and temporal authorities tend to suppress any cult that practises possession. Even so, many political authorities have had to watch helplessly while people have won social power through one form of possession or another and gathered followers who treated them as gods.

Lewis (1971) summarises this area of tension beautifully:

> Finally I would like to refer to our own religion. Traditional Christians depict God as almighty and omnipotent, which automatically implies that man is weak and unimportant. This, however, has made the Christian belief vulnerable in respect of human scientific and technological progress. Things that first were ruled

only by God begin to belong to the realm of man. This threatens to undermine God's inviolable position. Shamanistic religions, on the other hand, do not make this mistake. Their assumption is that there are moments when man can climb to God's level. Because man is originally seen as being able to participate in the authority of the gods then there is nothing more important to aim for than to become a holy authority, an equal of the gods. In general, what shamanistic séances demonstrate is that man and gods are both omnipotent. Shamanistic religions believe in an equal relationship with the divine, and so maintain a harmonious community of gods and people. In a community where they (Christians) have lost the ecstatic mystery (of possession) their myths of creation are their only nostalgic reminders of it and they desperately seek doctrines of personal beatification.

7.12 Therapeutic applications

Knowing the above patterns will be enough for most psychotherapists. A familiarity with them will be sufficient to help clients with religious or spiritual problems.

Techniques for speeding up the grieving process and to get along with the disruptive influence of ancestors will be followed in the rest of this chapter by methods for working with spiritual experiences and possession.

Technique 47: Dealing with grief

Indication: When complaints are rooted in a significant loss

1. In the social panorama, find the location of the dead person who is giving problems.
2. Find the peaceful locations of other dead people with whom there are no problematical feelings of grief.
3. Move the troublesome dead person to the peaceful location.

Possible problems (P) and solutions (S) by technique 48

P: The personification of the troublesome dead person is partly in the spiritual panorama and partly in the social panorama (bi-location).

S: Work only with the part that is still among the living. Find out why the client cannot 'let go'. Finish, in imagination, all uncompleted business with the dead. For instance, have a conversation with the ghost until it is satisfied and then it may move to the other side of its own accord.

P: The personification of the problematical dead person is in, or very near to, the body of the client.

S: Find out what abilities the dead person needs in order to be able to keep farther away. If that works, move the dead person to their last resting-place (the final destination in the spiritual panorama).

Technique 48: Reconciliation with ancestral spirits

Indication: Dead relative haunts the client

This technique is a minimal description of 'six-step reframing' (Derks and Hollander, 1996a; Bandler and Grinder, 1979)

1. Help the client to determine what the positive intention of the ancestral spirit is.
2. Together with the client, search for alternative behaviour that could help achieve the positive intention of the spirit.
3. Suggest these alternatives to the spirit and ask for a clear signal if it agrees.

Technique 49: Core state in the social panorama

Indication: In case of social conflicts

This method can be used as a guided fantasy with an individual or with a group. The idea is to solve social tension, of any sort, by using spiritual resources. This technique is based on Andreas and Andreas' 'core transformation' (1994).

1. In your mind, go to a beautiful, quiet place in nature.
2. Find somewhere to sit.
3. Think of all the people in the world surrounding you. Think for a little while about the social tension or conflicts that you sometimes experience.
4. Ask yourself what your worst characteristic is.

5. Imagine that a part of you is controlling that characteristic. What do you imagine that part is like?
6. Find out what the positive intention of that part is.
7. Ask the part what it is trying to achieve by that positive intention.
8. Find another, even more important positive intention behind the first one of the same part.
9. Go on searching until the part can think of no more important positive intentions. That means climbing up the hierarchy of positive intentions until you are right at the top. Name this highest positive intention.
10. In your mind, experience realising that ultimate positive intention.
11. Fill your whole body with the feeling associated with that. Surround yourself with a cloud of the colour that belongs to that state. Make the feeling as strong as possible by linking it to your breathing and to all your thoughts.
12. Take the feeling with you to your image of all the people in the world surrounding you. Think again, keeping hold of that feeling, of the social tension or conflict from step 3.
13. Keep hold of this combination of thoughts and feelings and think back to that beautiful, quiet place.
14. Come back to the here and now and bring with you any notions of this experience that will be useful to you.

Technique 50: Lowering the spiritual panorama

Indication: Reconnection with the world of spirits

1. Catalogue all the dead people, spirits and gods in your social panorama.
2. Find out, one at a time, where they are placed.
3. Stand so you can oversee the whole spiritual panorama.
4. In your mind, lower your spiritual panorama to your own level.
5. On that level, contact the dead people, spirits and gods with whom you want to communicate. Talk to them one by one.
6. Once you are satisfied, put the spiritual panorama back to the position that suits you best.

Technique 51: Creating a personal guiding spirit

Indication: The need for supernatural assistance

1. Which dead person would you like to have as your support or guiding spirit?
2. Visualise the personification of that person as it is now in your social/spiritual panorama.
3. Set the personification high and large in front of you.
4. Bring it to about four feet away from you.
5. Make contact with the personification; maybe even dance with it. Ask if it will support you in life. If it agrees, go on to step 6. If not, ask what conditions there are.
6. Put the personification in the closest position in your spiritual panorama.

Technique 52: Possessed until the alarm goes off

Indication: The need for safe supernatural connections

You want to have intensive contact with a personification in your spiritual panorama by means of unification. You can use this technique as a follow-on to Technique 51.

1. Set a timer for half an hour and tell yourself that, when it goes off, you will return to yourself by calling up a large self-image and speaking your own name. If necessary practise this a few times. As an alternative you can ask someone else to function as timer and, when the time is up, to bring you back by touching you and speaking your name.

2. Choose a spirit and ascertain where its personification is in your spiritual panorama.

3. Make your self-image large and close (Technique 11).

4. Practise making the spiritual personification larger and closer a few times.

5. Park that personification for now at a 'safe' distance (five mental metres).

6. Turn into yourself (Technique 11).

7. Make the spiritual personification as large and as close as pos-sible and allow yourself to be taken over. Stay in the experience until the alarm goes off.

Possible problems (P) and Solutions (S) by Technique 52

P: The intensity of the experience is low.
S: Take more time to visualise the spiritual personification.

P: The intensity is still low.
S: Put your self-image far away and make it small instead of turn-ing it into yourself. The disadvantage of this is that you have less control over the experience, but it is more exciting.

P: You don't know what this is for.
S: Choose an entity that has special powers and decide that you will have these powers as well during the possession. What would you like to be able to do?

P: You find the whole procedure ridiculous.
S: Realise that you have managed to read this book this far, which is quite an achievement. When I used this technique myself, I became possessed by the spirit of William James. That released an autonomous sort of creativity in me, which is responsible for, among other things, this chapter. For me this approach was nothing more than a very thorough answer to the question, 'How would James have presented the spiritual panorama in the year 2002?'

FOOTNOTE TO THE APPLICATION OF POSSESSION

As I have already said, possession is generally regarded as very serious and also potentially dangerous. I believe that it is safe to say that working with spirits is, indeed, dangerous for people who believe that spirits really exist. If you believe that they are internal cognitive constructions, then they are no longer as dangerous, but that also takes away a lot of the attraction. You will have the most success if you work with a sort of ambivalence in which you are aware that spirits are cognitive constructions while at the same time you behave as if they were autonomous beings. If you do that, there will be a bit of humour in the game, just enough to keep the devil away.

Chapter 8

Training, teaching and teams

8.1   *The trainer's panorama*

Arthur was an experienced trainer for a big software house. I had the honour to coach him while he was preparing for a new two days' sales seminar. The training programme contained many elements that were new to Arthur and there would have been far too many uncertainties if Arthur had not been assisted by his expert colleague, Peter. Together they were a formidable team of trainers but Arthur still became quite nervous when he thought about their freshly designed seminar. Especially when he realised that the try-out was next Friday and today was ... Tuesday!

I asked him to imagine standing in front of the try-out training group and to visualise the people just as he saw them now. What did he *see*?

Arthur explained in detail what he felt and how he thought the people might respond – their comments, wishes, fears and probable objections. He also made it clear that Friday's try-out seminar was very important because the company had invested a considerable sum in its development. He told me that the participants were all invited staff members with a high level of positive expectancy but also a healthy sense of criticism. 'They will decide whether or not to put the programme on the market.'

As was to be expected, my question, 'what do you *see*?' did not automatically cause Arthur to use any language describing the spatial characteristics of his representation of this group. As with most people, he did not spontaneously tell me how far away, high up or wide-ranged he saw this group. Only after I had stopped him from telling me about the context and content of the seminar could he be brought tentatively to describe his 'trainer's panorama' of the try-out group to me.

It was immediately evident that Arthur sensed this group only in his left visual field, in the shape of a half horseshoe. Arthur stood in front of it as if it were a whole horseshoe but he could only see its left side, which started about two metres in front of him.

One very prominent participant was straight in front of him at the toe of the horseshoe. 'That is Charles. I see him much bigger than the rest', commented Arthur.

I explained to him that many problems in education arise from teachers who feel controlled by authority figures. They often feel caught between the class and a headteacher who is looking over their shoulder. Headteachers push teachers to do things they don't like; the teachers in their turn compel the pupils to do things they don't want to do. 'It looks as if your headteacher is sitting in your classroom! Okay, let's do something about it'.

It would have been an easy task to improve Arthur's representation of the try-out group with only this information available. However, I had learned my lesson; I had already fallen prey, several times, to my eagerness to change social panoramas without a reference. By just shifting images left, right, up, down, back and forth, I had confused many of my clients and frequently endangered my rapport with them.

That was why I asked Arthur to think of an example of a training group he had really enjoyed.

It was easy for him to come up with examples of pleasant groups. We chose one that was similar in size and with similar types of participants. Arthur explained to me how he saw this reference group and soon we were able to compare the two groups by looking at the critical differences in sensory qualities.

The reference training group consisted of an entire horseshoe and he saw it a little lower than the try-out group. Movement and colour were more prominent in the reference group, and there were no dominating members.

We continued our work, changing the sensory characteristics of the try-out group bit-by-bit to make them more similar to those of the reference group. The most interesting part was the completion of the horseshoe.

Arthur, who was familiar with computer graphics, could simply 'mirror' the left part of the horseshoe over to the right-hand side. Once he had done that he continued by moving the whole group down a little, pulling everyone a bit closer, increasing the movement and adding more colour. In this way the try-out group started to look more like the reference group. It didn't take very sharp observation skills to see how much this affected Arthur's motivation. He started to smile and gave a sigh of relief. We had completed one of the oldest social panorama techniques, the trainer's panorama.

In the 1980s Richard Bandler did a lot of work with moving representations of people around. This inspired me to experiment with this process in the context of training groups. This application proved itself for the first time at a trainers' training at the University of Twente in the spring of 1988. From then on I was able to investigate how at least 500 trainers experienced difficult and favourite groups.

So when you ask me how trainers imagine their favourite groups, I can answer from experience – close by, just a little lower than they are, colourful, homogeneous and moving.

Contrasting the images of groups enabled me to make some remarkable discoveries. Most of all it became apparent that, by adjusting the sensory qualities of these group representations, a non-motivating group could be turned into a pleasant one. This discovery became a major tool in the workshops I presented for trainers. A lot of other social panorama work followed from this application.

Sometimes the phone rings and I hear a person say, 'Lucas, we have 12 people we want you to work with on leadership. Okay?'

Even when such a call does not provide me with any specific information about the participants, it still causes me to make a 'group image' in my mind. The sensory qualities of this image will, to a large extent, determine the pleasure I find in preparing myself for working with them.

Technique 53: Discover and change your trainer's panorama

Indication: Anticipation stress for a training group

How do you improve your image of the group in front of you? The answer is simple: look each and every participant in the eye and feel love and respect for him or her. To achieve this, however, it will be helpful if you go through the following steps when you are preparing yourself for a group session on your own.

1. Find the sensory qualities (distance, eye level, width, colours, movement, and sounds) of your image of the group you don't like to work with.
2. Compare these sensory qualities with those of a group you love to work with.
3. Find out what sensory qualities seem to be critical in motivating yourself for group work.
4. Change the critical sensory qualities of the group you don't like in the direction of those of the group you love to work with until your motivation is sufficiently improved.
5. Are there any remaining problems? (E.g. dominant individuals, controlling authorities, resistant alliances, etc.)

When you work with the trainer's panorama, it is likely that your representation of a training group will be dominated by disturbing individuals or subgroups. Just as Arthur discovered, he had this bloody Charles blocking him! What can you do about that?

Transferring resources to these disturbing individuals or subgroups is the most efficient remedy that I know of. It is not only effective, but quick and easy too.

Technique 54: Transferring resources to disturbing subgroups

Indication: Irritation or fear for group members

1. What resources does the subgroup lack that cause them to be disturbing to you?

2. Find a prominent example in your own life when you possessed this resource.

3. Fully associate with this example and intensify the experience as much as possible. Choose a colour that suits the experience of having this resource. Imagine being in a cloud of that colour while you continue to experience the resource.

4. Send the resource to the disturbing subgroup. This can be done by means of a cloud of coloured gas or a beam of laser light.

5. Check whether or not the subgroup can be moved to a better location in your trainer's panorama. If necessary, use the same method to add more resources.

Technique 55: Optimising the trainer's self-image

Indication: A trainer lacks positive self awareness

If you have read Chapter 3, about the self-concept, you will understand that trainers need a powerful self-image when they are working with a group. However, a self-image that is too dominant will have an overwhelming effect on the participants: they may find the trainer arrogant and reject their teaching. The trainer needs to find a balance between, on the one hand, playing a too insignificant role because of a small self-image and, on the other, appearing arrogant as a result of a self-concept that is too big.

Start with a self-image that is a little nearer than the closest participant and slightly bigger than life-size and adjust it to your particular
needs with this group.

8.1.1 *Dealing with objections by using the perceptual positions (and the out-framing of resistance)*

Let me tell you some more about Arthur. As soon as he had
restructured his trainer's panorama, he felt much more confident.
However, he soon started to frown again: 'But …' he said …
'But …'

He looked at the image of the group for a while and repeated,
'But …'

Of course I asked him, 'But what?' He said he didn't know. He kept on staring at the image of the group, his forehead creased.

I took three pieces of paper and wrote the figures one, two and three on them. 'Look,' I said, and I placed number one just in front of Arthur's feet. 'This symbolises the first perceptual position. That means that from here you look at the training as you see it through your own eyes.' Next, I placed the second piece about four metres in front of Arthur. 'This is the second perceptual position, the training as seen through the eyes of the trainees.' I placed the third perceptual position beside the line of interaction between the trainer and the trainees. It was the point of view of an observer, from the sidelines.

I took Arthur by his shoulders and placed him on the third perceptual position paper. 'Look at yourself and the group. Can you see what is wrong or missing?'

Arthur looked for some time, his head moving backwards and forwards from side to side. 'I'm putting far too much effort into this training,' he said, 'this will kill me. I'm far too active. I need to slow down. I need to give them a break.'

I didn't have to discuss the meaning of this with Arthur. As soon as he indicated that he had seen enough I told him to step back into first position.

It was quite visible from his posture and his breathing rate that he slowed down and relaxed in front of the imaginary group. He smiled at me and commented, 'The only way this seminar can fail is if I push everyone over their limits, including Peter and myself. I need to let go ...'

Now it was time to move Arthur to the second perceptual position. We placed a chair on the spot where he saw the group. He sat down. 'Be one of the participants and see yourself as the trainer ... What do you think of Arthur over there?'

'He is afraid of my criticism,' was Arthur's immediate response. 'He is afraid that the whole thing will be cancelled. I understand that, but it still worries me. Why does he doubt his own work so

329

much? Why does Arthur keep on trying to convince me of his qualities? I already know he is good!'

When Arthur was put back on the third perceptual position, he seemed to have a fit of creativity. He smiled, laughed and talked a lot to himself. I could not understand most of it. Then, spontaneously, he stepped back into the first perceptual position. He started to gesture and spoke in a soft tone of voice, but he was clearly audible to the imaginary audience in front of him.

Next I moved Arthur back into second position. I asked him, 'Imagine you are one of the most critical participants, what wishes and expectations of yours would *not* be fulfilled in this seminar?'

'I cannot air my own views and philosophies in this training programme.'

Back on the third perceptual position Arthur thought about how he could solve this but he failed to find a satisfactory answer. So I asked him to sit down and look at the following instructions.

Technique 56: The 'out-framing' of false expectations

Indication: Preparing a training

1. Put yourself in the place of one or more imaginary trainees and find out what expectations they may have and which of these will not be met by your programme. Make a list of these false expectations.

2. Now move to the observer's (third perceptual) position and start thinking about things you can say at the start of the training to 'out-frame' these false expectations. Use the list below for inspiration.

Some ideas for framing your training

FRAMING YOUR ROLE AS TRAINER

I am a guide
I am providing opportunities

I will let you nose around
I will show you some examples
I will help you to discover
Together we will explore
I want to invent with you

FRAMING THE PARTICIPANT'S ROLE AS TRAINEE

You will be guided step by step
You will have to make your own choices and decisions
You will provide us with cases and examples
You will teach one another
You will be confronted with your weak spots
You will be a consumer at a banquet
You will be stretched to your limits

FRAMING THE CONTENT OF THE TRAINING

These are basic tools
These are some recent ideas
This is a solid framework
This is an experiment
This is a metaphor
This is a jigsaw puzzle we must solve together
This is a fine-tuning of your skills

FRAMING THE PROCEDURES AND EXERCISES

We will simulate reality
We will play with some ideas
We will experiment with our limits
We will explore a new set of behaviours step by step
We will try out which tool does or does not fit our needs
We will be confronted with extreme situations
Together we will invent ways to learn

Arthur found two frames on these lists that suited his problems. 'I am going to start the seminar by telling them that I am going to show them some examples and some recent ideas …' he said. He explained that this would clearly tell the one problematic partici-pant that there would be not much room left for his own ideas and philosophies in the seminar. To compensate for this, Arthur decided to add an opening exercise in which the participants were invited to spend three minutes airing as many of their own ideas as possible about the subject matter of the training. 'That will do the job'. He smiled and said that he now felt solidly prepared.

8.2 *Identification in education*

With a few exceptions the word 'identification' is used with a similar meaning in all popular brands of psychology. This surprisingly high level of agreement as to what identification is suggests that the word is a label for a very robust psychological process. But, however valid this concept may be, the phenomenon itself is difficult to observe because it belongs to unconscious social cognition. All we can see are its behavioural results in people who have identified themselves with someone.

By using the social panorama model we can, as it were, make an x-ray of the process of identification. Seeing through it will help to reconstruct the underlying mechanism so we will be able to predict, understand and evoke identification. This is useful, because identification plays a crucial role in all areas of social influence and particularly in education.

A TRAGIC EXAMPLE

Let's explore the possible implications of such an identification. Imagine for a moment that in a parallel universe you are a 10-year-old boy. What will go on in your mind when your mother says, 'Oh boy, you are so like my younger brother, Eddy, who died when he was 13'?

You think, 'Hey! That's probably why Granny sometimes calls me Ed and then says, 'Sorry dear, I mean *you* of course! I'm pretty sure who *you* are, love!'

Now you are infected with the idea, the link between you and your dead uncle is imprinted on your brain tissue. Will it drive you to fuse the image of yourself with your concept of this dead youngster – a boy you never knew? Will you then merge his ghost with your self-image? Will you start to wrap his personification around your kinaesthetic self?

One Monday morning you look in the mirror and get a shock. You suddenly see his sad example and become aware of the fact that you share several personality traits with him. Then you will start having dreams in which you *are* him. When you are awake, you will even hear yourself talk to him out loud. But your problems really start when you start being afraid that you may meet a similar fate!

When this becomes a self-fulfilling prophecy and you also die very young, at your funeral your child therapist will explain to your relatives, 'He identified himself with his dead uncle'.

Thankfully, you are in this universe, you are your current age and none of this happened.

8.2.1   What is identification?

I wonder how this definition matches your own opinion:

'Identification is the process of thinking of person X as if he were person Y'.

In this definition the neutral term 'thinking' may vary in meaning from the total conviction that person X is the same individual as person Y to just noticing some similarities between X and Y. Beside this, we also need to distinguish between cases in which it is person X who believes himself to be person Y, and those in which it is a person Z who believes that person X and Y are one and the same. In the first case it could be John who believes himself to be his Uncle Eddy. In the second it is Fritz who may see that Bill has assimilated many traits that originate from his close friend Rick. Fritz may either express it clearly: 'I see so much of Rick in Bill, that I often confuse them' or he may make the comment: 'Bill identifies himself with Rick.' In the latter case, Bill may well deny this.

There is another notable dimension to identification. Most scientists believe that a person can either identify themself with someone on purpose, voluntarily, or that they may identify themself with someone when they fall victim to unconscious and compulsive dynamics. For instance, an actor, however totally absorbed in the role, is still consciously and voluntarily identifying. But the classical example of a psychiatric patient who believes himself to be Jesus Christ and acts the part demonstrates the other side of the coin; this person seems totally to identify without having had the intention of doing so. He will be doing some great acting, but a psychiatrist who calls out to him, 'Stop playing Jesus, for heaven's sake!' will not necessarily solve his patient's problem. A movie director can say the same thing to an actor with far more impact.

But neither voluntary nor involuntary identification is necessarily a problem. In fact, identification can be as absurd as it can be painful. Generally speaking, identification is regarded as funny when it appears to be intentional, but extremely serious when it is not. Role-play, mimicry and imitation can be hilarious, but multiple personality problems, communing with spirits or mediumistic trances are never considered funny. As I described in Chapter 6, being a substitute in a family constellation session can be dead serious, too. Voluntary identification is often of short duration while involuntary identification may last a long time and is often controlled by others. The reader who has read Chapter 7 on the spiritual panorama will recognise that possession is just another frame around the process of identification. Spirit possession is not considered to be funny either.

8.2.2 Identification with parents

An embryo shares its location with its mother – her body sensations and emotions will dominate its existence. That is why some psychologists argue that the womb is the cradle of identification. However, not all mammals are as good at identification as primates are, which proves that starting life in a womb does not automatically bestow the ability to identify. Many apes are masters at the art of guessing others' point of view. Some chimpanzees even seem to out-perform young children when it comes to knowing what others want and feel. That is why identification is still a great challenge for psychology.

From comparative primate research, Tomasello (2003) came to believe that identification is an innate faculty of humans. In line with Lakoff and Johnsons' reasoning, which I have followed throughout this text, I prefer to assume identification to be derived from bodily experiences in early life. But how is identification learned?

Though I do not support Tomasello in his genetic view of identification, I still like his concept of 'joint attention' because this idea helps to reconstruct the way in which identification can be generalised from basic experience.

In this reconstruction, 'joint attention' must be seen as the precursor of identification. For the development of joint attention, parents need first to direct their baby's awareness – move colourful objects over the cradle so the baby will stare at them. Once the child can be focused, the parents may join it in paying attention to the same thing. Joint attention will include talking to the baby and at the same time gazing at a toy until the child, too, looks at it. In this way the infant will learn to realise that it sees, hears and feels the same things as its parents do. Close physical contact will ensure that the baby will also experience some of the parents' emotions, which will be further promoted by the parents' frequent adjustments to the moods of their child.

The next stage will be the internalisation of this process. The child knows that the parent is thinking about the same things and has related feelings. After having experienced this regularly and for some period of time, the toddler will start to enjoy joint attention more independently. Even when the parent is actually looking elsewhere it may experience their unity of focus.

Joint attention is not yet identification, as we shall see from the analysis of the spatial (social panorama) patterns involved. For identification to appear, the feeling of self must be located inside the other personification.

So the next question is, how does a child learn to put its kinaesthetic self in another's place? In Chapter 3 we saw that the feeling of self is the core of identity, but that it is also quite dynamic, varying in both position and strength from context to context. In some situations (sleep, hypnosis, alert trance and some altered states of consciousness) the kinaesthetic self can be very weak or absent. The shift towards a sense of shared location with the parent may arise from the child having a flaw in its self-boundaries. Such a flaw is nothing special, since the contours of the self are not always sharp and clear. During relaxed episodes, in particular, the self-concept may have a vague outline only. When we are drowsy the boundaries of all our concepts become more fluid – something that seems to reach a maximum in dreams. In a deeply relaxed state the blending of self and other is not very far off and this seems to be very common in young children.

In a state of deep relaxation the child will learn to unite its self-concept with the parent personification at the same spot in mental space. This learning process may finally turn into the skill of identification. Later in life this will enable the person to shift back and forth into the second perceptual position with anyone.

In short, the first elements of identification are learned within the womb, expanded through close communication with parents and perfected in early childhood while playing with dolls and playing 'let's pretend'. On mother's lap you will experience almost the same as she does, especially when you take little naps in between her joining attention with you. To identify with her is just a small cognitive step; once you have mastered it you can share locations with any personification in your social panorama.

The fact that this blending of the two experiential spheres has proved to be easier for girls than for boys indicates the involvement of some genetic components. Some blame this on hormonal differences: girls share their mother's (sex) hormones and are more similar to her than boys are while they are in the womb. This could cause girls to develop a more diffuse kinaesthetic self, which would make the blending of identities easier.

In general it must be true that people with weak self-concepts will identify more frequently. This is because they will automatically identify with all dominating personifications (see Chapter 4, the law of the dominant personification) and the world is full of dominant personifications when you are a toddler.

When you are a child, your family consists of a number of big people with power over you. Since it may be difficult to keep your self-boundaries intact in such an intimidating environment, you will automatically identify a lot with your next of kin, as described in Chapter 6. This results in 'identification learning', which helps you to build a repertoire of family-characteristic behaviour.

To summarise the above we can say that identification with parents is largely automatic and a child will copy their behaviour without choosing to do so. At first, intimacy is necessary, but not for long. A child will later be able to learn from just observing its parents – or anybody else.

It is practical to see identification learning as a two-stage process. Once a behavioural example is memorised (stage one), it can be stepped into (stage two) at any time later. In other words, you make pictures with which you can identify at a later stage. A child may be forced to make the effort of identification by the challenges that life offers. In its inner search for answers to these challenges it will find the behavioural examples from others stored in its memory, ready to be turned into its own repertoire of behaviour.

The distinction between the moment of storage and the moment of identification is very helpful in understanding what is critical in identification learning. In real life the difference between these stages may be difficult to observe, especially when someone identifies with a model at the same time as the behavioural example is provided. For example, you may 'step into' your music teacher as soon as she plays for you. From the outside this will show in you slightly moving your body and your hands in about the same way she does.

8.3 *Identification learning in the social panorama*

Some psychologists (of whom Bandura is the best known) have observed how children automatically learn by identification at a very early age. Most social scientists agree that this is a fast, easy and unconscious way of learning. There is reason to believe that we acquire much of our behaviour by means of identification and that most social skills are learned in that way. Many famous artists and scientists identified themselves with their brilliant masters. That is how they all reproduced greatness.

Identification is a superb way to learn, but at times it can lead to problems. For instance, a person may acquire behaviour that is harmful, such as aggression, helplessness, mental problems, sexual perversions or criminality by this same type of unconscious learning. Examples get stored, unnoticed, and may lurk in the background until their time has come to be identified with. Can youngsters learn to be killers from TV? The answer seems to be, 'Yes they can.' Some people have, by means of unconscious identification, learnt lessons with destructive consequences. In Chapter 6 we met the family therapist Hellinger (1995) who specialises, among other things, in issues that stem from identification with bad examples within the intimate circle.

8.4 *Modelling identification*

Generally speaking, each personification occupies its own unique location in the social panorama, with the exception of personifications that are doubly or triply represented, bi-location and tri-locations (see Chapter 6). Another exception is when two personifications are placed on the same spot, shared locations.

Ten years of working with the social panorama model gradually revealed to me the mechanics of the process of identification. This model enables us to describe these mechanisms in detail. So what exactly does happen when person X identifies with person Y?

As must be clear to the reader by now, identification does not take place between 'persons' but between 'personifications'. Thus, if we see person X identify with someone, we may translate this into, 'One of the personifications in X's social panorama has blended with another.'

The core finding in the modelling of identification with the aid of the social panorama can be formulated as a simple pattern: Identification means that the two personifications involved occupy the same location in mental space. In other words, personification X and Y will be located at the same spot for as long as the identification lasts.

The fullest identification arises from a personification X that entirely and permanently unites with personification Y and can no longer be recognised as separate. Sometimes it is as simple as that. A client complains about compulsively acting like his mother, and, indeed, the mother-personification is located all round this client's body. Or in the same way, a client may find a very influential relative somewhere inside their head or chest. In many examples of identification, the person is aware that the other has great influence on his or her identity and may often report recurring confusion about who is who. But in many other cases the person clearly knows the difference between the self and the other. This extra complexity is caused by the fact that identification does not have to be a permanent state of affairs and may also sometimes involve only parts of the personifications.

In short, to experience two personifications as 'identical' one needs to see them on the same spot (see 'shared locations' in Chapter 6). Shared locations are found when clients see the other-personifications around, within or partially inside the boundaries of their bodies. As soon as the 'feeling of self' is included in the shared locations the person will be convinced that he or she is someone else.

In the theatre, this means that an actor who totally identifies with the role finds their self-experience located at exactly the same spot as the personification of the character they are depicting. However, if they are still aware that they are themselves and not the played personage, the personification of the role will not include their feeling of self ('his centre' as acting expert Keith Johnstone, 1979, calls it).

Someone who claims to be possessed by a spirit may point out that the location of this spirit is within their body boundaries and also includes their feeling of self. Such a person will tend to have amnesia for their own identity during the possession trance and will claim to have amnesia for the spirit-identity after the possession has stopped.

When we study the structure of identification in detail we will see that it can be very dynamic in the sense that a person does not need to hold the two personifications on the same spot for long. In the case of an actor it is quite clear that they will not be absorbed in their role on a permanent basis. Normally they will be able to step in and out of it very quickly and at will.

Multiple personality syndrome (MPS) seems to comprise the same patterns that we see in actors who switch between roles, save that an actor maintains a sense of 'real self', while a person diagnosed as having multiple personality syndrome does not. Actors and MPS-ers alike are surrounded by their potential roles and these role-identities (alters) need to be 'taken on' for identification to take place. When taken on, the image will be on the spot of the self-image (straight in front) and the feeling will be in the location of the kinaesthetic self.

It seems reasonable to believe that the difference between 'voluntary identification' as seen in actors and 'compulsive identification' as seen in multiple personalities, is marked by a strong or weak kinaesthetic self. However, some actors (Al Pacino is my favourite example) show a weak 'own self' when they are interviewed. When they act they produce much stronger personalities than their own.

8.5 *Counter-identification*

The opposite process to identification is counter-identification, in which person X is convinced that they are completely different from Y. This 'conviction' often means 'desire to be different from Y'. Take, for instance, a son who does not want to be like his aggressive father, a teacher who wants to be 'different from teachers', an Englishman who would hate to be taken for an American, a student who doesn't want to be similar to his teacher, or a macho man who fears to be accused of being homosexual.

Counter-identification helps people to create strong (counter-) identities but it may also lead to strange and severe symptoms. The problems that arise from counter-identification are caused by the rejection of many abilities that are, in fact, necessary, but are regarded as part of the rejected other-personification. In the example of father and son, this may prevent the son acting assertively because, if he did, he would be too much like his father.

The personifications with whom a person counter-identifies are quite often projected straight in front, a little higher than eye-level and at a distance of between five and 50 metres. Metaphorically speaking, the counter-identified personification works like the north in somebody's social compass. Because this spot is roughly where the self-image should be (also straight in front), the self-image is often obscured by the image of the personification with whom the person is counter-identifying and becomes attenuated. The person will end up with a stronger picture of what they are *not* than of what they *are*.

8.6 *Trainers in tears*

Imagine you are a trainer, and you have just given a superb demonstration of a mediation technique. Your demo had a dramatic impact: you solved an ancient conflict between two business partners. You showed all the steps in the right order and clearly explained their function. In short, an excellent job.

Armed with your accurate handout, your students went off to do the exercise. And after a breather and a cup of coffee it is time to see how much success they are having.

The first trio you observe tell you that they have not started the exercise because they needed to talk about something 'private'. The next couple is doing the exercise, but it is hard to see what step they are on. 'We prefer to do it in our own way', they explain and proceed without taking any more notice of you. To your great surprise you find another trio lying on the floor involved in what they call 'energy work' because they considered it more appropriate to the problem. To your relief you find a duo who indeed are using the right sitting arrangement, although they were meant to be doing the exercise with three people. But one of them is arguing about who should be blamed for the problem at hand .... You try to intervene; 'Do you remember how I talked to the parties?' Yes – no ... what ... really?

It is like a slap in the face when you are forced to conclude that your students have only a rudimentary recollection of your demonstration and that reminding them seems to have no effect.

In the bar you meet the remainder of the group. They are discussing whether or not negotiation is something that can be learnt at all – isn't it genetic?

Then you start to cry, but none of your students seems to notice. How in the world is it possible that the great behavioural example you just offered has gone up in smoke? Fortunately, it was just a 'Let's pretend' game, and your training exercises probably go just as you would like them to.

8.6.1 The four learning modes in training

On the neurological level, learning takes place at the synaptic endings of nerve cells (Sinclair, 1982) but for a trainer this is not a very useful piece of information.

In the trainers' training at the IEP-institute in the Netherlands, we differentiate between four modes of learning. These modes are modelled from observing and questioning trainees while they sit in the room and follow the training. What is it that goes on in a person's mind that we call 'learning'?

The first learning mode involves (1) **trying to memorise** the utterances of the teacher. This is what students usually try to do, often in vain – making notes and repeating everything to themselves. It is a very conscious activity which many educators consider, erroneously, as 'real' learning.

Another learning mode is (2) **drawing conclusions**. We see heads nodding and hear, 'Aah!' or, 'I see ...' The students make generalisations about what is happening in and around the training, generalisations that may turn into new beliefs. Drawing conclusions is also a largely conscious activity. Teachers often try to force their own conclusions onto the students, but this does not usually work because, however hard a teacher tries to influence them, students will draw their own conclusions, which is the best way to memorise anything. People tend to accept what suits them and to forget everything that does not. In general, beliefs that are formed earlier in life are always preferred to the ones that come later. New conclusions that contradict early beliefs provoke inner conflicts that must be solved by conscious mental effort. 'So I have been wrong all along ... which means ...'

The third learning mode is called (3) **the restructuring of earlier experience**. What a teacher says only makes sense if the words can be connected to the student's earlier experience; otherwise it is just meaningless sounds. This process necessarily involves the activation of memories that the student has already stored in his mind. Students build on their own life-long experience as the teacher talks. This means that learning mode (3), which is the restructuring of earlier experience, is a crucial one.

The fourth mode is (4) **learning by identification**. This is 'stepping into the shoes' of a role model and emulating them. It is the most effective way of learning behaviour, and the way that children learn their social skills.

8.6.2 *Categories of resources*

In the previously mentioned trainers' training program we focus a great deal on mode (3) learning. We recognise four (four again!) categories of experience into which a person may tap in order to learn. A person can either use actual memories of what they did or imagine what they could do. In the same way, a person may make use of earlier stored behavioural examples from others or fantasise about what others might be capable of. These four categories overlap with 'restructuring of earlier experience' (mode 3) and 'identification learning' (mode 4).

The categories of experience from which people learn are:

a. I have done it myself: actual memories of performing a skill.
b. I can imagine myself doing it: fantasies about how one may do it some day.
c. I saw others do it: actual memories of others performing the skill.
d. I can imagine others doing it: fantasies about how others may do it some day.

In the first two categories a person is tapping into their own experience: (a) has been done in reality while (b) is a product of imagination. In the categories (c) and (d) behavioural examples are drawn from the observation of others: (c) consists of actual observations while (d) contains imaginary observations.

Category (c) is prototypical identification learning. The imaginary examples in category (d) may work quite similarly, but it takes a lot of creativity to learn that way. The above matrix consists of the classical variables 'remembered & constructed' and 'self & other'.

In the process of identification learning, content from the category (c) or (d) is transferred to the category (b), finally to become category (a). In other words, skills belonging to others, real or imaginary, are assimilated by someone imagining himself doing it.

To sum up: for a person to learn by means of identification they must first store the examples and then step into them. Storage is the easy and fully unconscious part of the process. We must assume from coaching practice that people store a multitude of behavioural examples but identify with only a limited number of them. We can conclude that we all possess a massive potential of unused behavioural examples that are ready to be followed at any time.

We may state that both parts, the storage and the identification, largely depend on the relationship with the model (parent, teacher, peer). For storage to take place, the role model must be considered at least worthy of attention. The act of identification requires more mental effort and consequently the level of motivation needs to be a lot higher. A reasonably positive attitude towards the teacher seems to be a necessity; if the teacher is admired, identification may take place effortlessly and unconsciously.

8.6.3 *Teachers in the social panorama*

Most trainers believe that the making and keeping of a good relationship with the participants is crucial, but in the history of modern education the important role of the relationship between student and teacher is often neglected. In most school systems it is fairly normal for students to be obliged to learn from teachers whom they don't like. Many people believe that whether the scholar likes his tutor or not is irrelevant to the learning results. Some even believe that a harsh approach by an authoritarian professor works best and that a good teacher is an inconsiderate teacher. For the conscious learning modes (1) and (2) this may be correct – attention will be guaranteed by the threat of punishment – but unconscious learning will not work that way. Students are hardly likely to identify with teachers they do not like. When the teacher as a person is rejected, identification will be impossible and the entire mode of identification learning will be excluded.

To be more systematic about this I will describe the five basic variables in the student-teacher relationships:

1. The emotional attitude of the student to the teacher.
   – positive, neutral or negative.

2. The size of the teacher-personification in the student's social panorama.
   – bigger, equal to or smaller than the self.

3. Distance from student to teacher-personification.
   – near, at some distance or far away.

4. The size of the student's self-image.
   – bigger, equal to or smaller than the teacher.

5. The distance to the student's self-image.
   – near, at some distance or far away.

These five variables will help us to understand some crucial things about the role of relationships in education.

8.6.4 The emotional attitude of the student to the teacher

When a student loves the teacher, nothing will get in the way of their identifying with the teacher's behavioural examples. A trainer who is liked by the participants will see his or her demonstrations immediately reproduced in the exercises. If students don't like their teacher, they will not follow his or her example. They will not want to be like him or her, and they will resist

identification with a 'wrong', 'unethical' or 'evil' example; they may even counter-identify. The teacher will notice that the students do exercises 'in their own way', if at all. Some will show great creativity in inventing counter-examples and reasons why the teacher's ideas are wrong.

However, counter-identification learning must still be highly valued. Why? Because most progress in science comes from students who counter-identified with their authoritarian professors. New and creative hypotheses have come from trying to prove them wrong. Only an elite of great and totally independent spirits make themselves hated on purpose, to force their students to think for themselves.

8.6.5   The size of the teacher personification

The status of a person may result from many 'power sources' (Chapter 4). Celebrity status, money, dominant behaviour and the power to reward or punish are among the most common of these. Of course, how a teacher is represented in the social panorama of a student depends primarily on what the student considers important. Even if the teacher is a superstar or has a licence to kill, that must still impress the students if they are to put the teacher in a dominant location in his or her social panorama.

If the student sees the teacher as large it will increase the chances that the student will identify with him or her. If trainers are represented in a dominant fashion they will have great impact – as long as the students like them. Everyone will want to be like the trainer; wear his type of clothes, drive their brand of car, eat their sort of food and even do the exercises just the way they demonstrated them.

However, dominance combined with a negative emotional attitude will provoke the student to resist identification. For that, the students may arm themselves with very strong self-images; if their self-images are stronger than their representations of the teacher the students are safe. As a result the students will act with great self-confidence, which to the teacher, will appear as a combination of stupidity and arrogance. In such cases the power struggle between student and teacher will be a guarantee of lively teaching sessions.

8.6.6   *The distance from student to teacher personification*

We have reason to believe that the mental effort it takes to identify increases with the subjective distance at which a personification is experienced. If the teacher is seen close by, identification will be easy; the student will hop in and out of the teacher with small hops and identification will be a smooth, entirely unconscious process.

We already mentioned the tendency to protect one's integrity by means of placing dominant personifications at a great distance (Chapter 4). Students with small, negative or disrupted self-images may put dominant teachers at a great distance in their social panorama to avoid feeling submissive.

Some charismatic teachers (gurus) are admired, represented as being very dominant, and also actively support their students' self esteem, but they are too holy or mighty to be represented at close range. If such a guru is seen very far away, identification is nearly impossible, but the students' intake and storage of the behavioural examples offered by the guru will be great and the assimilation of information (learning mode 1) will be optimal. Students may memorise every utterance and expression of such a guru, but they will only be able to reproduce this knowledge in the form of citations: 'What he said was … and then he looked like that … he responded by saying …' The students will never ever reproduce this wisdom as if were it their own. As soon as the guru loses face and is pulled down from his pedestal all learning can at once be forgotten.

Charismatic trainers, who are represented too far away to be identified with, will never be short of work. Their students will never fully learn what they are taught because no identification occurs – they will always have to come back for more.

8.6.7   *The size of the student's self-image*

If a student has self-confidence, their self-image will be positive, stable and prominent and they will not automatically be overpowered by dominant teacher-personifications. They will be able to choose which of the teacher's behaviours they want to identify with, and we may expect a delay between the storage of the behavioural examples and the moment of identification, which will be absent in students with weak self-images. If such students happen to like the teacher they will be influenced immediately and will also pick up the teacher's irrelevant behavioural patterns. They may be quite dogmatic in following his examples.

Trainers and teachers have a great impact on the strength of their participants' self-esteem. If they have made them insecure and uncertain, they will have more influence as a role model, especially if they are still liked. A confrontational trainer who raises uncertainty in the participants may, of course, lose some of their regard, which will reduce the tendency of the participants to identify with them. The trainer will see little effect of their examples and this may cause an even more confrontational style that decreases identification even more.

8.6.8   Peer learning

Trainers often overestimate their own influence and underestimate the influence of peers. This may change when they are confronted with a group of students who show systematic aberrations from the examples offered by the teacher when tested on their practical skills. If all students make the same mistakes, these have probably been introduced by popular peers. The influence of the 'near peer' is great because they are easy to identify with.

When a peer is represented as insignificant in someone's social panorama (small and far off) identification learning will not take place, even if they are a great performer.

8.7   Team-building with the social panorama

Having been a mountaineer for over 30 years, I have come across pairs of very good friends who started to really hate each other in the mountains. Selfishness over limited food stocks, dangerous and unresponsive behaviour, alcohol, competition for women and stupidity caused by altitude sickness and exhaustion have been reasons for breaking up some of my own climbing friendships. I began to understand why some mountain accidents are suspected of actually being murder.

From this I have concluded that outdoor training activities cannot be guaranteed to bring people together. However much I love being out in nature, I am still rather sceptical about outdoor team-building programmes.

The reason I started the section in this way is to confront you with the essence of what the social panorama can mean in the field of team enhancement. Having participants undergo a certain set of group tasks is often mistaken for team-building. To build a team you must change the team members' minds about one another. In my opinion, many team-builders focus on programmes, activities and exercises but fail to see what teams are made of.

A TEAM IS A SET OF INTERACTING SOCIAL PANORAMAS

A team is created in the social panoramas of the individual team members. People's images of the other members in relation to themselves constitutes the team. In this book we will call these individual images 'team panoramas'. There are many abstractions in use about teams – team spirit, team culture, team interaction rules – they all spring from the same source, individual team panoramas influenced by other individual team panoramas.

So if we are confronted with a lousy team, we must assume that the social panoramas of the team members contain the elements that make the team that way.

FROM CURRENT TO DESIRED TEAM PANORAMAS

From my point of view, a team-building training must be directed towards restructuring the team members' team panoramas, which will engender feelings of togetherness, shared responsibility, loyalty and unity in all of them. In addition, as a result of such training, team members must find more enjoyment and pride in being part of the team. They should also be additionally motivated to put effort into maintaining a safe and productive atmosphere in the team.

The social skills required to work in a team should be already present in all team members before the training starts; any member who does not possess them will need individual counselling as part of the team improvement programme.

So we could say that a team-building project must lead the individual team members from the team panorama they have at present to their 'desired state' team panorama. What is the most efficient way to get them there?

As I have said earlier in this book, I prefer to change representations rather than interaction patterns. I see interactions as the result of social representations; it makes very little sense to teach people to say the right things if they still have negative images of one another.

So again: What is the most efficient way to change the social representations of team members?

WHAT DOESN'T WORK?
It is a naive idea to think that just getting team members round the table will do the job. Even if a team spends time in a luxurious resort with well-led and structured meetings, it will not necessarily improve their relationships. Conflicts often get worse when the parties are given time to develop them. The very setting of the resort may cause new conflicts, too – competition for rooms, waitresses or tennis courts may lead to more trouble that can come to a head late at night in the bar when the trainers are asleep. Moreover, interpersonal confrontations within large gatherings do not solve anything. If any interpersonal conflict was ever solved within a large group setting, it will have taken a lot of time and sheer luck. Conflicts between two people are best resolved between the two of them – possibly assisted by a consultant or mediator – but not in public. An arena is for fighting, not for resolving conflicts. Confrontations in front of groups tend to give rise to further polarisation. The audience is forced to take sides,

and they will both simplify and exaggerate the differences between the parties involved.

Putting the members of the team-to-be-built together in one room round a table is only effective if there are no conflicts at play, so, before designing any type of group team-building programme, it is absolutely necessary to make an in-depth conflict assessment.

Besides being aware of conflicts, a trainer needs to know the individual team members' motivation for being part of the team. Do they really want to become better members of that team?

It is often only the enthusiasm of management that carries a programme. It is worth remembering that if the management needs your help to improve a team, it means that they could not accomplish it themselves and this is often because management is not sufficiently in touch with their workers. They hope that a trainer will do the job for them. But leaving it to someone else often just turns people against their management. Before you know it, a team will find cohesion in criticising the management and that leads to a polarisation between management and workers – and will engender a very unproductive type of team spirit. If the management loses ground in the team members' social panorama, a team-building may do more harm than good to an organisation, even if the team itself may be empowered by it.

Often the trainer is seen as somebody who works for the management. When such a trainer puts the team members into a number of unpleasant, exhausting and utterly dangerous situations, they may well be seen as an 'executioner' in the service of the management. The team members will probably put the trainer on the same location as the management already occupied in their social panoramas, and will start openly to do what they cannot do with management – rebel. However good a trainer may be, if they are seen as 'someone who gets paid by the boss to manipulate us' they will not be very effective.

All this ground must be cleared to make things work. A team-building trainer needs to talk to as many individual participants as possible before designing the programme.

When they invite you to become their team-building trainer, the management will most often expect you to conduct a series of group activities and not a number of individual coaching sessions, but the latter may be the best thing to offer them. As everyone knows, superior products are sometimes the most difficult to sell.

Some team members have great influence on team panoramas; with individual coaching sessions you can get those people to change their panoramas first. As soon as they have an improved team panorama, these influential members can be stimulated to talk about it to the less influential members. A little individual training in how to use social panoramic language and group dynamic metaphors will help them to do the job. They will then spread the news on the wings of their social power. This kind of natural attitude change is probably the most elegant approach to team enhancement.

The identification and involvement of the leaders of the teams' social opinions may lead to short cuts in the process of team-building.

An experienced coach can be an effective team-builder with this book in one hand and a stack of classical NLP techniques in the other. Aided by these tools the coach will resolve traumas, reduce conflict and mistrust and enhance motivation by means of individual coaching. The coach will only bring the team together after the air is cleared and when spirits are high. Goal-directed coaching is probably the most effective preparation for a group session in team-building. Here is a brief outline of the steps to be taken.

Technique 57: Individual team-building

Indication: Team houses conflicts and negative relations

This outline provides guidance for working with individual team members in preparation for group activities.

Part One: Check the team members' motivation

1. Do you want to take part in the team?
2. Do you believe the organisational structure makes sense?

3. Are you involved in conflicts that go beyond the limits of the team, conflicts with the management, for instance?
4. Do you have any objections to the team, its people or the way it is organised?
5. Do you have any negative feelings about team-building as such?

When all objections are resolved, move on to formulate a clear personal outcome for the team member. 'What do you want team improvement to bring for you personally?' Put this in the near future on his personal timeline (see James and Woodsmall, 1988).

Go on with your coaching until each team member is congruent about their investment in the team and its future. Once all this is clear, proceed with the following steps.

Part Two: Coaching towards a desired team panorama

1. Ask for an experience of strong team spirit from the team members' life, preferably an experience that is not connected with the current team.
   Have the person explore the social panorama belonging to this experience of strong team spirit. Draw it on a piece of paper.

2. Ask for a typical experience of being involved in the current team. Then ask the team member to step into their present-state team panorama. Explore how they experience it. Ask them to draw this team panorama, too.

3. Ask the team member to fantasise about how the team should be built. Make use of the team explored in step one as an example of strong team spirit. Where would you have to see the other team members to enable you to feel team spirit? Ask the team member to associate in this desired state team panorama, and check it emotionally. Ask them to draw this new social panorama.

4. Now you have three drawings of team panoramas: a) a reference for strong team spirit, b) a present-state team panorama, and c) a desired state team panorama.
   Next you use the techniques from this book (mainly Chapter 5 and 6) to help to change the present-state team panorama into the desired state team panorama. Contrast the reference for strong team spirit with the present state to find the needed resources.

Repeat this approach with all relevant team players

This 'straight' approach will end as soon as all individual team members have overcome their mistrust and hatred. For some of them you may need to change limiting beliefs (Technique 17), empower self-esteem (Chapters 3 and 4) or resolve traumatic experiences from early childhood. Whatever is necessary for that, do it and it will pay off.

Using the Kweekel approach

Wim Kweekel is a distinguished team-builder in the Netherlands. In an extensive interview with him, he argued that the best team-building approach focuses strictly on the job, the team's tasks – it turns their work into an exercise. Kweekel is very directive in getting the team members to plan their future work down to the last detail, leaving no room for uncertainty. He believes that if everyone knows exactly what to do, many interpersonal problems will automatically be resolved. To create the optimal certainty, the team has to commit themselves to a work-plan that takes them months, or even years, into the future. They need to decide exactly who will complete which task and when and everything is written down on special worksheets. Kweekel himself returns regularly to check the progress of the team in the execution of the plans and meetings are held when deadlines are missed. In his very effective team-building approach he makes no mention of any other social engineering. 'They do what they are paid to do, and in the role that suits them'. For Wim Kweekel the social panorama is irrelevant.

However, any trainers and consultants who want to intervene more on the social-emotional level will find three techniques for that purpose on the pages ahead.

Technique 58: Building a team

Indication: Lacking spontaneity and intimacy

Clear a room of furniture. Invite the team to come in. Hand each member a sheet of paper. Tell the team to explore together what the smallest number of sheets is, on which the whole team can stand. (No further questions must be answered.)

This exercise introduces physical closeness as a way to deepen group feelings. It also provides a diagnostic tool: individuals who cannot share the group feelings will refuse to take part in such an exercise.

Technique 59: Team panorama exploration in a group session

Indication: Team members need insight in their relations

This technique was first carried out in 1996, but it comes close to the creation of 'sociograms' as they were developed in the sixties on the basis of the Social Field Theory of Kurt Lewin (1951). The second part of the procedure is based on Bert Hellinger's (1996) method, except that here no representatives are used. This approach tends to be highly confrontational, so it is prudent only to use it with groups and teams where there are no conflicts. Groups can be occupied in this way from 15 minutes up to two hours, depending on their involvement in the team. On all levels it is a very useful diagnostic tool. Observe how a group performs this task and you will know your next step of intervention.

Part One: On paper

In 1996, I gave them all a piece of paper and told them to draw a small circle in the middle of it. 'This circle represents you,' I said, 'draw your nose upwards. Now close your eyes and think of all the people in the world as they surround you. Visualise those members of the team that are relevant to you. Who are they? Where do you see them? How far away? Are they to your left or your right? Now, make a drawing that shows how you experience the positions of these team members in relation to yourself.

An example on a flip chart clarified a lot, but some participants still needed assistance. Eventually everyone had made some representation of his or her experience of the team. Everyone showed the direction of gaze by the direction in which the nose was pointing. Only the vertical dimension was missing but we found a solution for that, too. It was very simple; people who were seen as higher or lower were marked with a little arrow, upwards or downwards. The length of these arrows showed how far up or down a person was seen.

Next, everyone was instructed to draw the same team, but this time, as they would like it to be. If they wanted to, they could also explain why the changes were needed.

Part Two: In flesh and blood

After all the participants had done this I asked them to take their drawings to another room. Here there were chairs placed against the walls and everyone sat down on one of them. 'It looks just like a teenage dancing party,' one person commented.

One member, Astrid, was chosen to bring her social panorama to life by getting the real team members to stand and sit according to the spatial configuration of her first drawing, the one of the current state of affairs. She moved people around for a while until their positions matched her drawing. She ended up with two members standing on tables, one of them lying on the ground and another one kneeling.

Finally Astrid sat down on a chair in the middle, her own spot, and checked if everything looked right. She seemed satisfied; 'This is how it all feels to me,' she said. Not much comment was needed, since everyone could easily give his or her own interpretation to this landscape.

Towards improvement

Next, Astrid picked up her second drawing. By moving some people and chairs, and having some sit down, she was able to show everyone how she preferred things to be. Some people she wanted closer, while others had to move from the right to the left.

I allowed some time for them to discuss what would be needed to make these changes happen in reality. Repeating this process with another team member clarified even more the needs within the team.

Technique 60: Taming the dragon

Indication: If the team feels threatened by outside forces

In another team-building training a group version of Technique 7 was developed. A volunteer, one of the more stable elements of the team, wore a dragon's head that was made out of a flipchart sheet with eyes drawn on it. He adopted the role of symbolic dragon, representing every outsider who threatened the functioning and well being of the team. (A particular highly placed executive seemed to be seen as the real threat.)

The taming pattern

1. Verbal abreaction
    The team was placed in a wide circle round the dragon and everyone was given the opportunity to express his or her aggression verbally to the dragon. It was stressed to everyone that this dragon represented a person outside the room.

2. Positive intentions.
    All explored what they thought the dragon's positive intentions might be. 'What is he trying to accomplish by this dragon-like behaviour?'

3. Lacking resources
    Each team member explored on his own what qualities the dragon-person lacked. 'What resources does the dragon need in order to be able to act agreeably and effectively?'

4. Activation of these resources
    Now the whole team was asked to direct their attention inwards and find an example of a time when they possessed and used these resources. Once an example had been identified, the suggestion was given to associate fully with this example and relive it as intensely as possible.
    Next they were asked to imagine that these resources were something you could put in your hand and make into balls. As soon as this was done the next step was introduced.

5. Transferring resources
    The group members were invited to throw their resources (balls) to the dragon, and see how these transformed it. In this way the dragon changed into something different.

Technique 61: Dreaming a team

Indication: To improve the climate in a training group or team

Sit down quietly. Create a meditative atmosphere by means of hypnotic language that goes like this:

'Orient yourself in the here and now. Feel your seat, your feet, your head on your neck ... Breathe slowly and deeply. Relax, listen to what

I say and listen, too, to the sound of the birds, the wind, the cars...
Listen to everything ... So, take a look around you and then close
your eyes and explore what you can still see of it in your mind's eye.
Who do you see around you in your memory image, what are they
wearing, how are they sitting? What colours, light and shade, movements, shapes ....

Now look at all the members of the team, as you see them inside your
head. Take your time.

Once you have observed the members of the team in your head,
open your eyes again and look at the real people here ... look around
... Is there any difference? Did you forget anybody? Who was closest
to you? Who was farthest away? Who is big, small, tiny or tall?

Close you eyes again, relax, and remember how you saw the team in
your head ... Well ... Some team members may have been far away
or forgotten. Take your time and put them in place, maybe bring them
closer to you. Make them clear and the right size for you. Maybe you
understand why some team members need to be kept at a distance?
Do you want to change that? Take your time .... (Pause)

You are dreaming about the team – what colour are the connections
between you and the other team members? Maybe it is coloured light
that binds you together. Look at the strongest bonds ... the weakest
bonds ... With whom would you like to connect more strongly?
Imagine that connection growing stronger ... (Pause). See how all the
members are connected together. Draw coloured lines between yourself and the others.

Now, fly above the team ... and see all these connections from above
... (Pause). Does it look right like this? Do you want some connections to be changed? Take your time ... (Pause).

Now feel free to find the best example of togetherness, camaraderie
and friendship from your life ... (Pause). Re-experience this situation.
Feel it again. Be there with those people again ... (Pause). Enjoy it
for a while ....

Keep this feeling inside you and float down into yourself, as you are
now, in the middle of this team.

Now, feel the strength of the new connections ... (Pause).

Step outside the team and see yourself in the middle of it from the side. What do you look like? Are you involved in the team? Does it look good to you? See yourself interacting with the other members from this distance.

Now place yourself in the position of one of the least influential members of the team. What do you see through his or her eyes? How do you think this person sees you ...? (Pause).

Leave this position and move towards the position of the most dominant team member; look through his or her eyes, see the team and look at yourself ... (Pause).

If necessary, move up members who are too far down, and push those who are too high a little downwards. Feel what is difficult about this. Feel what is good about it.

Float back into yourself. Is there anything more that you would like to improve in your picture of the team? Take your time to complete your picture, and ask yourself what this means for how you will communicate and get along with the other team members in the future. What problems must be solved? (Long pause).

Take your time to come back to the here and now and share, if you want to, what has happened in this dream.'

Postscript

My friend and colleague, Wolfgang Walker from Berlin, has applied the family panorama pattern with over 70 psychiatric patients (May 2004). He also claims that in many cases this has improved his clients' lives. That is great news! The enthusiasm of workers in the field is the best promotion for a tool like the social panorama. It helps me every day in my own work with clients and I cannot imagine how I could work without it.

For me personally it is a stream of surprising new insights that has fuelled my motivation to move on with this long-term project.

However, writing a book like this seems a never-ending story. One can always improve on every sentence or consider changing the whole concept. It can be more scientific, more a casebook or more narrative …. But it is just what it is: The first book on the subject ever to see the light of day.

It took 10 years from the invention of the term 'social panorama' to this English edition and I have to admit that every step was hard. But having been a mountaineer for most of my life, I know that a summit that has had to be bitterly battled for is the one that is most marvellous.

I have led you up the mountain of this text but even the best of guides cannot carry a climber to the summit and back. If you have reached this high point with me, I congratulate you. You followed in my steps, but it was you who kept on placing one foot in front of the other until you reached the summit, this last page.

Bibliography

Abram, D., 1997, *The Spell of the Sensuous,* Vintage Books, Random House, New York.

Abrams, R., 1999, *When Parents Die: Learning to Live with the Loss of a Parent*, Routledge, East Sussex, England.

Adorno, T. W., Frenkel-Brunswik, E., Levinson, D. J., and Sanford, R. M., 1950, *The Authoritarian Personality*, Harper, New York.

Ahsen, A., 1968, *Basic Concepts in Eidetic Psychotherapy*, Random House, New York.

Ahsen, A., and Lazarus, A. A., 1972, Eidetics: An Internal Behaviour Approach. In: Lazarus, A. A., *Clinical Behavior Therapy*, Brunner Mazel, New York.

Akstein, D., 1991, *Un voyage a travers la transe: La Terpsichore-Transe-Thérapie*, Editions Sand, Paris.

Allport, G. W., 1954, *The Nature of Prejudice*, Addison-Wesley, Reading, MA.

Alstadt, D., and Kramer J., 1993, *The Guru Papers: Marks of Authoritarian Power*, Frog Press, Berkeley.

Andreas, S., 2001, Building Self-Concept, *Anchor Point*, July 2001, Vol. 15, No. 7.

Andreas, S., and Andreas, C., 1989, *Heart of the Mind*, Real People Press, Moab, Utah.

Andreas, S., Faulkner, C., and McDonald, R., 1994, *NLP: The New Technology of Achievement*, William Morrow, New York.

Andreas, T., and Andreas, C., 1994, *Core Transformation: Reaching the Wellspring Within*, Real People Press, Moab, Utah.

Augoustinos, M., and Innes, J. M., 1990, Towards an integration of social representations and social schema theory. In: *British Journal of Social Psychology*, 29, 213–31.

Baars, B. J., 1983, Conscious Content Provide the Nervous System with Coherent, Global Information. In: Davidson, G., Schwarz, G., and Shapiro; *Consciousness and Self Regulation: Advances in Research and Theory*, Vol. III, Plenum Press, New York.

Bailey, D., 1997, *Computational Model of Embodiment in the Acquisition of Action Verbs*, PhD dissertation.

Bakan, P., 1978, *Two Streams of Consciousness: A Typological Approach.* In: Pope, K., and Singer, J. (eds.), *The Stream of Consciousness*, Plenum Press, New York.

Baker, R., and Oram, E., 1998, *The Great Baby Wars*, Fourth Estate Limited, London.

Baldwin, J. M., 1987, *Social and Ethical Interpretations in Mental and Social Development*, Macmillan, New York.

Ballif, B., 1981, *The Significance of the Self-Concept in the Knowledge Society.* In: Lynch, M., and Norem-Hebeisen, A., Computer Science Division, EECS department, University of California, Berkeley.

Bandler, R., 1985, *Using Your Brain for a Change*, Real People Press, Moab, Utah.

Bandler, R., and Grinder, J., 1975a, *Patterns of the Hypnotic Techniques of Milton H. Erickson, MD, Part 1,* Meta Publications, Cupertino, CA.

Bandler, R., and Grinder, J., 1975b, *The Structure of Magic I*, Science and Behavior Books, Palo Alto.

Bandler, R., and Grinder, J., 1979, *Frogs into Princes*, Real People Press, Moab, Utah.

Bandler, R., and Grinder, J., 1982, *Reframing: Neuro-Linguistic Programming and the Transformation of Meaning*, Real People Press, Moab, Utah.

Bandler, R., Grinder J., and Satir, V., 1976, *Changing With Families*, Science and Behavior Books, Inc., Palo Alto, CA.

Baron-Cohen, S., 1991, The Theory of Mind Deficit in Autism: How specific is it? In: *British Journal of Developmental Psychology*, 9, 301–314.

Bateson, G., 1972, *Steps to an Ecology of Mind*, Ballantine, New York.

Bateson, G., and Mead, M., 1942, *Balinese Character: A Photographic Analysis*, New York Academy of Sciences, New York.

Beahrs, J., 1982, *Unity and Multiplicity: Multilevel Consciousness of Self in Hypnosis*, Brunner Mazel, New York.

Bem, D. J., 1967, Self-Perception: An Alternative Interpretation of Dissonance Phenomena, *Psychological Review*, 74, 183–200.

Bertalanffy, L., 1968, *General Systems Theory*, Braziller, New York.

Bolstad, R., 2002, *Resolve: A New Model of Therapy*, Crown House Publishing Ltd, Carmarthen, Wales.

Bolstad, R., and Hamblett, M., 1999, The Unanswerable Question. In: *Anchor Point*, Vol. 13, No. 7, July 1999.

Bolstad, R., and Hamblett, M., 2001, Why the Moon Changes Size: The Neurology of Submodalities. In: *NLP World*, Vol. 8, No. 1.

Boon, S. and Draaijer, N., 1995, *Screening en diagnostiek van dissociatieve stoornissen*, Swets & Zeitlinger bv, Lisse.

Bostic St. Clair, C., and Grinder, J., 2001, *Whispering in the Wind*, J&C Enterprises, Scotts Valley, California.

Boszormenyi-Nagy, I., 1987, *Foundation of Contextual Therapy: Collected Papers of Ivan Boszormenyi-Nagy*, Brunner Mazel, New York.

Bourguignon, E., 1968, World Distribution and Patterns of Possession States. In: Prince, R. (ed.), *Trance and Possession States*, R. M. Bucke Memorial Society, Montreal.

Braun, B., 1986, *Treatment of Multiple Personality Disorder*, American Psychiatric Press, New York.

Brown, R., 1988, *Group Processes*, Blackwell, Oxford.

Burgoon, J., 1991, Relational message interpretations of touch, conversational distance, and posture. In: *Journal of Nonverbal Behavior*, Vol. 15, 4, 1991.

Cameron-Bandler, L., 1978, *And They Lived Happily Ever After*, substantially revised as *Solutions*, 1985, Real People Press, Moab, Utah.

Cameron-Bandler, L. and Lebeau, M., 1986, *The Emotional Hostage: Rescuing Your Emotional Life*, Future Pace, San Rafael, CA.

Campbell, J., 1964, *The Masks of God*, Viking, Penguin Books, New York.

Chekhov, M., 1953, *To the Actor*, Harper & Row, New York.

Chen, M., and Bargh, J., 1997, Nonconscious behavioural conformation processes: The self-fulfilling consequence of automatic stereotype activation, *Journal of Experimental and Social Psychology*, 33, 541–560.

Cipoletti, M. S., 1989, *Langsamer Abschied; Tod und Jenseits im Kulturvergleich*, Museum fuer Voelkerkunde, Frankfurt am Main.

Social Panoramas

Cladder, H., 2000, *Oplossingsgerichte korte psychotherapie*, Swets & Zeitlinger, Lisse.

Cladder, H., 2001, Metenweten. In: *De Eekhoorn*, negende jaargang, nummer 2, maart 2001.

Cotkin, G., 1990, *William James and Psychological Discourse of Heroism*, Lezing op het Principles Congress 1990, William James Foundation, Amsterdam.

De Shazer, S., 1989, *Wege de erfolgreiche Kurztherapie*, Stuttgart, Klett-Cotta.

Dekkers, M., 1997, *De Beste Beesten 2*, Uitgeverij Contact, Amsterdam.

DeLozier, J., and Grinder, J., 1987, *Turtles All the Way Down: Prerequisites to Personal Genius*, Bonny Doon, California.

Demer, M., and Pyszczynski, T., 1978, Effects of erotica upon men's loving and liking responses for women they love. In: *Journal of Personality and Social Psychology*, 1978, 36, 1302–1309.

Derks, L., 1984, *Geheime Psychologie; een theoretische basis voor de therapeimethode van Bandler en Grinder*, William James Foundation, Amsterdam.

Derks, L., 1988, *Creativiteitsmanagement. IEP publicaties, Nijmegen.* Later: SON Repro service, Eindhoven.

Derks, L., 1989, *Psychotherapie een kwestie van wennen*, William James Foundation, Amsterdam.

Derks, L., 1992, *De Postume Colleges van Herman Blaas.* In de Knipscheer, Amsterdam.

Derks, L., 1995, Exploring the Social Panorama. In: *NLP World*, Vol. 2, No. 3, 28–42, November 1995.

Derks, L., 1996, Teambuilding met het Sociaal Panorama. In: *NVNLP informatiebullitin*, November 1996.

Derks, L., 1997a, Family Systems in the Social Panorama. In: *NLP World*, Vol. 4, No. 1, March 1997.

Derks, L., 1997b, Personifikaatio ihmisten keskeisessa kanssakaymisessa. In: *NLP Mielilehti*, N:0 2/97, Finland.

Derks, L., 1998a, *Gedachtenmonsters: Gesprekken over de beleving van bodemverontreiniging*, Rapporten Programma Geintegreerd Bodemonderzoek, Deel 18, Wageningen.

366

Derks, L., 1998b, Families in the Social Panorama. In: *Anchor Point*, Vol. 12, No. 2, February 1998.

Derks, L., 1998c, *The Social Panorama Model: Social Psychology meets NLP*, SON Repro Service, Eindhoven.

Derks, L., 1998d, *De Levenlijn*, Son Reproservice, Eindhoven.

Derks, L., 1999a, Perheet The Social Panorama Mallissa. In: *NLP Mielilehti*, 2, 1999, Finland.

Derks, L., 1999b, *Spoken in de kop; de sociaal panorama gids*, Son repro service, Eindhoven.

Derks, L., 2000a, Das Soziale Panorama bei Verhandlungen: NLP-Friedensgesprache. In: *Multi Mind*, 6, 9, 2000.

Derks, L., 2000b, Iedereen is voor een schone bodem. In: Bodem, tijdschrift voor duurzaam bodembeheer, jaargang 10, nummer 4, augustus 2000, Samson bv, Alphen aan de Rijn.

Derks, L., 2000c, De verkenning van het spirituele panorama. In: *Inzicht*, nummer 5, zomer 2000.

Derks, L., 2000d, *Das Spiel sozialer Beziehungen; NLP und die Structur zwischenmenschlicher Erfahrung*, Klett-Cotta, Stuttgart.

Derks, L., 2002, *Sociale Denkpatronen: en het veranderen van onbewust social gedrag*, Servire, Utrecht.

Derks, L., 2003, Alien Lessons, *Anchor Point*, Vol. 17, No. 5, May 2003.

Derks, L., and Goldblatt, R., 1985, *The Feedforward Conception of Consciousness: A Bridge between Therapeutic Practice and Experimental Psychology*, The William James Foundation, Amsterdam.

Derks, L., and Hollander, J., 1996a, *Essenties van NLP*, Utrecht, Servire.

Derks, L., and Hollander, J., 1996b, Exploring the Spiritual Panorama. In: *NLP World*, Vol. 3, No. 2, July 1996.

Derks, L., and Hollander, J., 1998, Systemic Voodoo. In: *Anchor Point*, Vol. 12, No. 3, March 1998.

Derks, L., and Sinclair, J. D., 1990, *Racing the Turbo Brain*, William James Foundation, Amsterdam.

Derks, L., and Sinclair, J. D., 2000, Expanding the Neuro in NLP, *NLP World*, Vol. 7, No. 2, July 2000.

Devine, P. G., 1989, Stereotypes and Prejudice: Their automatic and controlled components, *Journal of Personality and Social Psychology*, 56, 5–18.

Diener, E., 1980, Deindividuation: the absence of self-awareness and self-regulation in group members. In: P. B. Paulus (ed.), *Psychology of Group Influence*, Erlbaum, Hillsdale, NJ, 209–42.

Dilts, R., 1990, *Changing Belief Systems with NLP*, Meta Publications, Cupertino, California.

Dilts, R., and DeLozier, J., 2000, *Encyclopedia of Systemic Neuro-Linguistic Programming and NLP New Coding*, NLP University Press, Santa Cruz, California.

Dilts, R., and Epstein, T., 1989, *NLP in Training Groups*, Dynamic Learning Publications, Santa Cruz, California.

Dilts, R., and McDonald, R., 1996, *Tools of the Spirit*, Meta Publications, Cupertino, California.

Dilts, R., Hallbom, T., and Smith, S., 1990, *Beliefs: Pathways to Health and Well-Being*, Metamorphous Press, Portland, Oregon.

Duba, R. M., 2000, *Links-rechts aandacht patron*, Cursus materiaal in de SETH hypnose opleiding.

Edelstein, M. G., 1981, *Trauma, Trance and Tranceformation*, Brunner Mazel, New York.

Ellis, A., 1973, *Humanistic Therapy: The Rational Emotive Approach*, McGraw Hill, New York.

Erickson, M. H., 1967, *Advanced Techniques of Hypnosis and Therapy*, Selected papers, edited by Haley, J. Grune & Stratton, Inc., Orlando, Florida.

Erickson, M. H., and Rossi E. L., 1983, *Exploraties in Hypnotherapie*, Van Loghem Slaterus bv, Deventer.

Erickson, M. H., Rossi, E. L., and Rossi, S. I., 1976, *Hypnotic Realities: The Induction of Clinical Hypnosis and Forms of Indirect Suggestion*, Irvington Publishers, New York.

Evarts, E. V., 1967, Mind Activity-Sleep and Wakefulness. In: Quartor, G.C., Melnechuk, J., and Schmitt, O. (eds.), *The Neuro Science Study Program*, Rockefeller University Press, New York.

Fauconnier, G., 1997, *Mappings in Thought and Language*, Cambridge University Press, New York.

Fauconnier, G, and Turner, M., 2002, *The Way We Think: Conceptual Blending and the Mind's Hidden Complexities*, Basic Books, New York.

Faulkner, C., 1994, *Metaphors of Identity: Operating Metaphors & Iconic Change*, 3 audio cassettes, Genesis II, www.AchievingExcellence.com.

Ferguson, M., 1990, *Book of PragMagic: Pragmatic magic for everyday living*, Pocket Books, New York.

Fernando, S., 2003, *Cultural Diversity, Mental Health and Psychiatry: The Struggle Against Racism*, Brunner-Routledge, Hove, Sussex, England.

Fiske, S. T., and Taylor, S. E., 1991, *Social Cognition*, McGraw-Hill, New York.

Fitzgerald, M., 2003, *Autism and Creativity: Is there a link between autism in men and exceptional ability?*, Brunner-Routledge, Hove, Sussex, England.

Flanagan, B., 1999, Logical Levels and Systemic NLP by Wyatt Woodsmall. Letter in: *NLP World*, Vol. 6, No. 2, July 1999.

Folette, V. M., Ruzek, J. I., and Abeug, F. R., 1999, *Cognitive-Behavioral Therapies for Trauma*, Guilford Press, East Sussex, England.

Frijda, N., 1986, *The Emotions*, Cambridge University Press, Cambridge.

Fuller Torrey, E., 1975, *De Dood van de Psychiatrie*, Bert Bakker, Den Haag.

Fuller Torrey, E., 1986, *Witchdoctors and Psychiatrists*, Harper and Row, New York.

Gergen, K. J., 1998, *The Saturated Self: Dilemmas of identity in contemporary life*, Basic Books, HarperCollins Publishers, USA.

Gershon, M., 1998, *The Second Brain*, HarperCollins, New York.

GGZ Nederland, 2001, *Aktieplan Intercuturalisatie Implementatievoorstel 2001*, Postbus 8400, 3503 RK, Utrecht.

Giel, R., 1978, *Vreemde Zielen: Een sociaal psychiatrische verkenning van andere culturen*, Boom, Assen.

Glaudemans, W., 2002, *Het Wonder van Vergeving*, Uitgeverij Ankh-Hermes bv, Deventer.

Goleman, D., 1996, *Emotional Intelligence: Why it Can Matter More Than IQ*, Bantam, New York.

Greene, R., and Elffers, J., 1998, *The 48 Laws of Power*, Penguin Putnam, London.

Greenspan, S. I., 1997, *The Growth of the Mind and the Endangered Origins of Intelligence*, Nederlandse vertaling: (1998) De Ontwikkeling van Intelligentie. Uitgeverij Contact, Amsterdam.

Grinder, J., 1998, Key Note lecture, DGNLP kongress 1998, Bad Neuheim, Duitsland.

Grinder, J., and Bandler, R., 1976, *The Structure of Magic Vol II*, Science and Behavior Books Inc., Palo Alto, CA.

Grinder, J., and Bandler, R., 1981, *Trance-Formations: Neuro-Linguistic Programming and the Structure of Hypnosis*, Real People Press, Moab, Utah.

Grochowiak, K., 1996, *Da NLP-practitioner Handbuch, 2. Auflage*, Junfermann, Paderborn.

Grove, D., 1998, The Philosophy and Principles of Clean Language, talk given at the Clean Language Research Day in London, 13 November 1998.

Grove, D. J., and Panzer, B., 1989, *Resolving Traumatic Memories: Metaphors and Symbols in Psychotherapy*, Irvington, New York.

Gunn, J., 1991, Human Violence: A biological perspective. In: *Journal of Criminal Behavior and Mental Health*, Vol. 1.

Haley, J., 1976, *Problem Solving Therapy: New Strategies for Effective Family Therapy*, Jassey-Bass, Inc. Publishers, San Francisco.

Hall, E. T., 1966, *The Hidden Dimension*, Doubleday, New York.

Hall, M., 1996, *Dragon Slaying: Dragons to Princes*, E. T. Publications, Grand Junction, Colorado.

Hall, L. M. and Bodenhamer, B.G., 1999, *The Structure of Excellence: Unmasking the Meta-Levels of Submodalities*, E. T. Publications, Grand Junction, Colorado.

Hancock, G., 1995, *Fingerprints of the Gods*, Heinemann, London.

Hanson, J. L., 1995, *Invisible Patterns: Ecology and Wisdom in Business and Profit*, Quorum Books, Westport, Connecticut, London.

Hart, van der O., 1991, *Trauma, Dissociatie en Hypnose*, Swets & Zeitlinger, Amsterdam.

Heider, F., 1958, *The Psychology of Interpersonal Relations*, Wiley, New York.

Hellinger, B., 1995, *Ordnungen der Liebe; Ein Kurs-Buch von Bert Hellinger*, Carl Auer Verlag, Heidelberg.

Hellinger, B., and Beaumont H., 1998, *Love's Hidden Symmetry. What makes love work in relationsships*, Zeig, Tucker & Co, Phoenix, Arizona.

Hermans, J. M., 1988, On the integration of idiographic and nomothetic research method in the study of personal meaning, *Journal of Personality*, 56, 785–812.

Hermans, J. M., 1990, *The Significance of William James for Modern Self-Psychology*, Lezing op het 1990, Principles Congress, William James Foundation, Amsterdam.

Hilgard, E., 1977, *Divided Consciousness*, Wiley, New York.

Hoenderdos, H. T. W., 1994, *Toepassing van Veranderingstechnieken*, Stichting voor Hypno-, Gedrgas en Verbaaltherapie, Velserbroek.

Hoffmann, G. L., 2001, *Beyond the Reality Principle of Convention*, Eigen publicatie binnen Avatar, Zwitserland.

Hogg, M., and Vaughan, G. M., 1995, *Social Psychology: An Introduction*, Prentice Hall/Harvester Wheatsheaf, Hemel Hempstead.

Hollander, J., 1997, *Trance & Magic*, Becht, Haarlem.

Hollander, J., 1999, NLP and Science: Six recommendations for a better relationship. In: *NLP World*, Volume 6, No. 3, November 1999.

Hollander J., Derks, L., and Meijer, A., 1990, *NLP in Nederland*, Servire, Utrecht.

Hollander, J., Derks, L., and Tanebaum, B., 1996, The Modelling of Magic. In: *NLP World*, Vol. 3, No. 3, November 1996.

Hubble, M. A., Duncan, B. L., and Miller, S. D., 1999, *The Heart & Soul of Change: What works in Psychotherapy*, American Psychological Association, Washington, DC.

Isert, B., and Rentel, K., 2000, *Wurzeln der Zukunft; Lebensweg-Arbeit, Aufstellungen und systemische Veraenderung*, Junfermann, Paderborn.

Jacobson, S., 1986, *Meta-cation: New improved formulas for thinking about thinking*, Meta Publications, Cupertino.

James, T., and Woodsmall, W., 1988, *Time Line Therapy and the Basis of Personality*, Meta Publications, Cupertino, California.

James, W., 1890, *The Principles of Psychology*, Dover Publications, New York.

James, W., 1907, *Pragmatism: A New Name for Some Old Ways of Thinking*, Longmans, Green & Co, New York.

James, W., 1956 [1897], *The Will to Believe and Other Essays in Popular Philosophy*, Dover, New York.

James, W., 1961 [first edition 1902], *The Varieties of Religious Experience*, Collier Books, New York.

James, W., 1992, *De Hoofdsom van de Psychologie: Een Selectie uit de Principles of Psychology, samengesteld door Douwe Draaisma*, Swets & Zeitlinger bv, Amsterdam – Lisse.

Janet, P., 1889, *L'Automatisme Psychologique*, Felix Alcan, Parijs. Heruitgave: 1971, Societe Pierre Janet, Paris.

Jaynes, J., 1976, *The Origin of Consciousness in the Breakdown of the Bicameral Mind*, Houghton Muffin, Boston.

Jenner, K. D., and Wiegers, G. A., 1998, *Heilig boek en religiues gezag: ontstaan en functioneren van canonieke tradities*, Kok, Kampen.

Johnstone, K., 1979, *Impro: Improvisation and the Theatre*, Methuen Drama, London.

Kalma, A., 1991, Hierarchisation and dominance assessment at first glance. In: *European Journal of Social Psychology*, Vol. 21, 2, 1991.

Kampenhout, D. van, 2001, *Die Heilung kommt von ausserhalb; Schamanismus und Familien-stellen*, Carl-Auer-Systeme Verlag, Heidelberg.

Klass, D., 1999, *The Spiritual Lives of Bereaved Parents*, Brunner Mazel, London.

Klinger, E., 1978, Modes of Normal Conscious Flow. In: Pope, K. and Singer, J. L. (eds.), *The Stream of Consciousness*, Plenum Press, New York and London.

Koch, H., 1955, *The Relation of Certain Family Constellation Characteristics and the Attitude of Children towards Adults*, Child Development, 26, 13–40.

Koch, H., 1958, *Der Einfluss der Geschwister auf die Persönlichkeitsentwicklung Jüngere Knaben*, Jahrbuch Psychologie und Psychotherapie, 5, 211–225.

Koomen, W., 1992, Stereotypen en vooroordeel. In Meertens, R. W., and Grumbkow, J. von, (eds.) *Sociale Psychologie*, Wolters-Noordhoff, Groningen.

Krakauer, S. Y., 2000, *Treating Dissociative Identity Disorder*, Brunner Routledge, East Sussex, England.

Kunda, Z., 1999, *Social Cognition: Making Sense of People*, MIT Press, Cambridge, MA.

Kunda, Z., and Sinclair, L., 1999, *Motivated Reasoning with Stereotypes: Activation, Application and Inhibition*, Psychological Inquiry.

Lakoff, G., 1987, *Woman, Fire and Dangerous Things*, University of Chicago Press, Chicago.

Lakoff, G., and Johnson, M., 1980, *Metaphors We Live By*, University of Chicago Press, Chicago and London.

Lakoff, G., and Johnson, M., 1999, *Philosophy in the Flesh*, Basic Books, Perseus Book Group, New York.

Lamers, I., 2000, He, wie ben jij? Spel contact met autistische kinderen. In: Poel, L. (ed.), Spel Werkt. Sociale beroepen reeks 13, HvU Press, Utrecht.

Lange, A., 2000, *Gedragsverandering in Gezinnen*, Wolters Noordhoff, Groningen.

Lankton, S. R., and Lankton, C. H., 1983, *The Answer Within: A Clinical Framework of Ericksonian Hypnotherapy*, Brunner Mazel Publishers, New York.

Lawley, J., and Tompkins, P., 2000, *Metaphors in Mind: Transformation Through Symbolic Modeling*, The Developing Company Press, London.

Lawley, J., and Tompkins, P., 2003, Clean Space: Modeling Human Perception through Emergence, *Anchor Point*, Vol. 17, No. 8, September.

Lewin, K., 1951, *Field Theory in Social Science*, Harper and Row, New York.

Lewis, I. M., 1971, *Ecstatic Religion: A Study of Shamanism and Spirit Possession*, Routledge, London and New York.

Lewis, R. D., 1997, *When Cultures Collide: Managing Succesfully Across Cultures*, Nicholas Brealey Publishing, London.

Lewis, T., Amini, F., and Lannon, R., 2000, *A General Theory of Love*, Random House, New York.

Lorenz, K., 1961, *Evolution and Modification of Behavior*, Harvard University Press.

Mandell, A. J., 1980, Towards a Psycho-biology of Trancedence: God in the Brain. In: Davidson, J. M. and Davidson, R.J. (eds.), *The Psychobiology of Consciousness*, Plenum Press, New York.

Mandler, G., 1979, Thought Processes, Consciousness and Stress. In: Hamilton, V. and Warburton, D. M., *Human Stress and Cognition*, Wiley, New York.

Markus, H., Smith, J., and Moreland, R. L., 1985, Role of the Self-concept in the Perception of Others, *Journal of Personality and Social Psychology*, 49, 1494–1512.

Martin, L. L., and Clark, L. F., 1990, Social cognition: exploring the mental processes involved in human social interaction. In: M. W. Eysenck (ed.), *"Cognitive Psychology": An International Review*, Vol. 1, 266–310, Wiley, Sussex.

Matzken, R., 1995, *Met fantasie naar de nieuwe tijd*, Moria, Hilversum.

Matzken, R., 1996, *NLP in een Bijbels perspectief*, Amersfoortse studies, Amersfoort.

Mavromantis, A., 1987, *Hypnagogia: The Unique State of Consciousness Between Wakefulness and Sleep*, Routledge, New York.

McDonald, R., 1997, Brief Therapy: An Introduction to NLP and Emotional Transformation, Workshop handouts: 29, 30 & 31 oktober 1997, IEP, Nijmegen.

Mead, G. H., 1934, *Mind, Self and Society*, University Press of Chicago, Chicago.

Meertens, R. W., and Grumbkow, J. von, 1992, *Sociale Psychologie*, Wolters-Noordhoff, Groningen.

Merlevede, P., Bridoux, D., and Van Damme, R., 2001, *7 Steps to Emotional Intelligence*, Crown House Publishing Ltd, Carmarthen, Wales.

Mervis, C., 1984, Early Lexical Development: The Contribution of Mother and Child. In: Sophian, C. (ed.), *Origins of Cognitive Skills*, Erlbaum, Hillsdale, New York.

Minuchin, S., and Fishman, H. Ch., 1981, *Family Therapy Techniques*, Harvard University Press, Cambridge, Mass.

Mithen, Stephen, 1996, *The Prehistory of the Mind: The Cognitive Origins of Art, Religion and Science*, W. W. Norton, New York.

Mol, H., 1996, *NlsPel*, Son Repro, Eindhoven.

Mol, H., 1998, Kijk eens om je heen. Pesten en het Sociaal Panorama. In: Buys, O., and Poel, L., (eds.) Spel werkt. Sociale beroepen reeks 10, HvU Press, Utrecht.

Moreno, J. L., 1991, *Die Grundlagen der Soziometrie*, Westdeutscher Verlag.

Morris, B.G., 1992, Adolescent leaders: Rational thinking, future beliefs, temporal perspective, and other correlates. In: *Adolescence*, Vol. 27, 1992, 105.

Moscovici, S., 1983, The phenomenon of social representations. In: Farr, R. M., and Moscovici, S. (eds.), *Social Representation*, Cambridge University Press, Cambridge, 3–69.

Mulder, M., 1977, *Omgaan met macht: ons gedrag met elkaar en tegen elkaar*, Elsevier, Amsterdam.

Narayanan, S., 1997, *Embodiment in Language Understanding: Sensory-Motor Representations for Metaphoric Reasoning About Even Descriptions*, PhD Dissertation, Department of Computer Science, University of California, Berkeley.

O'Connor, J., and McDermott, I., 1997, *The Art of Systems Thinking*, Thorsons, Hammersmith, London.

Ostrom, T. M., 1989, *Three Catechisms for Social Memory.* In: Solomon, P. R., Goethals, G. R., Kelly, C. M., and Stephens, B. R. (eds.), *Memory: Interdisciplinary Approaches*, Springer-Verlag, New York, 201–20.

Ötsch, W., 2000, *Heider light: Handbuch fuer Demagogie*, Czernin Verlag, Wien.

Ötsch, W., 2001, *Demagogische Vorstellungs-Welten; Das Beispiel der FPÖ*, Johannes Kepler Universität Linz: In druk.

Ötsch, W., and Stahl, T., 1997, *Das Wörterbuch de NLP*, Junfermann, Paderborn, Duitsland.

Palmer, H., 1987, *Creativism: The Art of Living Deliberately*, Star's Edge International, Longwood, Florida.

Palmer, H., 1994, *Leven vanuit vrije wil*, Bruna, Utrecht.

Pannekoek, L., 1983, *Aandacht, sympatie en liefde*, Ank Hermes, Deventer.

Peirce, C. S., 1876, On a new list of categories, *Proceedings of the American Academy of Arts and Sciences*, 7, 287–298.

Peirce, C. S., 1877, The Fixation of Belief, *Popular Science Monthly*, 12th November 1877, 1–15.

Perls, F., 1969, *Gestalt Therapy Verbatim*, Real People Press, Moab, Utah.

Piaget, J., 1965, *The Child's Conception of the World*, Littlefield, Adams & Company, New Jersey.

Pinker, S., 1997, *How The Mind Works*, W.W. Norton, New York.

Pouwel, J., 1992, *De voorouders en haar Winti*. In eigen beheer, Amsterdam.

Prochaska, J. O., 1984, *Systems of Psychotherapy: A Transtheoretical Analysis*, The Dorsey Press, Homewood, Illinois.

Raven, B. H., 1965, Social Influence and Power. In: Steiner, I. D., and Fishbein, M. (eds.), *Current Studies in Social Psychology*, Holt, Rinehart and Winston, New York, 371–82.

Roberts, J., 1978, *The Afterdeath Journal of an American Philosopher: The World View of William James*, Prentice-Hall Inc, New York.

Rosch, E., and Lloyd, B. B., 1978, *Cognition and Categorization*, Erlbaum, Hillsdale, New York.

Rosenblatt, P. C., 2000, *Parent Grief: Narratives of Loss and Relationships*, Brunner Mazel, East Sussex, England.

Rubin, Z., 1970, Measurement of romantic love. In: *Journal of Personality and Social Psychology*, 1970, 16, 265–273.

Rychlak, J. F., 1988, *The Psychology of Rigorous Humanism*, New York University Press, New York.

Sargent, A. C., 1999, *The Other Mind's Eye: The Gateway to the Hidden Treasures of Your Mind*, Success Design International Publications, Malibu, CA.

Satir, V., 1972, *Peoplemaking*, Science and Behavior Books, Palo Alto.

Schaffer, H. R., 1996, *Social Development*, Blackwell Publishers, Oxford, UK.

Schneider, W., and Shiffrin, R. M., 1977, Controlled and Automatic Human Information Processing; Detection, Search and Attention. In: *Psychological Review*, 84, 1–66.

Schwarz, R. C., 1997, *Internal Family Systems Therapy*, Guilford Press, East Sussex, England.

Selman, R. L., 1980, *The Growth of Interpersonal Understanding*, Academic Press, New York.

Shapiro, F., 1995, *Eye Movement Desensitization and Reprocessing: Basic Principles, Protocols, and Procedures*, Guilford Press, East Sussex, England.

Sheldrake, R., 1988, *The Presence of the Past*, Times Books, London.

Sherif, M., and Hovland, C. I., 1961, *Social Judgement: Assimilation and Contrast Effects in Communication and Attitude Change*, Yale University Press, New Haven, Connecticut.

Sinclair, J. D., 1982, *The Rest Principle: A Neurophysiological Theory of Behavior*, Lawrence Erlbaum, New York

Singer, J. L., 1974, *Imagery and Daydreaming: Methods for Psychotherapy and Behavior Modification*, Academic Press, New York.

Singer, J. L., 1990, A Fresh Look at Repression, Dissociation, and the Defenses as Mechanisms and as Personality Styles. In: Singer, J. L. (ed.), *Repression and Dissociation*, The University of Chicago Press Ltd, London.

Sokolov, E. N., 1977, *Inner Speech and Thought*, Plenum Press, New York.

Souget, F., 1985, *De achterzijde van de menselijke geest*, Swets & Zeitlinger b.v., Lisse.

Sparrer, I., 2001, *Wunder, Loesung und System. Lösungsfocussierte Systemische Structuraufstellungen fuer Therapie und Organisationsberatung*, Carl Auer Systeme, Heidelberg.

Sperry, L., 2001, *Spirituality in Clinical Practice*, Brunner-Routledge, East Sussex, England.

Spiegel, H., and Spiegel, D., 1978, *Trance and Treatment: Clinical Uses of Hypnosis*, Basic Books, New York.

Stam, J. J., 1998, Bringing the Roots of Organizations to Light, *Anchor Point*, July 1998, Salt Lake City, Utah.

Steens, R., 1995, *Menselijke Communicatie*, De Interactie Academie, Schonebekestraat 33, Antwerpen.

Stephen, H. J. M., 1995, *Winti en Hulpverlening*, Uitgave, Stephen, ISBN 90-800960-2-4.

Temple, R., 1989, *Open to Suggestion*, Aquarius Press, Thorsons, Wellingborough, Northamptonshire, England.

Toivonen, V. M., and Kauppi, T., 1993, Persoonlijke communicatie over: Interconnectedness of NLP-modes (personal communication, Helsinki, 1993).

Toman, W., 1960, Haupttypen der Familienkonstellation, Psychologische Rundschau, 11, 273–284.

Toman, W., 1961, *Family Constellation*, Springer Publishing Company Inc., New York.

Tomasello, M., 2003, The Key is Social Cognition. In Gentner, D., and Kuczaj, S. (eds.), *Language and Thought*, Mit Press, Chicago.

Turner, M., 1995, *The Literary Mind*, Oxford University Press, New York.

Varga von Kibet, M., 1995, *Ganz im Gegenteil: Querdenken als Quelle der Veraenderung*, Graphic-Consult, München.

Varga von Kibet, M., 2001, Systemische Kreativitaetstraining. In: Weber, G. (ed.), *Derselbe Wind laesst viele Drachen*, Carl Auer Systemen, Heidelberg.

Varga von Kibet, M., and Sparrer, I., 1998, *Structuraufstellungen*. Weber, G. (ed.), Praxis des Familien-Stellens. Carl Auer Systeme, Heidelberg.

Veldman, F., 1987, *Haptonomie: Wetenschap van de affectiviteit*, Erven Bijleveld, Utrecht.

Walker, W., 1996, *Abenteuer Kommunikation. Bateson, Perls, Satir, Erickson und die Anfaenge des Neurolinguistischen Programmierens (NLP)*, Klett-Cotta, Stuttgart.

Walker, W., 2004, personal communication in September 2004 at the Prenzl-Komm Training in Berlin.

Walsh, A., 1996, *The Science of Love: Understanding Love and Its Effects on Mind and Body*, Prometheus Books, New York.

Watkins, M., 1986, *Invisible Guests: The Development of Imaginal Dialogues*, Erlbaum, Hillsdale, NJ.

Watzlawick, P., Beavin, J., and Jackson, D., 1967, *Pragmatics of Human Communication*, W. W. Norton, New York.

Watzlawick, P., Weakland, J., and Fisch, R., 1974, *Change: Principles of Problem Formation and Problem Resolution*, W. W. Norton, New York.

Weber, G., 1994, *Zweierlei Glueck; Die systemische Psychotherapie Bert Hellingers*, Carl Auer Verlag, Heiderberg.

Weber, G., 1998, *Praxis des Familien-Stellens; Beitraege zu systemische Loesungen nach Bert Hellinger*, Carl Auer Systemen, Heidelberg.

Weber, G., 2000, *Praxis des Organisationsaufstellung*, Carl Auer Systemen, Heidelberg.

Weber, G., 2001, *Derselbe Wind laesst viele Drachen steigen*, Carl Auer Systemen, Heidelberg.

Wessler, R. L., 1990, *Beyond Cognitive Therapy: Innovations in Treating Disorders of Personality*. Lezing, ter gelegenheid van het 100 jarige uitkomen van `The Principles of Psychology': William James Foundation, Amsterdam.

Wessler, R. L., and Hankin-Wessler, S., 1989, Emotion and Rules of Living. In: Plutchik, R., and Kellerman, H., (eds.), *Emotion: Theory, Research, and Experience*, Vol. 5, 231–253, Academic Press, San Diego.

Wilber, K., 1997, *Een beknopte geschiedenis van alles*, Lemniscaat, Rotterdam.

Wolberg, L., 1948, *Medical Hypnosis: Volume 1 and 2*, Grune & Stratton, New York.

Woodsmall, W., 1999, 'Logical Levels' and Systemic NLP. In: *NLP World*, Volume 6, No. 1, March 1999.

Wrycza, P., 1996, *Living Awareness: A course in open-heart learning and perception*, Gateway Books, Bath, England.

Zeig, J. K., 1980, *A Teaching Seminar with Milton H. Erickson*, Brunner Mazel, New York.

Zimbardo, P. G., 1970, The Human Choice: Individuation, Reason, and Deindividuation, Impulse and Chaos. In: Arnold, W. J., and Levine, D. (eds.), *Nebraska Symposium on Motivation 1969*. University of Nebraska Press, Lincoln, Vol. 17, 237–307.

Zimbardo, P. G., and Leippe, M. R., 1991, *The Psychology of Attitude Change and Social Influence*, McGraw-Hill, New York.